THE VATICAN REVOLUTION

Geddes MacGregor is the Rufus Jones Professor of Philosophy and Religion at Bryn Mawr College. He is the author of *Aesthetic Experience in Religion* (1947), *Christian Doubt* (1951), *Les Frontières de la morale et de la religion* (1952), *From a Christian Ghetto* (1954), and *The Thundering Scot: A Portrait of John Knox* (1957). An Oxford Doctor of Philosophy and a Fellow of the Royal Society of Literature, he also holds degrees from Edinburgh, and the French State Doctorate in Letters from the Sorbonne. He was ordained to the ministry of the Church of Scotland in 1939. Ten years later, when he came to the United States, he was voted the privilege of retaining his place in the ecclesiastical courts of Scotland.

THE VATICAN REVOLUTION

by Geddes MacGregor

BEACON PRESS   *Beacon Hill*   Boston

© 1957 by Geddes MacGregor
Library of Congress catalog card number: 57-6524
Printed in the United States of America

CONGREGATIONI FIDELIUM

"A radical and essential revolution in the con-stitution of the Church."

—MGR. MARET, Dean of the Faculty of Theology, Paris, and Bishop *in partibus* referring to the proposed definition by the Vatican Council

CONTENTS

ACKNOWLEDGMENTS

My debt to writers who have already labored in this field will be obvious to scholars. I wish also to express my thanks to two of my graduate students: to Miss Sarah Ann Caner for her patient and devoted assistance in the preparation of the typescript, and to Miss Ann Fox for her lively help with the proofs.

GEDDES MacGREGOR

Ard Choille
Kennedy Lane
Bryn Mawr
Pennsylvania

INTRODUCTION

"There is not, and there never was on this earth, a work of human policy so well deserving of examination as the Roman Catholic Church." So wrote the great English historian Lord Macaulay over a century ago, and a generation before the Vatican Council. Macaulay's observation is even more apposite today than it was when he made it.

Historically, the term "Roman Church" is applied, on the one hand, to the diocese and See of Rome and the government there seated, and, on the other hand, to the whole body of Roman Catholics everywhere that acknowledges that Roman Church to be, in the words of the Council of Trent, "mother and mistress of all churches." In the Middle Ages, the term was used in both these senses. Modern scholars use the term "Roman Communion" to designate the wider society. Although this usage may not be familiar to all American readers, I have followed it where clarity seemed to demand it.

This book is certainly in no sense "against" the Roman Church. Intelligent Roman Catholics, who are more acutely concerned than other persons can be to know whether the best or the worst elements in their own tradition are in evidence today, will find the treatment not unsympathetic.

From early times there were in the Roman Church two tendencies. There was, especially from the age of Hildebrand in the eleventh century, a papalist party. Popes are, of course, as likely to be papalists as kings are inclined to be royalists. Some medieval papalists maintained extreme views about the papacy (for example, that the Pope can legally do anything God can do), beside which modern papal pretensions are mild. There was also an important

constitutional theory among the learned in the Middle Ages: the
political doctrine of the sovereignty of the people under God. Associated with this, though to be carefully distinguished from it, was
the great conciliar movement that was so lively on the eve of the
Protestant Reformation. The work of the Protestant Reformers
arose largely out of despair at the failure of the efforts of the conciliarists. The gulf between papalism and conciliarism was very
great. I do not seek to underestimate the historical importance of
either party, though I will try to show that conciliarism, which
appeared to suffer defeat at the Vatican Council in 1870, had an
immense weight of learned opinion on its side throughout the later
Middle Ages; so much so that Maret's phrase, from which I have
taken the title of my book, was justified. The measure of its justification may be determined by the reader on the basis of the facts
I shall produce in evidence of the unconstitutional character of the
proceedings of the Council.

Conciliarism is not democracy in the modern, secular sense; nor,
indeed, was the medieval doctrine of popular sovereignty democratic in this sense. No ideals that might be held by a theocentric
society such as the Christian Church (for instance, universal suf-
frage or literacy) could be quite the same as they are in secularist
hands. But I am of the opinion that Christianity was from the first
essentially democratic in tendency, and that the tendency has always been realized wherever spiritual activity has been sufficiently
vigorous. The process of realization may be slow, as in the case of
the gradual abolition of slavery—an institution that was accepted,
faute de mieux, both in New Testament and much later times. But
though the practice of democracy was difficult in the Middle Ages,
democratic ideals in both Church and State were fostered by the
liveliest minds as they were cherished in the most generous hearts.
I therefore cannot accept the supposition, widespread even among
scholars, that the papal autocracy commonly associated with Roman
Catholicism is an inevitable development and the only effective
form of government the Roman Church could have. It seems to me
that to acquiesce in this view is to capitulate to the indoctrination

of the papalist party, which has always depended for its success on the psychological fact that most people evidently find it easier to yield the reins of government to others than to bear the responsibility of sharing them. The realization of a Christian democracy is not easy; no easier than the realization of Christian love, the *agape* that St. Paul exalted above the other virtues. But its enemies have exaggerated the difficulties, because they wished men to despair of its possibility.

For instance, in the thirteenth century, Pope Innocent IV wrote that it was sacrilegious even to question the plenitude of the papal power (*plenitudo potestatis*). By this power the Pope was able, according to Huguccio, Bishop of Pisa and ablest of the twelfth-century canonists, to exercise over all dioceses the same "ordinary" jurisdiction that each bishop exercised over his own. A very different conception of the government of the Church was, however, developed by other learned men, notably after the close of the thirteenth century, at which time there had been a faction of cardinals in open revolt against Boniface VIII, impugning the legality of his election as well as his personal integrity. Giles of Rome wrote at that time on the subject of such rebellion, but without pressing his arguments to the conclusion adopted by his great contemporary, John of Paris. This scholar, canonist as well as theologian, took a principle that the lawyers had already applied to corporations generally, and applied it to the corporate structure of the Church. The authority in a corporation was not, he held, concentrated in the head only, but was diffused among the members. The power of jurisdiction was conferred on a prelate by human delegation in the act of election, and so must be distinguished from the sacramental powers that inhere in bishops by virtue of their consecration, and priests by reason of their ordination. The application of that principle to the Church was of immense influence. It taught the learned, at any rate, to regard prelates as proctors (*procuratores* or *dispensatores*), not masters (*domini*). Authority (*dominium*) rests, therefore, in the "congregation of the faithful" (*congregatio fidelium*), and all prelates, including the Pope, are only entrusted with the duty of administration. In answer to papalist assertions that no human authority could take away the powers of a Pope, John maintained that the authority that was diffused among the members of the Church was at least equal to that which was concentrated in the papacy. In all this John was restating an earlier writer's doctrine that the Pope, though enjoying an authority greater than that of any single member of the corporation, did not enjoy an authority greater than that of all the members together. Prelates, moreover, did not derive their authority from the Pope; they derived it from God directly, and by the election and consent of the people.

I mention this at the outset so that readers who are unfamiliar with the technicalities of the subsequent widespread development of this tradition may have some indication of what lay behind the events to be recounted in the first chapters of this book. On the eve of 1870, the doctrine of Papal Infallibility was far from being universally held. In 1825, for example, with a view to the proposed emancipation of English Roman Catholics from their political disabilities (eventually achieved by the Roman Catholic Relief Act, 1829), a British government commission asked a panel of Irish Roman Catholic bishops whether it was held that the Pope was infallible. The bishops correctly replied that this was no part of Catholic teaching. Forty years later, however, it became an essential doctrine for all Roman Catholics throughout the world.

In view of the venerable tradition against the doctrine, and the association of this with a fanatical ecclesiastical party, it is questionable, to say the least, whether the Roman Church could, constitutionally, repudiate the conciliar, democratic, and liberal elements in its own tradition, and yield itself up to the dominion of the papalist faction. At any rate, the circumstances of the Vatican Council demand scrutiny. What was done at that Council is of the greatest importance in the history of ideas. *How* it was done is, moreover, instructive study in papalist methods.

The chief actor in the drama, Pope Pius IX, who reigned longer than any other pontiff in history, is a fascinating character, representing the best and the worst in the papalist mind. To his detractors he appeared an unscrupulous schemer; to his admirers a veritable saint. He was neither.

This book is intended to be within the scope of those general readers who are interested in the history of Roman Catholicism and its impact on modern society, especially that of the United States. For their convenience, therefore, explanations have been occasionally introduced that would be unnecessary in a work designed exclusively for specialists. To assist such readers in verifying the facts without having to consult other works, there is an appendix setting forth the text of the Decrees of the Vatican Council, together with an English translation of this document. There is also another appendix providing brief critical commentaries on the two doctrines that must now be considered closely connected, historically, with the promotion of the doctrine of Papal Infallibility, namely, the doctrines of the Immaculate Conception and of the Assumption of Mary. For those who, on the other hand, wish to consult the primary sources and the other vast literature on the subject, there is a select bibliography, with some annotations, of nearly two hundred works.

Not all scholars will agree with my view that many of the ideals underlying modern democratic government, for example, those of the United States, Britain and France, have roots in Biblical and patristic doctrine. By no means will all ecclesiastical historians agree with my opinions concerning the growth of government in the Christian Church of the first centuries. Such questions are highly controversial, and they are much too technical to permit of fair discussion within the scope of the present book. I wish, however, to make it clear that I am not writing in any sectarian interest whatsoever; still less am I writing against any such interest. If one were doing so, I suppose one would more discreetly disguise one's sympathies. It will be abundantly evident that mine are, at any rate, anything other than secularist. Nevertheless, I do not believe there is sufficient evidence for holding that any one modern church polity is, or need be, wholly in accordance with the practice of apostolic times. I incline, rather, to the view expressed by the late provost of my Oxford College, Canon Streeter, in a lecture given in the United States many years ago, that the "early" Church was not Congregationalist or Episcopal or Presbyterian, but was Congregationalist and Episcopal and Presbyterian and much else besides.

I would therefore ask of those Anglican and other scholars who think differently such toleration of my opinion on these matters as I have of theirs. Some Anglicans will also dislike certain terminology I use; for instance, they will feel that by including them among Protestants I am putting them in a class to which they do not wish to belong. In all this I am only following ordinary American usage. I do not think that the term "Protestant" need be, as the late A. P. Herbert called it, a "witch-word," any more than the term "Catholic" need be. In my vocabulary both terms are encomiastic. Too often we Christians deserve neither term.

1

"LONG LIVE THE INFALLIBLE POPE '

AT NINE o'clock in the morning, Monday, the eighteenth of July, 1870, in the largest church in the world, His Eminence Cardinal Barili began to say his Mass. It was a low Mass, but a high occasion.

St. Peter's, Rome, is an immensely impressive church. It is impressive even if you know no history. It is twice the size of St. Paul's, London. It is also longer and very much larger than the still unfinished Anglican Cathedral in New York, whose cornerstone was not laid till twenty-two years after the date of the scene now depicted, and whose now completed and enormous nave is longer than that of any cathedral in England, even Winchester. But St. Peter's is much more impressive to the historian, for though, after the hundred and twenty years of its building, it was consecrated as recently as 1626, it supplanted an older St. Peter's, built some thirteen hundred years earlier on the site of Nero's circus, where the apostle was believed to have been martyred. At Christmas in the year 800, in that historic church Charlemagne received the imperial crown of Rome from the hands of Pope Leo III. The circular slab of porphyry on which he and other emperors were crowned has been wrought into the pavement of the present church, whose massive dome, four hundred and thirty-five feet high, sits like the panoply of heaven itself above a hundred and fifty gigantic columns.

At the end of the Mass, a small throne bearing a copy of the Bible was placed on the altar. Outside, black clouds eclipsed the light and color of Rome. The crowded church was curiously sombre. Presently, amid the hundreds of venerable prelates from all over the world, whose white mitres gleamed in the lightning as they reverently turned their heads, the distinguished figure of Pope Pius IX appeared in view. An Italian of noble birth, seventy-eight years of age, he had reigned for a quarter of a century—longer than any pontiff in history. There had been for long a superstition that no pope would ever "see the years of Peter," and Pius had already by the length of his reign defied this popular belief.

The Pope, after kneeling for a few moments at the *prie-dieu,* proceeded to his throne in the apse of the right transept and recited the usual prayers. The Litany of the Saints was sung. Its wistful beauty can speak to the simplest heart, while to the more thoughtful it calls to remembrance the great procession of the holy heroes of the Roman Church from the glorious days of her persecuted infancy. In those far-off days, her members had foregathered in secret as a group of subversives who, refusing to burn incense before the image of the deified Emperor, talked instead about their Lord Christos, in loyalty to whom they were ready to suffer torture and terrible death. Now that same Roman Church commanded the loving allegiance of millions. Though in the course of her long history many had separated themselves from her and sought their Christian salvation beyond her fold, she was spread more widely over the face of the earth than ever before. No dawn, from London to Melbourne, from Boston to Bombay, now rose without there rising with it the uplifted hands of one of her priests, offering to God the Very Body and Blood of his own Son in the holy sacrifice of the Mass.

In a reverent hush came the inbreathing of the assembled multitudes for the thousand-year-old hymn to the Breath of God: *Veni Creator Spiritus!* The sonorous words spoke directly to many, not least to the assembled prelates of the Church, of the Church's condition in those very troubled times and of the assurance she had ever claimed that God himself would always guide the Ship of Peter and safeguard her in the face of Christ's many enemies:

Keep far our foes; give peace at home:
Where Thou art Guide no ill can come.

One of the bishops ascended the pulpit and, above the vast array of other dignitaries, read the schema, a document setting forth the business before the meeting. It was the last day of a General Council of the Church that looked as though it might be the last Council ever to be held. Many felt an immense sense of relief that the business was almost over. The bishop asked the conventional question—whether what had been put before the Fathers pleased them. Then Monsignor Jacobini called out the names of each of the five hundred and thirty-five prelates present. It was the most momentous decision in the history of the Roman Church. Five hundred and thirty-three answered in the affirmative: *Placet*. Two answered in the negative: *Non placet*. One hundred and six members of the Council were absent. The absence of one hundred and six members, including many of the most distinguished and learned bishops in the world, of so important a Council on the day of its final sitting was a very remarkable circumstance. That circumstance is among the mysterious affairs that the present book is intended to examine and explain.

There was a violent thunderstorm over Rome that morning. The voting of the prelates was punctuated by vivid flashes of lightning and awful bursts of thunder. In later years these were to be variously interpreted as signs of God's approval or of his wrath. The storm outside continued as the Pope, who had meanwhile awaited in silence the result of the voting, arose and, having announced the Council's decision, defined, confirmed, and approved, by his own apostolic authority, the decrees the Council had voted. The Council had acknowledged that for all ages to come there was nothing that such a world-wide, age-hallowed assembly such as itself could do that the Pope could not do by himself.

Then, like the murmur of the sea before it breaks itself into tumultuous uproar on the rock, came the throbbing voice of the crowds of Italian spectators, bursting as if on the very Rock of Peter, into a tremendous shout of exultant applause: *Viva Pio Nono Papa infallibile!*

Pius, for all his faults, was a warm-hearted and generous man, with a disarming geniality, a cheerful wit, and a pleasantly mischievous sense of humor. He had indeed all the most captivating Italian virtues, and had for long stolen away the people's hearts. He was their idol, the priest-prince.

Three days earlier, on Friday, goaded by Bismarck's provocative telegram, the French Emperor, Napoleon III, who was the Pope's political ally and supporter, had declared war. It was a war that in a few weeks demolished not only the French Empire but also what remained of the Papal States over which the Popes had reigned for centuries. The temporal dominions of the papacy were gone.[1]

The decree published and approved on that memorable Monday in July, 1870, is contained in a document entitled *The First Dogmatic Constitution Concerning the Church of Christ*. This consists of a brief proem or introduction and four short chapters.[2] The first of these is called "The Institution of the Apostolic Primacy in Blessed Peter." The following excerpt will suffice to indicate its character and claims:

> We therefore teach and declare that, according to the testimony of the Gospel, the primacy of jurisdiction over the universal Church of God was immediately and directly promised and given to blessed Peter the Apostle by Christ the Lord. . . . At open variance with this clear doctrine of Holy Scripture as it has ever been understood by the Catholic Church are the perverse opinions of those who . . . deny that Peter in his single person, preferably to all the other Apostles, whether taken separately or together, was endowed by Christ with a true and proper primacy of jurisdiction; or of those who assert that the same primacy was not bestowed immediately and directly upon blessed Peter himself, but upon the Church, and through the Church on Peter as her minister.

[1] Nominal territory was restored to the papacy by the Lateran Treaty, 1929, under Mussolini's Government.

[2] For the full text, see Appendix I.

If anyone, therefore, shall say that blessed Peter the Apostle was not appointed the Prince of all the Apostles and the visible Head of the whole Church Militant; or that the same directly and immediately received from the same our Lord Jesus Christ a primacy of honour only, and not of true and proper jurisdiction: let him be anathema!

To those who knew the history of the Roman Church these were indeed stupendous claims. Henceforward, any Catholic scholar who, while admitting the primacy of Peter, affirmed that he got that primacy only from the Church as the Church's elected Head, would share in the same anathema as that awarded to unbelievers who repudiated the whole Christian faith. Yet the Pope was and still is an elected Head, though the electors (the College of Cardinals) cannot be said to be a body truly representative of the whole Roman Communion.

The second chapter is on "The Perpetuity of the Primacy of Blessed Peter in the Roman Pontiffs."

. . . For none can doubt, and it is known to all ages, that the holy and blessed Peter . . . lives, presides, and judges, to this day and always, in his successors the Bishops of the Holy See of Rome. . . . Whence, whosoever succeeds to Peter in this See, does by the institution of Christ himself obtain the Primacy of Peter over the whole Church. . . .

If, then, any should deny that it is by the institution of Christ the Lord, or by divine right, that blessed Peter should have a perpetual line of successors in the Primacy over the universal Church, or that the Roman Pontiff is the successor of blessed Peter in this primacy: let him be anathema.

The third chapter describes what is claimed concerning "The Power and Nature of the Primacy of the Roman Pontiff." His primacy is over the whole world, and by divine appointment the Roman Church has a superiority of power over all other churches: that is to say, all persons and groups are both individually and collectively bound to submit to the Roman Pontiff

. . . not only in matters which belong to faith and morals, but also in those that pertain to the discipline and government of the Church throughout the world. . . . This is the teaching of

Catholic truth, from which no one can deviate without loss of faith and of salvation. . . .

And since by the divine right of Apostolic primacy the Roman Pontiff is placed over the universal Church, we further teach and declare that he is the supreme judge of the faithful.[3] . . . Wherefore they err from the right course who assert that it is lawful to appeal from the judgments of the Roman Pontiffs to an œcumenical Council, as to an authority higher than the Roman Pontiff.

The breath-taking implications of the claims of the preceding chapters of the document are confirmed. There is no appeal from a papal judgment. So absolute is the papal authority that not even the entire Church may dare to review or modify a pope's judgment in any way. If the whole of the rest of the Church should disagree with the Pope, the whole of the rest of the Church would be in error. It is true that such a situation is unlikely; but it is at least theoretically possible. After all, the Pope is the Universal Doctor, the teacher of all Christians, and a teacher's pupils do need to be taught; that is to say, without his instruction they might be in error.

What sort of a Council was it that came from all over the world to stay for the better part of a year in Rome in order to conclude by acknowledging that it had no function to perform that could not be performed as well or perhaps even better by the Pope alone? In the anathema that inevitably ends the chapter, those are condemned who would say that the Pope's office is one of inspection or direction only; also those who would admit that he has the principal part of the Church's supreme power, but not the whole of it. Herein lay the novelty. From early times the immense authority of the Bishop of Rome had been very widely recognized. But this extreme papalist interpretation of it had been very far indeed from being universal. It had been as much a party view as was, in Stuart times in England, the "Divine Right" of kings a party view in English constitutional theory.

People today have become so accustomed to associating such

[3] See Appendix I, n. 39.

uncompromising papal absolutism with the Roman Church that to many at the present day there is nothing here that will be much of a surprise. "Is it not the nature of the Roman Church to be under the absolute dominion of a pope?" they may ask. Every historian knows, however, that the constitutional basis of the Roman Church had for eighteen hundred years been in question. That the Pope's office was a very high one had certainly for long been recognized. Men do, however, tend to exalt their own office. This is not necessarily a bad thing, nor is it only bad men who do it. Popes, good and bad, had, especially from the eleventh century, made some extreme claims for theirs, and there had been extravagant support for such claims. But the apparently almost completely docile acquiescence, by what purported to be a General Council of the Church, in a papal claim so uncompromisingly expressed, was startling. The most tremendous claim of all, however, was yet to come.

It came in the fourth and last chapter, in which the document sets forth the Decree concerning "The Infallible Teaching of the Roman Pontiff."

> Therefore faithfully adhering to the tradition received from the beginning of the Christian faith, for the glory of God our Saviour, the exaltation of the Catholic religion, and the salvation of Christian people, the sacred Council approving, we teach and define that it is a dogma divinely revealed: that the Roman Pontiff, when he speaks *ex cathedra*, that is, when in discharge of the office of pastor and doctor of all Christians, by virtue of his supreme Apostolic authority, he defines a doctrine regarding faith or morals to be held by the universal Church, by the divine assistance promised to him in blessed Peter, is possessed of that infallibility with which the divine Redeemer willed that his Church should be endowed for defining doctrine regarding faith or morals; and that therefore such definitions of the Roman Pontiff are irreformable[4] of themselves, and not from consent of the Church.[5]
> But if any one—which may God avert—presume to contradict this our definition: let him be anathema.

[4] That is, no one may review the judgment of a pope when it has been made in the circumstances described. See Appendix I, n. 52.

[5] The last words, "of themselves . . ." were added before the final voting. They were peculiarly odious to many members of the Council.

Given at Rome in public Session solemnly held in the Vatican Basilica in the year of our Lord one thousand eight hundred and seventy, on the eighteenth day of July, in the twenty-fifth year of our Pontificate.

It must be noted, since Monsignor Fessler, the papal Secretary at the Council, mentioned the point in reply to a severe criticism published immediately after the Council by the learned historian Schulte, Professor of Canon Law at the University of Prague,[6] that this final definition should be understood in the context of the historical explanations that precede it. These explanations themselves, however, are carefully selected from the most favorable sources that could be found in the records of the Church over a period of about eighteen hundred years. It was not claimed in the Vatican Decree that a pope can *change* Christian doctrine. The *whole* Christian doctrine was given to Peter as a "deposit of faith." A pope can never say, therefore, that anything he defines was unknown to preceding ages. On the contrary, when a pope speaks officially to the Church, defining a doctrine as one that all Christians must henceforward believe, he acknowledges that the doctrine he defines has always been, implicitly at least, the teaching of Christ and part of the heritage the Church received from the beginning. If the doctrine appears to contradict Scripture, the seeming contradiction needs to be explained.

For instance, Pius IX himself had declared in 1854 that while all humankind is born into an inheritance of "original sin," the Virgin Mary was miraculously excepted from this. This declaration was given out as infallible teaching. Mary, alone among human beings, was exempted from that taint of original sin, that spiritual disease, from which all other creatures suffer. At the time of her conception in the womb of her mother, Anna, she was, by a special miracle of God, conceived without original sin. This, the doctrine of the Immaculate Conception, was proclaimed, not as something new that the faithful were required to believe, but, rather, as a part

[6] Johann Friedrich von Schulte, *Das Unfehlbarkeits-Decret v. 18 Juli 1870.*

of the Christian heritage of faith that had always been implicitly held by faithful Christians from the time of the apostles themselves, so that all that the Pope was doing in 1854 was drawing this to the attention of the faithful, in case there should be any doubt in their minds on the subject. Before his pronouncement doubt on the subject was permissible, since there was no clear guidance on it; after his pronouncement it would be apostasy to question the doctrine. It was proclaimed that the doctrine had always been according to the Mind of the Church; but the Church had not always clearly expressed her mind. Why the expression of the Church's mind had not always been clear was itself, however, far from being clear.

The Church had in fact so ill expressed her mind on the subject that practically all the Church Fathers who touched on the subject of original sin, including St. Augustine, wrote so as to make it clear that they did not suppose the Virgin Mary to be exempt from it, and in the Middle Ages the most revered authorities, including the great philosopher St. Thomas, and the great mystic St. Bernard, were explicitly opposed to it. Indeed, so strong was St. Thomas's opposition to the doctrine that it became almost a point of honor throughout the Dominican Order to oppose the notion as theologically untenable. The Franciscans, however, following Duns Scotus, were more inclined to foster the notion, and the Jesuits, later on, made it one of their special concerns to do so. If Pius IX was right, let alone infallible, it seems regrettable that the learned theologians of Christendom should have been left for eighteen hundred years with such a marked lack of guidance on the subject that they not only erred on it but erred almost in proportion to their stature as the leaders of the Church's intellectual life, the luminaries in the firmament of her mind.[7]

Almost a century later, the doctrine of the Assumption of Mary, which had been even more widely acknowledged to be based on an apocryphal legend (and so acknowledged in days when men were naturally much less critical about history than they are to-

[7] See Appendix II.

day), was to be likewise proclaimed by Pius XII as part of the original "deposit of faith" given by Jesus Christ to the Apostles.[8]

It is a matter of some importance, not least for Christians, whether inside or outside the Roman Communion, to determine the constitutional legality of what happened at the Vatican Council. While it is true that no change of view regarding the constitutional legality of that assembly's acts would of itself immediately alter the general attitude of most other Christians towards the Roman Church, it would certainly open up considerable possibilities for the future welfare of Christendom if the modern Roman Communion could be seen to be constitutionally reformable. No historian or canonist can fail to appreciate the vast difference between a society that is legally autocratic and one that is illegally so. The difference is not merely theoretical. One cannot without revolution reform a purely autocratic institution; but one may very well reform a *de facto* autocracy if there are grounds for believing such autocracy to be constitutionally questionable. If it could be shown, for instance, that the triumph of the papalist party in 1870 was an illegal triumph and that the opposition had law and history on its side, the prospect of a richer, purer, reunited Christendom would be much brighter. The bitterness of much feeling in America and other democratic countries towards the policy of the Roman Communion is due in large measure to the fact that it appears under the guise of an international ecclesiastico-political autocracy with headquarters on foreign soil.

That there should have been some gerrymandering and other irregularities will surprise no one. No democratic assembly, secular or otherwise, is free from these. Everyone who knows anything of the habits of a certain type of ecclesiastic will expect some intrigue as a matter of course. There is, however, the question: how much corruption does it take to vitiate the legality of an assembly? How free must an assembly be in order that its proceedings be constitutional? A few irregularities of procedure, one or two shabby moves, or even a great, deliberate fraud need not nullify every-

[8] See Appendix II.

thing an assembly does. But how many such acts does it take? How much corruption kills a Council? In particular, how free in mind and pure in heart and morally unanimous need a Christian Council be when, having the assured guidance of the Holy Ghost in making its decision, it decides to acknowledge its own dispensability and recognize that the Pope has no need of it, since he is personally invested by God with every power a Council could have?

Even the most ardent upholders of the papalist view admit that, due to the human element common to all assemblies and including even those believed to be so specially guided by God, the Vatican Council had shortcomings. The Benedictine Abbot B. C. Butler, for instance, in a recent defense of the papalist position, admits that there was intrigue,[9] and that it was by a "coupon" election that the most important committee of the Council [10] was chosen. No one denies that there were irregularities. But how bad were they? Not so bad as the devilry alleged by the more unenlightened annalists on the anti-papalist side; worse, no doubt, than we hear of from Jesuit sources and the like. It is impossible to discover exactly how bad any assembly's proceedings really are. It would be sufficient if we were to discover that they were in this case bad enough to make the Council unconstitutional.

[9] B. C. Butler, *The Church and Infallibility,* p. 95 f.
[10] The "Deputation on Faith."

2

THE BACKGROUND OF THE VATICAN COUNCIL

IT IS commonly said that Pius IX began his pontificate as a Christian liberal and ended it as a reactionary. The period of his interest in liberal political reform in the States of the Church was, however, brief. His own brother had said of him that if he were cut into pieces there would grow from each, as from a polypus, a priest. The Bishop of Volterra, who had given him the tonsure, called him stiff-necked. It is unlikely that his sympathies with any sort of political liberalism were ever firmly grounded in his mind, and there was much in the temper of the liberalism of mid-nineteenth-century Europe to repel all but those whose faith in liberal ideas had very deep foundations indeed. He seems, moreover, to have had a peculiarly strong personal conviction from the first concerning the infallibility of the Pope and the supremacy of the Roman See over all the rest of the Church.

When Pius began his long pontifical reign in 1846, he talked pleasantly of all sorts of reforms. He spoke of introducing gaslighting in the streets of Rome. Wherever he went he always gave the impression of one who was fully alive to the needs of the people and eager to make use of every modern idea for the glory of God and the welfare of his Church. In all this Pius was perfectly sincere. He was, indeed, a most lovable man.

But the Italian crowds expected too much of him. They anticipated, for instance, that he would drive the hated Austrians out of Venice and Milan, where they had ruled since 1815, and unify

Italy at last. What could be more natural for their excited imaginations than that they should dream of him as the first president of such an Italy? In his benign face, his disarming eloquence, and, above all, his genuine simplicity, they saw their ideal leader. Here was a man everybody could understand; not a theologically-minded ecclesiastic, nor yet a politically-minded statesman, but a man who shared the simple faith of the people, speaking to their hearts and praying the way they liked to pray. Everything that endears an able, lively, gentle parish priest to the hearts of his flock seemed to be found in this most fatherly of men. And he it was whom God had made Pope, the man who now sat on St. Peter's throne in Rome at a time when Italy badly needed a great leader. The ideal of imaginative Italian piety had been actualized. One had but to wait for the fulfillment of the promise that seemed unbounded.

In all this there was no cynicism or bitterness such as has characterized popular devotion to some modern political dictators. The people expected no more of Pius than parishioners are entitled to expect of the new rector of a parish, except for the much grander scale. Nor was there anything in the heart of the new Pope that was unworthy of this kind of devotion. He was an ingenuous man in many ways, and it was a right instinct that prompted the crowds to love him for his simplicity and priestliness. He was not without ability: on the contrary, he was endowed with many of the qualities of mind that make a good bishop. He had not, however, a sufficient sense of his own personal limitations, particularly in the realm of learning. A bishop, even a pope, need not be a man of extraordinary learning, but he does need the wisdom to know his limitations: if he is on the papal throne he needs this wisdom most abundantly.

The simple notions of good and evil that are sufficient for a parish priest are by no means enough for a pope, who has to cope, both inside and outside the Church, with a range of influences far beyond the capacity of any one human being properly to understand. Wisdom in such an office depends largely on a pope's ability and readiness to take every kind of counsel he can get, listening not only to those whose opinions may seem congenial to him, but also to those whose opinions are less welcome. The very qualities that endear such a man as Pius to the people when he comes to them at what seems a providential moment are just the qualities that are most dangerous unless they are joined to an extraordinary open-mindedness and eagerness to hear the counsels of those who are learned in the history of the institution in which he has been called to his high place. It is not enough that he should be humble enough to kneel with his people at the altar of the Virgin; he must be sufficiently humble to seek out and hear the opinions of specialists who, though they may be much less endowed than he with the gifts that make a great ruler, may, however, be very much better equipped to understand legal and constitutional questions, let alone theological ones. Pius not only lacked such a disposition; he was more than ordinarily deficient in the will to seek advice. His method was, rather, to make up his own mind first and then muster as many opinions as he could in those quarters where he had reason to expect that they would agree with his own mind. The most that may be said in his favor in this regard is that he seems to have been remarkably sincere in his prejudices and frank in the manner in which he sought counsel that would agree with them. It was only after some experience on the papal throne that he acquired the political ability to make maneuvers that would have come more easily to a wilier man. Duplicity was foreign to his nature, for to be capable of duplicity one must have a gift for thoroughly understanding both sides of a question. Pius was far too much guided by his personal feelings to be temperamentally equipped for that.

Such considerations do much to explain his advent as a liberal pope, friendly to all ideas of reasonable reform, and his exit as an apparently intractable autocrat, having been obliged not only to relinquish all notions he may have entertained of introducing obvious reforms, but also to cede to his political enemies even the possibility of doing so. They explain no less his promotion of the interests of that ecclesiastical party whose ideas seemed to be most congenial to himself. After his death, when his body was being carried through the streets of Rome by stealth, anticlericalists threw the mud of the

Tiber at his coffin. Only a man who had given himself over so completely to his own personal feelings of piety could have evoked so much love and so much hatred. His superficial mind, linked to his simple heart, knew no doubt, and therefore could learn no wisdom. That same temerity that had enabled him to proclaim, on his own authority, and against that of the most revered doctor of the Roman Church, the doctrine that Mary, unique among creatures, was immaculately conceived in the womb of her mother, had led him to lend his support to a party that desired to mould the entire Church into an army modeled as far as practicable on the ideals of the Jesuit Society.[1]

In his political struggles with the secular Italian powers, Pius associated these more and more with the Devil and himself with God. Sincerely convinced of his own divine mission, and impressed, no doubt, by the length of the pontificate that God had accorded him, he became obsessed with the notion that God had called him to establish once and for all the doctrine that the Pope has in his own right the whole authority of the Church. By this time he had learned many diplomatic arts. He might have simply announced what he believed about papal infallibility. Many would have been prepared for this and would have rejoiced at his official proclamation of it. But Pius knew enough to recognize something of the place and authority that councils had enjoyed in the history of the Church. How much more impressive and unassailable in practice would be his pronouncement if only it could have the appearance of being sought by a General Council, rather than of emanating from himself, the Pope. Such a council would be, historically, his only constitutional rival. He would, therefore, call one and contrive to get it formally to relinquish all its powers in his own favor. Knowing that a considerable element in the Church was well prepared for the result of such a maneuver, he would patiently ascertain the extent and influence of the opposition and gradually deal with this, using, of course, all the might of his own party against his possible adversaries.

[1] See Appendix II.

The principal organ of the Jesuits, the *Civiltà Cattolica,* and that of the Papal Court, the *Moniteur,* as well as the pastoral letters of Manning, Dechamps, and other archbishops, predicted the passing of the Decree on the infallibility of the Pope. Yet this part of the business of the forthcoming Council was not even mentioned in the Bull of Convocation and other official preliminary acts.

The declared object of the Council was to crush the power of infidelity and settle all that belongs to the doctrine, worship, and discipline of the Church, and man's eternal salvation. Protestants and other alleged heretics, as well as the ancient schismatic Eastern Orthodox Church, were invited by two special letters of the Pope, written on September 8 and September 13, 1868, to return to "Christ's only sheepfold." Some respectfully declined the invitation; others ignored it. The Patriarch of Constantinople refused even to receive the letter from the papal messenger (though it was bound in red morocco and emblazoned with gold letters bearing his own name), on the ground that he had already read it in the *Giornale di Roma* and found it contained principles contrary to the Gospel and to the doctrines of the ecumenical councils and Fathers of the Church. The Metropolitan of Chalcedon returned the letter with the word *Epistrephete,* a fair modern colloquial paraphrase of which would be "scram." Other oriental bishops either declined or returned the papal letter. Dr. Cumming of London, a Presbyterian, indicated that he would be willing to accept the invitation if the Pope would allow discussion of the reasons for the separations from Rome. He was duly informed by the Pope, through Archbishop Manning, that the discussion of such questions would be inconsistent with the supremacy of the Holy See.

Meanwhile, Roman Catholic scholars and leaders such as Bishop Dupanloup of Orleans, Bishop Maret, who was Dean of the Theological Faculty of Paris, a number of German bishops, and many others viewed the prospect with dismay. Some felt that even though there might be, in the Roman Catholic world, a vaguely general belief in the Pope's infallibility in matters of doctrine and the like, the raising of such a question, at such a time, by such an assembly, could not but be disastrous for the reputation of the Roman Communion, to say the least, in a world in which the more extravagant forms of nineteenth-century liberalism had made that reputation already thoroughly suspect. The extremists were speaking and writing with recklessness that could not but justify such fears in the mind of any reasonable man, not least that of a convert like John Henry Newman, who had led the movement from Oxford to Rome in the forties, when men still remembered the evidence that had been given before a royal commission in 1825, by the Irish bishops who affirmed, in view of the proposed bill to free Roman Catholics in England from their disabilities, that papal authority was strictly limited by the councils of the Church without which the Pope could pass no decree that would be binding on the faithful.

Newman wrote to a friend in 1869, comparing the impending Decree with the definition of the Immaculate Conception in 1854:

> As to the Immaculate Conception, by contrast there was nothing sudden, or secret, in the proposal. . . . This [Papal Infallibility] has taken us all by surprise.
> The Protestant and Infidel Press, so far from taking part with Mgr. Dupanloup, have backed up all along the extreme party—and now all through the country are taking an argumentative position against me.[2]

Writing to Bishop Ullathorne privately on January 28, 1870, after the Council had met, Newman deplored what seemed imminent. "What have we done to be treated as the Faithful never were treated before?" he asked. "Why should an aggressive and insolent faction be allowed to make the hearts of the just to mourn whom the Lord hath not made sorrowful?"[3] Yet he had unbounded trust that God would continue to look after the Church. In a rosier mood he wrote a friend on February 22: "I don't think much will come of the movement for Papal Infallibility, though something very mild may be passed."[4]

[2] Wilfrid Ward, *The Life of John Henry Cardinal Newman*, Vol. II, p. 283.
[3] *Idem*, p. 288: "aggressive" and "insolent" are strong terms in Newman's vocabulary.
[4] *Idem*, p. 285.

Those who spoke thus of the inopportunity of the proposed Decree were naturally labeled "inopportunists." Later, the papalist party sought to interpret all opposition to their views as of this character.[5] But we shall see there were many who, less gentle and pacific by temperament than Newman, contemplated with horror what they believed to be the overthrow by a papalist party of the constitutional rights of the Holy Roman Church. As Newman observed, the only other persons who looked with unsurprised satisfaction at what was going on were among the "Protestants and Infidels" who thought they saw in it the final exhibition of the wickedness they had always attributed to Rome. But even in such quarters there were many whose hearts also were saddened by what they were to see.

On the Feast of the Immaculate Conception, December 8, 1864, exactly six years before the opening of the Vatican Council, the Pope had issued an encyclical, *Quanta Cura*. This document was no hurried letter; it had been in preparation for ten years, which, even as ecclesiastical time is computed, may be accounted a long period. The root of the evil of the modern world, declared the Pope, lies in the "impious and absurd principle of naturalism," which holds to the view that "human society should be constituted and governed without regard to religion." Liberty of conscience and worship and freedom of the press in religious matters are all condemned in the most bitter terms as a "liberty of perdition." To this document was appended the notorious *Syllabus of Errors* in which were set forth eighty propositions believed to be characteristic of the modern liberal spirit. These propositions, which are condemned "by virtue of the Apostolic authority," include some which every Christian must obviously deplore and others which many Christians cannot but welcome. The view, for instance, that was being much canvassed among liberal-minded Roman Catholics—that there should be freedom to worship and that the Roman Church need not be the only State religion—is condemned on equal terms with the view that the "prophecies and miracles set forth and

[5] See Chapter 4, "The Inopportunist Legend."

narrated in the Sacred Scripture are the fictions of poets." Likewise, communism and societies for the diffusion of the Bible among
the laity are condemned under the same head and described as
"pests" (*pestes*). Another of the eighty propositions condemned is:
"The teaching of those who compare the sovereign Pontiff to a
free sovereign acting in the universal Church is a doctrine which
prevailed in the Middle Ages." There is no question of deference
to historical evidence, even evidence that might become available
at some future date. History itself must be in error if it conflicts
with what is said by a pope who is speaking "by virtue of the
Apostolic authority." Nor is it only history that must conform or
else be dubbed erroneous; contemporary events and circumstances
known to all men may likewise be condemned by the Supreme
Pontiff. For example, if anything was known to the educated
classes in continental Europe in the middle of the nineteenth century, it was the empirical fact that there was disagreement among
Roman Catholics about the compatibility of the spiritual and the
temporal powers. But it is explicitly declared in the *Syllabus* that
it is an error to attempt to maintain that "the children of the
Christian and Catholic Church are not agreed upon the compatibility of the temporal with the spiritual power." [6]

It was the last item in the *Syllabus* that most shocked the world.
The proposition that "the Roman Pontiff can and should reconcile
and harmonize himself with progress, liberalism and recent civilization," was condemned. The antecedent document referred to was
an allocution issued in 1861 in which the Pope had closed the door
to all negotiations with Cavour about the possibility of anything
such as a concordat with him on the question of the Temporal
Power. No doubt Pius had his political enemy in mind when he
included this item in the *Syllabus*. But the governments of England, France, Belgium, and other countries did not interpret the
Pope's utterance as relating only to his quarrel with the Piemontese
government. Nor is there any reason why they should have so in-

[6] The full Latin text of the *Syllabus* is to be found in *Acta Pii Papae IX*,
vol. III, 701 ff.; also in Mirbt, *Quellen* (see Bibliography).

terpreted it. The whole document was indeed directed against the Pope's Italian enemies, Cavour, Mazzini, Garibaldi; but it was addressed to all Christendom. The fears behind it were fears of the increased influence of anticlerical Freemasonry, especially in Milan and Turin in the north, and to a lesser extent the not inconsiderable progress of the Waldensians, whose form of heterodoxy had existed since the twelfth century. The Pope's position in Italy was threatened on all sides, and naturally he was concerned about it. But the governments of Europe's great powers saw in the Pope's attitude to his immediate environment and the manner in which he dealt with his political problems there a token of the papal attitude towards the world at large. And it can hardly be said that their misgivings were ill founded.

Two days before the *Syllabus* was issued, Pius had asked twenty-one cardinals for their written opinion on the advisability of summoning a General Council of the Church. Nineteen had answered in the affirmative; two in the negative. In April of the following year, highly confidential letters were addressed to thirty-four bishops asking for their opinion on subjects that it would be desirable for such a Council to discuss. Two years later, on June 26, 1867, appeared an official announcement of the intention to hold the Council. This announcement was made to some five hundred bishops, who evidently received the news with acclamation. The only question that seriously troubled the minds of many churchmen was whether the Pope intended to use the occasion for pronouncing himself infallible. Everyone knew that there were some who desired this, and it was rightly assumed that the Jesuits would be doing all in their power to bring it about.

It is difficult to tell how many, at this stage, welcomed such a prospect and how many viewed it with horror. That there were a considerable number, at any rate, who did not welcome it is attested by the fact that some able observers on the papalist side felt that it might be in any case "inopportune" *because it would reveal disunity in the Church.* How could it have revealed disunity if there was none?

At last, on June 29, 1868, the official document was published, proclaiming the date on which the deliberations of the Council would begin—December 8, 1869, the Feast of the Immaculate Conception. There was some gratification that nothing was on the agenda about Papal Infallibility at all. But as preparations went on, no one could fail to note that the various commissions being appointed—which would play a vital part in the running of the Council—consisted largely of men who had quite obviously been chosen for their papalist polity rather than for their scholarly achievement. Contrary to tradition, the bishops as a whole were given no real share in the work of preparing the Council. But *was* it contrary to tradition if, as Pius is said to have exclaimed, *La tradizione son' io* ("I am tradition")? From the extreme papalist point of view there could be nothing contrary to tradition if the Pope decided it wasn't.

Then, early in 1869, there was consternation in many quarters in the Church to discover, in the *Civiltà Cattolica*, an article boldly predicting that the Council would quickly confirm the *Syllabus*, declare the Pope infallible, and go home. Bishop Dupanloup, though loyal to the Pope, publicly deprecated such attempts to anticipate the findings of so solemn an assembly of the Church. But, of course, from a Jesuit point of view there was no impropriety in anticipating what councils might do. The only impropriety would be to anticipate what the Pope might do. They knew, of course, as most people did by this time, that what they predicted was also the Pope's long-cherished and dearest wish.

In the Middle Ages it had often been the practice for the civil rulers to take a great interest in the work of councils and exert influence and pressure on them. The papalist party now plainly feared that some European nations might seek to interfere, for this party well knew what direction such interference would take. The very existence of such fears demonstrates the ostrich-like attitude of the leaders of the party. For already the intransigeance of the papacy had so changed the mood of Europe that the civil governments were giving up all hope of treating the papacy as other than a reactionary force. So, they contended, Papal Infallibility was a "spiritual" matter, in which they should have nothing to say. From the papalist standpoint, however, even the temporal claims of the papacy were "spiritual" matters. France alone among the great nations went so far as to make important comment. She pointed out that any interference with the existing settlement between her and the Vatican might have very serious results, and she expressed the hope that if any doctrine such as Papal Infallibility were to be promulgated at the Council, it would be presented in some very moderate form.

But not even the Pope's political enemies disturbed him more than did his critics within the Roman Church. Döllinger had written against papalism.[7] Maret did not entirely repudiate the notion of Papal Infallibility. But he pointed out what was well known to every historian, that according to the tradition and constitution of the Roman Church there could be no question of the infallibility of the Pope when he was acting apart from the episcopate. Otherwise the Church would be given over to an absolutist government quite alien to her character and historic constitution.[8]

On December 2, by which time over five hundred prelates (including forty-three cardinals) were already in Rome, notices were posted on the doors of St. Peter's and several other important buildings announcing that the book, *The Pope and the Council*, by "Janus," had been, on November 26, added to the Index.[9] On the same day a sort of informal preliminary meeting was held in the Sistine Chapel at which Pius addressed the prelates without yet informing them what the Council's program was to be. A papal brief, however, was read indicating the manner in which the Council would be conducted. From this it was made abundantly clear that, contrary to what had been the practice at previous councils of the Church, including Trent, the Pope claimed the sole right of initiating proposals. By way of fatherly benevolence, however, he

[7] See Bibliography.
[8] See Bibliography.
[9] It was mainly the work of Döllinger.

had decided to permit that any member who wished to make a proposal might submit it to a committee appointed by the Pope. The Pope would then decide whether the proposal might be discussed or not.

This was in itself indeed such an outrageous arrogation by the Pope of the traditional rights of the Council as to deprive the latter of its legal effect. By assuming the sole legislative authority, Pius was exercising beforehand the independence from the Council that the Council had yet to recognize. This action of the Pope's is the more interesting when it is noticed that an *attempt* had been made at the Council of Trent to depart from the unquestionable tradition of the Church on this point and assign to the Pope the right of initiating the discussions. This attempt had been thwarted by the resistance of the Tridentine Fathers on obvious legal and constitutional grounds.

At the Council of Trent, decrees had been passed with the following beautiful and impressive words of introduction: "The Sacred Synod, lawfully assembled in the Holy Spirit, under the presidency of the legates of the Holy See, ordains." But the Brief of Pius IX announced that decrees passed at the Vatican Council would be introduced by the words: "Pius, bishop, servant of God, with the approbation of the Sacred Council, ordains." [10] The implication of the change was tremendous.

Such innovations would hardly have been possible had the Church been holding regular ecumenical councils even every fifty years or so. But when there had been a lapse of three hundred years, the papalist party had a great advantage. Even so, the innovations could not and did not go undetected. Most astounding of all innovations, however, were the measures of extreme secrecy ordered by the Pope. The prelates were to reveal to no one any business discussed at the meetings, or any opinions of individual members. As a special precaution to enforce this, the post office was empowered to stop letters so that these might be censored. No one was to print anything whatsoever on the subject of the Council.

[10] Appendix I.

If a bishop wished to consult a theologian or other scholar in his own diocese, which almost every conscientious bishop was likely to feel bound to do sooner or later, he would find this difficult. Even some of the French and German bishops who had come to the Council ready to toe the Pope's party line were dismayed at the indignities imposed by the Brief. Various other arrangements were also made that could not but hinder the activities of historically-minded critics. Nevertheless, as we shall presently see, some astonishing scenes took place; scenes that could not but amuse casual observers as much as they pained loyal children of Rome.

3

THE DRAMA OF THE COUNCIL

RAIN was pouring on the Tiber when, to announce the opening of an ecumenical Council of the Holy Roman Church, cannon roared from the Castel Sant' Angelo, the seventeen-hundred-year-old fortress built over Hadrian's tomb. It was the eighth of December, 1869; once more, the Feast of the Immaculate Conception. Bells were pealing all over Rome. Of the crowds that poured into the Piazza San Pietro, some eighty thousand managed to get inside the basilica.

The Castel Sant' Angelo was indeed a symbol of the Pope's mind. Standing guard by the river beneath the Vatican hill, it had been used more than a thousand years before, to repulse the Goths. In 590, a terrible plague visited Italy, reducing the population of Rome by half. Gregory, one of the greatest of all popes, ordered a votive procession and took part in it himself. As the procession crossed the bridge that spans the Tiber, an angel in great might and splendor, says tradition, appeared on top of the round fortress, in the act of sheathing his sword. It was a sign that the visitation of God had come to an end. A bronze statue now depicts the angelic visitant. As recently as about the year 1500, the covered passage was added that leads from the Vatican to this great river fortress. Several popes increased the Castle's defensive walls and transformed the interior into splendid apartments. There were gloomy dungeons too, and from one of these Benvenuto Cellini, having with his masterly hand drawn a crucifix in charcoal, escaped with the aid of strips of his coarse bed-sheets, breaking his leg on the last rampart.

The Fathers of the Council assembled above the portico of St. Peter's about half-past eight in the morning. Singing the *Veni Creator,* they moved in procession into the basilica, past the specially bedecked statue of St. Peter, and past Very God Himself present in the consecrated Host exposed for adoration on the High Altar under the twisted columns of the *baldachino,* the work of Bernini.

This was exactly the sort of occasion Pius loved. His voice was strong as he sang the prayers at the High Altar. Some bishops pontificate dutifully; others enjoy doing so. Pius certainly enjoyed his liturgical function as Head of the Church, offering the Church's prayers to Almighty God with hundreds of bishops standing around him. It was an experience no pope had enjoyed for three hundred years, and it fell to a pope on whom it was by no means wasted.

The procession veered towards the right transept, which had been prepared as the Council Chamber. Here the prayers, ceremonies, sermon, and the formalities connected with the opening of the Council lasted well into the afternoon.

The Pope had given special instructions that the doors of the Council Chamber should be left open so that the crowds could see something of the ceremonies, and join, as far as possible, in the responses. It was an impressive sight. Probably no sight fired the vivacious imagination of the Italian spectators more than the patriarchs and bishops of the eastern rites, whose exotic garb and long, flowing beards could not but excite awe. These oriental bishops came from the banks of the Nile where Moses had been cradled, from the valley of the Euphrates, and from the Jordan where they had trodden in the very paths of Christ himself. Their serene faces reminded the onlookers of the pictures they knew of Abraham and the prophets of Israel. The pictures had come to life, all resplendent in the robes of Pastors of Christ's earthly flock— robes such as one did not often see in western Europe, even in Rome.

Latin was, of course, a convenient as well as traditional language for such an assembly. All but a few of the oriental prelates knew enough to understand something, at least, of the speeches. Some, no doubt, fancied they understood more than they did; nevertheless, many had studied at seminaries where the lectures were still given in Latin and were accustomed to listening to speeches in this language. But each spoke Latin with the accent of his own country—the French nasalizing it, the English mouthing it, the Italians caressing it. Was not all this a re-enactment of the Pentecostal miracle, by which Parthians, Medes, Elamites, and the rest heard, each in his own language, "the wonderful works of God"?

For the first time in human history there were mitred prelates from the American continent. At the time of the last Council, that of Trent, America had been discovered only half a century before, so that not a single representative of North or South America was among the Tridentine Fathers. Australia had not even been discovered at all. Now the Americans and Australians mingled with the rest. A Chinese bishop had traveled over twenty thousand miles, taking weeks to journey through the interior of China to the Yangtse-Kiang, and thence down the river and by sea for a voyage of many months to Rome. Was not this truly the most representative Council of the Roman Communion the world had ever seen?

Let us see how representative it was in fact. Out of 1,037 prelates eligible according to the papal view, over 700 were present on the first day of the Council, and within a short time there were 766.[1] Of these 766 prelates, 541 came from Europe, and of these the number coming from present and former States of the Church was 206. The number of prelates from the island of Sardinia was 25, while the whole of Germany was represented by 19. The little Kingdom of Naples had 65, and together with Venice (8) and the islands of Sicily and Malta (13) had two representatives more than the whole of France—the "eldest daughter of the Church," which at that time had a population of thirty-four millions. The islands of Sicily, Sardinia and Malta had almost as many as the whole of

---

[1] Cf. the numbers at the first session of Trent: according to Cardinal Pallavicino (Le Plat and Sarpi give slightly different figures), 3 legates, 4 archbishops, 20 bishops, and 5 generals of religious orders.

Spain. The Kingdom of Naples had actually more than twice the representation of the entire continent of South America, preponderantly Latin and Catholic, and more than ten times that of the very loyal Roman Catholic kingdom of Belgium. Ireland (20) had more than three times the representation accorded to Belgium, and twice that of Austria and the Tyrol together. Most striking of all, perhaps, out of the 541 prelates from Europe, the Italian peninsula, with a population of 27 millions, was represented by 276, 11 more than the whole of the rest of the continent including Britain and Ireland. How small Italian dioceses can be may be judged from the fact that the distance between the cathedral city of Amalfi and the cathedral city of Ravello is little more than half the length of Central Park in New York City.

Even more horrifying is the fact that those of the Papal States that had not at that time yet been seized, and which had a population of less than three-quarters of a million, were represented by sixty-two bishops, while five million Roman Catholics elsewhere were represented by three bishops—those of Paris, Cambrai and Cologne—all three critical of the standpoint of the papalist party.

But let us concede that it was not according to the tradition of the Roman Church that dioceses should all be the same size. Let us suppose that it just so happened that Italian dioceses were small compared with even the parishes of some other countries. After all, who dare lay down any inflexible rule that to every shepherd ought always to be assigned a fixed proportion of the sheep? Might it not be in the wise Providence of God that Belgian sheep needed but half a dozen shepherds, while the Neapolitan sheep might have strayed headlong into the Gulf of Sorrento had they had fewer than sixty-five crosiers to hold them back?

In many cases, however, since the shepherds were not in charge of any sheep at all, they could hardly be called shepherds. It is true that, as we learn from Dom Cuthbert Butler, Protestant controversialists tended afterwards to exaggerate the number of the bishops without dioceses.[2] But there were many. There were, more-

[2] *The Vatican Council*, Vol. I, p. 262.

over, many prelates who were not even in the episcopate. Apart from some of the cardinals not in episcopal orders,[3] there were six abbots *nullius dioceseos*, twenty-three abbots-general of monastic orders, and twenty-nine generals and vicars-general of congregations of clerks regular, monastic orders, and mendicant orders, who were accounted entitled to be present,[4] and of these over fifty were present in fact. It was calculated in an anonymous pamphlet circulated in Rome after the Council had been in operation for five months and attributed to Mgr. Darboy, Archbishop of Paris, that one hundred and ninety-five members of the Council had no constitutional right to be there at all. "The Council includes," affirmed this document, "besides diocesan bishops, whose right alone is beyond dispute, bishops with no dioceses, vicars apostolic dependent on Rome and removable at will; cardinals who are not bishops and in some cases not even priests, and superiors of religious orders." It is also mentioned that "a considerable number of bishops are being maintained by the Pope, which increases the difficulties of real independence."[5] There were at the very least forty bishops who may be suspected of having been in this unenviable position, and of twenty-three cardinals *in curia* and the fifty or more prelates who came as monastic superiors and the like, many were more closely tied to Rome than even the least independent bishop. Nor is it likely that *all* the eighteen bishops from Hindustan and Cochin China were bishops in the sense in which, say, the Bishop of Cambrai was a bishop.

Georges Darboy, to whom the anonymous pamphlet was attributed, merits respect. He was born in Haute Marne in 1813. He became Bishop of Nancy in 1859, and Archbishop of Paris in 1863. A strong defender of episcopal independence, he may be said to have been representative of the old Gallican tradition. He actively

[3] Cardinals, though many of them are bishops, need not even be priests.
[4] The full list, showing the disposition of the prelates invited, according to office and rank, is set forth in the *Lexicon geographicum* in the *Acta et Decreta*. See Bibliography. Objections had been raised at the first session of the Council of Trent, three hundred years earlier, to the voting powers of such non-bishops. See Chapter 6.
[5] See Bibliography.

sought to suppress the activities of the Jesuits within his jurisdiction, and at the Vatican Council his opposition to the doctrine of Papal Infallibility was undisguised. Afterwards, in the Franco-Prussian War, he remained at his post in Paris while the city was under siege, and during the brief victory of the Communards, who, in April 1871, arrested him as a hostage. The following month he was shot in prison, with some others, and died uttering words of blessing and forgiveness. His body was eventually recovered and given a public funeral. He had commanded such great personal respect during his life that it was not only as a high dignitary of the Church that his testimony was weighty.

The composition of the Council, then, was not only very Italianate,[6] but included at least a hundred dignitaries whose right to be there was, to say the least, questionable. Of these at least thirty or forty (probably many more) were in a position of such extreme dependence on the Pope that they could hardly have expressed views against Papal Infallibility.

At a generous estimate, not more than one hundred and fifty of the prelates knew Greek well enough to understand the sense of the original text of those passages of the Greek Fathers that were used in the course of the discussions. Nor was a genuine reverence for history anywhere predominant in the deliberations of the Council. Archbishop Manning had already said that appeal to history was "a treason and a heresy," and wherever such an appeal was made in criticism of the papalist position, it was met with extreme coldness, if not something worse.

No assembly of seven hundred persons can work without committees, and it was natural that such should be appointed. Commissions of experts in theology and canon law had prepared the agenda of the Council, the schemata. The plan was that these schemata would be discussed in the General Congregation of the Council, but when difficulties arose, as they were certain to do, these would be referred to four committees, called, respectively,

<hr />

[6] Not only were there more Italian members than members of any other European race or nation; eventually, the five presidents of the Council were Italian.

(1) the Deputation on Faith, (2) the Deputation on Discipline, (3) the Deputation on Regulars,[7] and (4) the Deputation on the Eastern Churches and the Missions. Of these by far the most important was the Deputation on Faith.

Even Dom E. C. Butler admits that, when the extremist parties had met to try to get their nominees on the Deputation on Faith, the inner ring of infallibilists drew up a list of twenty-four names and gave out this list to the members of the Council as being approved by Cardinal De Angelis who was a member of great influence and who later became president of the Council. As a result of whatever one may care to call this remarkable maneuver, the whole list was elected, so that the Minority party had not a single representative on it. This E. C. Butler regarded as "the one serious blot" on the doings of the Council.[8] It was certainly not an inconspicuous blot that the election of the most important committee in a General Council of the Roman Church was secured by means of a trick. The fact that the trick did nothing to mollify the minority and may even have hampered the cause, as Abbot B. C. Butler suggests,[9] does not improve one's confidence in the Council's methods, or increase one's admiration for the papalist party. Abbot Butler says that a balanced historian, though he may find "his sense of propriety is offended" by such doings, ought not to be unduly affected by all this.[10] Elsewhere, however, and even in secular assemblies, there is a tendency to discredit men who behave even once in such a fashion.

During the early months, the Council was officially occupied with setting forth the attitude of the Church concerning views such as rationalism and pantheism, and the faith of the Church concerning her own nature. This involved lengthy discussion about the relations between Church and State, and the question of the Tem-

[7] Regulars are priests living under monastic vows, contradistinguished from priests living in the world and bound only by their ordination vows of celibacy.
[8] *The Vatican Council*, Vol. I, p. 158 f.
[9] *The Church and Infallibility*, p. 96.
[10] *Op. cit., loc. cit.*

poral Power of the papacy. Many observations and amendments were, in the course of the Council's proceedings, sent back to the Deputation on these subjects. The question of infallibility, which was uppermost in the minds of the Fathers, was being discussed only behind the scenes, between the formal sessions. The papalists were becoming very impatient. It looked as though the all-important subject might not come on till the summer, when the heat of Rome might make an adjournment a practical necessity. The Pope, however, upheld his policy of determining to say nothing officially to influence the Fathers. "I, Giovanni Mastai, believe in and accept infallibility, but as Pope I do not ask anything of the Council. The Holy Ghost will enlighten it." [11]

At the same time he lost no opportunity of expressing his own private opinion on the subject, and the views he so expressed were blazed abroad in the press of almost every civilized country in the world. For the Pope himself was now growing impatient. An out-spoken letter by Montalembert against the infallibilist position had annoyed Pius, and in March he wrote to the Abbot of Solesmes a very remarkable letter in which he called those who were express-ing such views on the subject instead of waiting patiently for the outcome of the divinely inspired Council "bold, foolish, irrational, impudent, uncharitable and violent." [12] He especially deplored the fashionable use of the term "ultramontane." It was "the general-ity" [13] of the Church, he objected, that was being so dubbed by its adversaries.[14] By the following month the Pope was becoming so enraged by the activities of those whose opinions differed from his own on a subject which the Council had not yet even debated, that he at last favorably received the request of Manning and his asso-ciates that the question of Papal Infallibility be taken out of turn and, after the preparation of the necessary papers, discussed at

[11] Pelcząr, *Pio Nono e il suo pontificato*, Vol. II, p. 525.

[12] This seems unnecessarily strong language for a Pope who believed not only in the infallibility of the Council, but that he had this infallibility him-self, even without it. See Chapter 8.

[13] *reliquam omnem Catholicorum familiam.*

[14] *Civiltà Cattolica*, VII, Vol. X, p. 222 *et al.*

the earliest opportunity. This debate was opened in the General Congregation on May 13.

In the meantime, the Minority had been no less active than the Majority. But their field of action was, in the nature of the case, different. The Majority knew well they had few supporters in the civil governments of the world. Their work was done, therefore, mainly in episcopal huddles in Rome. The Minority, on the other hand, while not underestimating the strength of the ecclesiastical forces on the side of the Pope, staked considerable hopes on political influence from the world outside to bring pressure to bear on the Council and so prevent the passing of the Decree.

The Minority were by this time well organized under the leadership of Mgr. Dupanloup, Bishop of Orleans, a figure of impressive dignity and a genuinely able and wise man whose breadth of vision was matched by his persuasive eloquence. His humanitarian and internationalist sympathies are shown in his *Letter on Slavery*, written on the occasion of the American Civil War. His influence in high circles in France was due in no small measure to the respect that his moderation and personal dignity commanded. Born out of wedlock in Savoie, in 1802, Félix-Antoine-Philibert Dupanloup was taken by his devoted mother to Paris at the age of seven to help him avoid the stigma of illegitimacy. There she toiled to keep him at the Collège Sainte-Barbe, so that he might have an education that would equip him for whatever profession he might be led to by his own inclinations. Her sacrifices for her son were repaid by his lifelong gratitude and devotion. Eventually choosing the priesthood, he was ordained on December 18, 1825, and became curate at the Madeleine and religious instructor to the Duc de Bordeaux and the Princes d'Orléans. Both before and after his appointment as a Canon of Notre Dame de Paris in 1845 he enjoyed a great reputation as a preacher and spiritual director, and from 1849 till his death in 1878 he was widely renowned for his zeal and eloquence as the Bishop of Orleans, and for his immense literary output. Throughout his life one of his most dominant interests was the education of the young, and in his educational work he anticipated modern developments in a way that showed him to be far in advance of his time. Deploring the notion that education is a mere infusion of knowledge into the brains of pupils, he regarded it as a process of developing mental activity, and insisted, therefore, that teachers must respect the freedom of their pupils. The methods he advocated may even be said to have foreshadowed the modern American "honor system." The sincerity of his role as leader of the Minority at the Vatican Council was all the more evident by reason of the zeal with which he had for long defended the papacy against its detractors. But he was set against the infallibilists, and labored indefatigably against them behind the scenes.

Behind the scenes also were what Louis Veuillot called the *Commères du Concile*, the ladies who, in fashionable Roman society, talked gaily and wittily about the question of Papal Infallibility. Such unofficial assemblies were too useful to be ignored by any prelate who had the interest of either party at heart. They were important arenas of combat, not least for the papalist side, for these ladies were predominantly inclined to infallibilist opinions. A word skilfully dropped into the proper ear could bear fruit in the Council. Many of the Fathers who had come to Rome with no strong views on either side and no special knowledge of the intricacies of the subject were unmoved, except to boredom, by the long disquisitions of the eloquent leaders in the official debates of the Council. In the less somber, more genial atmosphere of a *salon*, however, they might be convinced by a few persuasive words when hours of Latin argumentation had failed.

The Minority bishop who, according to Dupanloup, was the one man in the Council whose speeches and incisive observations were making the suppression of the Minority impossible, was Mgr. Strossmayer, Bishop of Bosnia, on the Turkish frontier. Born in 1815 of German peasant stock, Joseph Strossmayer was ordained to the priesthood in 1838 and raised to the episcopate in 1850. He was, politically, a supporter of the Croatian National Party and a Panslavist. Coming from eastern Europe he was deeply conscious of the feelings there against anything that savored of papal autocracy, for it was such feelings, as much as anything else, that had kept the Eastern Church for eight centuries separated from the Latin West. Strossmayer, in his endeavors to win over the separated Eastern Christians and bring them within the Roman fold, made use of the Old Slavonic Liturgy, which had been used in some churches in Dalmatia since the ninth century. His loyalty to Rome was therefore as manifest as was that of Dupanloup; but his opposition to the infallibilists was even more vehement.

On March 22, the Council had under its consideration a schema, the introduction to which referred to modern rationalism as one of the errors that Protestantism had brought in its train.[15] This was so absurd as to be not even good anti-Protestant pamphleteering. Cardinal Prince Schwarzenberg, a prelate of commanding appearance, handsome features and great eloquence, objected to this gratuitous attack on Protestants, and thanked God that the days of mutual cursings between Catholics and Protestants were now passed. Then Bishop Strossmayer ascended the tribune. In a remarkable speech, Strossmayer expressed his view, as a loyal Roman Catholic bishop, that while Protestants had indeed been guilty of great errors, nevertheless the germ of modern rationalism was to be found in the humanistic Renaissance which, as every historian knows, was even more distasteful to the Protestant Reformers than it was to the medieval Roman Church. "This judgment," he said, referring to the historical blunder contained in the schema under discussion, "seems to me to be consistent neither with truth nor with charity." He also reminded the Council that modern rationalism originated in the contempt for the faith (a contempt they all of course deplored) that arose, not in a Protestant country, but in France. By way of contrast, he went on to speak of those who, though nurtured in Protestant error, were nevertheless good men. Despite their misguided opinions, they championed Christian truths that Roman Catholics and Protestants hold in common. Paraphrasing St. Augustine, he said the Protestants erred, but erred in good faith. He drew special attention to the fact that to the very errors

[15] Modern rationalism had been explicitly condemned in the *Syllabus*.

the Council was now bound to consider, Roman Catholics had never given any more vigorous refutation than had Protestants such as Leibniz and Guizot, to whom all Christians were deeply indebted.

The bare mention of these two famous names in the history of thought evoked indignant murmuring, and the president rang the bell and remarked that this was not the place to praise Protestants. (*Non est hicce locus laudandi Protestantes.*) In spite of this comment on what was, after all, only a routine observation such as any honest historian would have felt it natural to make, Strossmayer went on to show that there were a great many people in Protestant countries such as England and America and Germany who erred in good faith.

"Shame, shame! Down with the heretic!" cried some of the prelates.

Strossmayer continued. He went on to criticize the methods of the Council, as he had already done on previous occasions, not without some effect even on such an assembly. The Council, he said, lacked both freedom and truth. "A Council that disregards the old rule of the necessity of moral unanimity, and begins to decide propositions that concern faith and morals by a majority of votes, will, according to my deepest conviction, forfeit the right to bind the conscience of the Catholic world on condition of eternal life and death." [16]

To the papalist party, these were indeed fighting words, and there were fresh shouts from all sides: "Get down from the pulpit, heretic! Heretic! Heretic! We condemn him! (*Damnamus eum.*)"

According to some reports, several of the prelates got up from their seats at this point and shook their fists in his face.

One voice was heard, however, out of harmony with their shouts. It was that of Mgr. Place, the Bishop of Marseilles, who was on the side of the minority. "*I* do not condemn you," he said.

This evoked a concerted and emphatic shout that seemed to come

[16] The Latin text of the salient parts of Strossmayer's speech is given in Acton's *History of Freedom and other Essays,* p. 541 f.

from every side: "*All* of us, *all* of us condemn him! (*Omnes, omnes illum damnamus.*)"

So history that was only an instant old could be repudiated too.

The president had been ringing his bell almost continuously throughout the uproar, and the bishop who had appealed to history at last descended, shouting above the din: "I protest! I protest! I protest!"

Of this scene Cardinal Gibbons later wrote:

His [Strossmayer's] name figured conspicuously during and after its [the Council's] proceedings, and he felt obliged to repudiate certain hostile sentiments towards the Holy See that had been falsely imputed to him.[17] His discourses were always sure to captivate, if they did not convince, his hearers. His periods flowed with the grace and majesty and musical rhythm of a Cicero. By a masterly arrangement of words, which the genius of the Latin tongue allows so much better than our own, he would bring out the strong points of his discourse at the close of each sentence in some well-rounded phrase. Occasionally in the heat of his oration he would wander from his subject *into a forbidden field.*[18] An expression of disapproval would come from some Bishops, and then the patient President, yielding to the remonstrance, would stretch his hand toward the bell, the ringing of which was the signal that the speaker was out of order. When the Bishop would see the hand in close proximity to the bell he would dexterously return to his subject, and thus avoid the humiliation of an admonition.[19]

It is a fascinating picture that the American cardinal draws. One can almost see the eloquent prelate hard at work trying to distract the attention of the president (Cardinal de Angelis, a zealous infallibilist), eyeing him perhaps to detect signs, it might be, of somnolence. Then the quick-change by stealth from the grandiose parts to a few sharp blasts of historical criticism, all with one eye on the president's fist. For within the time it took for the latter to get the directive from the presidential brain and reach the bell

---

[17] Strossmayer was the last of the protesting bishops to submit to the Decrees of the Council. He refused his consent till December 26, 1872. *Infra,* p. 63.

[18] Italics mine.

[19] From an article in *The North American Review,* 1894, reprinted in *A Retrospect of Fifty Years,* Vol. I, p. 26 f.

whose ping was law, the intrepid Bishop of Bosnia must have the dexterity to hare back from his run of freedom to his wicket of papal orthodoxy, and end up by unsmilingly acknowledging the decision of the umpire of Vatican cricket.

The sequel to the Strossmayer incident is illuminating. The following day a written protest was submitted, demanding a plain answer to the question of how far moral unanimity was required. Strossmayer went so far as to say that if a plain answer were not forthcoming, then he should have to face the question whether he could remain in a Council where the freedom of bishops was suppressed and where dogmas were to be defined in a fashion that was new and alien to the indisputably established and ancient practice of the Church of God. This protest was signed by several bishops.

At length, after the great ceremonies of Holy Week and Easter, the third public session of the Council took place on April 4, the first Sunday after Easter. The prelates were in their places by nine o'clock in the morning. The Noble Guard and the Knights of Malta[20] were on duty. High Mass was celebrated by Cardinal Bilio. Once again the *Veni Creator* was sung and prayers offered with the doors of the Council Chamber open, so that the crowds might see the resplendent scene. Pius, wearing a richly-embroidered cope, was seated on a throne. On either side of him sat the cardinals, mitred and in their most gorgeous robes, and in front of them the patriarchs. The other archbishops and bishops wore white mitres and copes of red lama, except for the orientals in their multicolored copes and multijewelled tiaras. In sombre contrast were the heads of the religious orders in their plain black, white, or brown habits.

Monsignor Valenziani ascended the pulpit and read, in his strong, clear voice, the Dogmatic Constitution.[21] It took forty-five minutes, at the end of which he asked the formal question: did the Most

---

[20] The Knights of Malta belong to a Sovereign Order standing in a special relationship to the Holy See. On its present status in international law, see article "The Sovereign Order of Malta in International Law" by C. D'O. Farran, in *The International and Comparative Law Quarterly*, April, 1954.

[21] That is, excluding *Pastor Aeternus*, the Constitution on the Primacy and Infallibility of the Pope, which was still to be debated. See Appendix I.

Eminent and Most Reverend Fathers approve of the canons and decrees they had heard?

Descending, he gave place to Monsignor Jacobini, who called for the votes. As the prelates signified their approval, some in a weak, aged voice, giving their "aye" in the customary word, *placet*, first one usher and then a second repeated the word clearly, so that soon there was a chorus of *placets*. When Strossmayer's name was called the ushers replied *abest*. He had stayed away that day. But not one vote was cast in the negative. The voting took about two hours, at the end of which the Pope addressed the Fathers:

> Most reverend brethren, you behold how good and sweet it is to walk together in concord in the Lord's House. Ever walk thus! And as our Lord and Saviour Jesus Christ on this day said to his apostles, "Peace," I, his unworthy vicar, say unto you, in his Name, Peace. Peace, as you know, casts out fear. Peace, as you know, closes our ears to evil words. May that peace go with you all the days of your life. May it console you and give you strength in death. May it be to you everlasting joy in heaven.

Prayers followed; then the *Te Deum*. The third session of the Council was closed, in an atmosphere of complete unanimity. The preamble and the first four chapters of the Dogmatic Constitution[22] had now been irrevocably passed by the Fathers. There remained to be discussed, at a further session, the highly controversial subject of Papal Infallibility.

On May 13, the great debate was opened by Mgr. Pie, Bishop of Poitiers,[23] who, in the name of the Deputation on Faith, expounded the proposed text of the Decree on the Primacy and Infallibility of the Roman Pontiff—a document also consisting of a preamble and four chapters. The text had already been distributed to the Fathers. They had made their observations on it to the Deputation, which sent a printed report of their opinion to each prelate. Next day, the discussion was begun by Cardinal Patrizi, followed by the Archbishop of San Francisco and others.

By far the most important papalist actor in the drama, excepting

[22] See Appendix I.
[23] Mansi, LII, 722.

only Pius himself, was the English convert, Henry Edward Manning. Manning's father had been a rich West Indian merchant who in later life drove daily from his country seat into London, where he was a Governor of the Bank of England and a Member of Parliament. Born in 1807, Manning was brought up in an atmosphere of Evangelical piety and had at first found his father's plans for making him into a churchman very much against his grain. At Oxford he was Gladstone's senior by a year and was a success at the Union, the training ground of English politicians and statesmen. But, like many another young Englishman of his time, he was led, perhaps more from force of circumstance than any positive sense of vocation, into taking Holy Orders in the Church of England, in which, after his wife's premature death, he became an archdeacon. He had a gift for administration and the prospect of a bishopric in due time. Under the influence of those of the English Tractarians who had followed Newman's leadership and gone over to the Church of Rome, he began to think of such a way for himself. It was not, however, an intellectual compulsion that led him to be received, on April 6, 1851, into the Roman Church. Not long before this event he had written in his diary: "I feel as if a light had fallen upon me. My feeling about the Roman Church is not intellectual. I have intellectual difficulties, but the great moral difficulties seem melting." Manning never claimed to be a learned man. In later life, speaking of his own writings, he said: "I am not, like Newman, a poet, or a writer of novels, or of an autobiography, but a priest and a priest only." He had indeed many affinities with Pius himself and, sharing the latter's ecclesiastical romanticism and unconcern with history, he was in many ways a living translation into English of the Italian Pontiff's mind. Conceiving of intellectual controversy only as a game, he once declared: "We must be able to play dominoes with those with whom we argue." In his personal weaknesses he likewise exhibited the Pope's temper, anglicized. One of his admirers, W. G. Ward, noticed that Manning was strongest when being attacked in the *Times,* and that when he was, on the contrary, praised by the *Times,* he tended to vacillate and hold up the silver side of the shield. "We ought therefore to pray," Ward added smilingly, "that Manning may be attacked every morning by the *Times*." By the time Manning, now Archbishop of Westminster, had launched into the debate on Papal Infallibility in public session at the Vatican Council, he had not only been widely attacked, but had earned for himself the nickname of "the Devil of the Council" (*il diavolo del Concilio*), and it betrays the attitude of his mind that he delighted in the name, accepting it as a compliment. The office of Compline reminds priests that the Devil "goes about like a roaring lion, seeking whom he may devour," and Manning, thinking perhaps of his own attitude towards the anti-infallibilists, liked the analogy. Certainly when he read his nickname in the Italian newspapers, he called it "the noblest of titles."

By a series of complicated moves, Manning succeeded in presenting a case to Mr. Odo Russell, the British Agent in Rome, which so convinced the British cabinet that Papal Infallibility was a matter of merely ecclesiastical interest, not of political concern, that, despite Gladstone's protests, the British Government declined to interfere. Other governments generally took a similar attitude.

The discussion that Dom Cuthbert Butler calls "the Crucial Debate" began on May 25, when Manning opened his speech by asserting that Papal Infallibility had been "taught by the common and constant *magisterium* of the Church" and had been recognized *in practice* by the Third Council of Constantinople and the Second of Lyons. He cited Bellarmine and other Jesuit writers. He admitted that there had been for two centuries many who were guilty of the grave error of denying Papal Infallibility, and from the fact that this denial had led to controversy and uncertainty, he argued, it seems, that the remedy was obvious: proclaim the doctrine now! He reminded the Fathers of the large number of converts to Rome that had been coming over for a generation, and urged that nothing could hinder the progress of the Roman Church in England more than controversies among her members, especially any dispute about the foundation of the certainty of faith, namely, the infallible *magisterium* of the Pope. Since the publication of the *Syllabus,* he lamented, not only Protestants but Catholics also had derided Papal Infallibility as a novel doctrine invented since the Council of Constance.[24]

Manning then proceeded to quote the English Protestant press, which, he showed, believed that Papal Infallibility was the logical consequence of Roman doctrine. One might have supposed the Protestant press to be an inapposite authority for a Roman Catholic archbishop to quote in support of a doctrine he wanted promulgated at the Vatican Council. But Manning knew his audience. He was more concerned to win his case than to put a good argument on record.

The Council of Florence, he held, had plainly *implied* Papal Infallibility, though it had not defined it. Nevertheless, perverse interpretation had distorted the truth so as to admit the juridical power of the Pope in the Church without recognizing his doctrinal *magisterium.* If only doubt on the subject had been removed at Trent, the Church would have been spared the "bitter fruit" of Gallicanism.

Beginning with the assertion that Papal Infallibility *is* true doctrine, he had, of course, no difficulty in showing that it was a pity the truth had not been more speedily recognized. Even some of the infallibilists could not swallow this whole, and two bishops protested against Manning's statement that the doctrine was already an article of Faith in the Roman Church. Manning took no notice of the fact that the almost unanimous proclamation of the Council of Constance against Papal Infallibility,[25] and the vehement affirmations against it by generations of French divines, had gone unrebuked by the papacy in any clear utterance such as it would have been so easy for the papacy to make.[26] He was concerned, as was

[24] The Fathers of Constance had ordained in 1415 that "This Holy Synod . . . has received immediately from Christ a power to which all persons, of whatever rank or dignity, not excepting the Pope himself, are bound to submit in matters concerning the Faith." See Mansi XXVII, 590 f.; also *infra.*

[25] *Supra.*

[26] See Chapter 8.

the Irish bishop who followed him in debate,[27] to demonstrate the practical advisability of promulgating the doctrine, rather than to establish an historical, constitutional case for it.

The next speech came from the Opposition. The speaker, Bishop Clifford of Clifton, turned Manning's own arguments against him. Manning had said that the infallibility of the Pope and the infallibility of the Church were inseparable questions. Clifford objected that it was, therefore, a mistake to separate them as the schema did. Referring to Manning's allusion to the conversion of England, Clifford pointed out that the first thing one had to show an Englishman was that the Roman Church was not despotic in character, since it was a primary contention, among English Protestants, that she was. If the proposed Decree were promulgated it would confirm this English Protestant prejudice. He went on to point out that all the Roman Catholic catechisms in England insisted on the infallibility of the Church, but assumed that no doctrine could ever come to be accounted infallible unless it had first been discussed and passed by a General Council. It was thus, he said, that converts in his own diocese were instructed, and his clergy, in so instructing them, were following the method of Cardinal Wiseman's[28] famous lectures, *The Teaching and Practice of the Catholic Church.* The doctrine now proposed was irreconcilable with that which his people had hitherto heard concerning the infallibility of the Church. It would appear to be new to them as well as to Protestants. He had been bombarded with protests from both clergy and people, from both converts and born Catholics, and he had assured them all that Rome never acted too hastily.

Moreover, the hope of the Roman Church seemed to lie more in converts than in born Catholics. The countries which caused most grief to the Church were Italy, Spain, and South America, while in England, Germany, and North America, the Church was vigorous. In these latter countries she was more free than she was

[27] Mgr. MacEvilly, Bishop of Galway.
[28] Wiseman was Manning's predecessor as Archbishop of Westminster.

in those of the Mediterranean. In France the freedom of teaching had, furthermore, been vindicated. Most of this was due to the efforts of bishops and clergy whose opinions on Papal Infallibility would be condemned by the proposed Decree. He went on to allege that those who wished to promulgate the Decree had no idea how, in England and America, the faithful lived among Protestants, depending much upon good will between these and themselves.

When the Council began, he continued, one of the most important assurances was that it would be fully admitted that the bishops in Council were real judges, and that it was for them to judge matters of faith together with the Pope. The Bishop of Edessa, however, had just published a book in Rome which denied this. There was, he observed, great confusion in discussions on the subject, for often, though the Fathers were discussing the same point verbally, they were really talking about different things. He ended with a plea that the Opposition bishops, many of whom were struggling to propagate the Faith in heretical lands, should be treated as the brethren of the others, not simply as subjects for conversion.

The assembly was then prorogued for three days, and on May 28 the discussion was resumed in a speech by Senestréy, Archbishop of Regensburg, who was on the infallibilist side. The thirteenth-century Albertus Magnus, whose authority he invoked, affirmed only the supremacy of the Pope, not his infallibility. The other authorities he cited were mainly Jesuits.

He was followed by Vérot of Savannah, who gave evidence from Scripture and from the Fathers of the Church down to recent times. Vérot's speeches in the Council were often amusing, and indeed he was rebuked on more than one occasion for his jests (*facetiae*) and tomfooleries (*scurrae*). But there was profound wisdom in his jests, many of which were barbed, so that they were naturally distasteful to the infallibilists, who affected to treat him as a jester instead of taking his arguments with the seriousness they certainly demanded. Dom Cuthbert Butler, in his account in

The Vatican Council, would have us believe that Vérot was justly rebuked. It is difficult to see why. His demands for arguments to refute what he was saying went largely unheeded by the infallibilists, and these demands were eminently reasonable to anyone who was approaching the subject with an open mind as the Fathers were, in theory, undertaking to do.

There is much evidence that the infallibilists used their influence to make it impossible for the Opposition to publish anything in Rome while the Council was sitting, although they encouraged or allowed their own party to publish there. This would seem to be an outrage against the most elementary freedom to which the members of the Council were entitled. The infallibilist Bishop of Edessa had published a book in Rome while the Council was sitting. But anything that the Opposition bishops wrote had to be published elsewhere and then circulated in Rome as well as their authors could contrive. One of the most devastating criticisms of the doctrine of Papal Infallibility was written by the American Archbishop Kenrick of St. Louis.[29]

Peter Richard Kenrick was a remarkable man. He had come to America as a young Irish priest at the invitation of his brother, also a priest. When his brother became a bishop he appointed Peter, despite his youth, president of his diocesan seminary. During the next seven years Peter Kenrick labored with his brother, producing at the same time theological writings that brought him a considerable reputation for learning. When he was in Rome, at the age of thirty-four, he met Rosati, the Bishop of St. Louis, who was so impressed by him that he petitioned to have him raised to the episcopate as his associate (coadjutor). Rosati died soon afterwards and Kenrick, succeeding him, found himself in charge of a diocese whose affairs were in a very grave condition in every way: there was a heavy debt, for example, on the Cathedral, and little zeal among the faithful towards the process of diminishing it. There were few churches, and not enough clergy even for these. The diocese was enormous, and Kenrick often had to ride hundreds of

[29] See Bibliography.

miles on horseback, lodging by the way in log cabins and huts. By his energy and able administration, Kenrick not only paid off the debt on the Cathedral in gold, but so immensely developed his diocese that it was raised to an archdiocese of such a flourishing condition that it eventually had to be divided up into sixteen separate dioceses. By the time of the Vatican Council, Kenrick was sixty-four years old.[30] Gibbons recalls the ease and elegance of his Latin, when he was speaking, without notes, in the Council's deliberations.[31]

Kenrick's speech, published at Naples during the Council, was a masterpiece in the presentation of scholarly evidence. He was not allowed to deliver it, on the ground that it was too long. It is true that in such assemblies one cannot be expected to endure all the harangues that long-winded speakers may inflict on the patience of the members. But Kenrick's speech contained less than 13,000 words, and in view of his high rank as an archbishop, his recognized eminence in character and learning, and, above all, his indefatigable service to the Roman Church in a lifetime of difficult missionary endeavor and his spectacular success, he was surely entitled to be heard. His published but undelivered speech is well worth the most careful scrutiny. But let us here examine only a few specially interesting points.

While acknowledging the primacy of the Roman Pontiff over the whole Church, a primacy both of honor and of jurisdiction, Kenrick insists, "but when I say primacy, I do not mean domination." He goes on to deny that there is any authority in the early Fathers for the modern interpretation of Scripture that gives Peter the kind of independence that the modern theory of Papal Infallibility implies. "I do indeed admit that Peter was granted a privilege beyond all the rest, on the testimony not of Scripture but of all Christian antiquity, but on condition that he shall take counsel of his brethren, shall be helped in judgment by these colleagues in this supreme office, and being their head and mouthpiece, should speak

[30] He died at the age of eighty-five.
[31] *A Retrospect of Fifty Years*, Vol. I, p. 22 f.

in their name." After considering certain rather technical questions he proceeds to deny that the doctrine of Papal Infallibility, in the sense indicated in the schema, *could* (that is, constitutionally) be proposed:

I hold that it is no doctrine of faith, nor can be proposed as such even by conciliar definition.

Definitions of faith are not a stimulus to piety; still less are they triumphal flourishes of scholastic decisions on one side or the other. They are authoritative expositions of dogmas of the faith, generally warning us against the aberrations of innovators. They never impose a new faith. I say, on these grounds, that papal infallibility is not a doctrine of faith.

1: It is not in the Creeds; nor is it mentioned in the Catechisms as an article of faith; nor is it found in any liturgical record. Therefore the Church has not hitherto taught it as something which must be accepted *de fide*. Yet, if it had been a doctrine of faith, the Church ought to have handed it down and taught it.

2: The Church not only has never taught it in any public document; she has permitted it to be controverted, not everywhere, but in almost every land except Italy, and for long. All this is well known and beyond contradiction. Innocent XI gave approval on two occasions to Bossuet's *Exposition of Faith,* in which infallibility is not only never mentioned but seems plainly alluded to by what is said concerning " 'free' matters that are disputed among theologians." I may say of all the English-speaking peoples that this opinion is not mentioned among the verities of faith in any of their books on the Creed or the Catechism.

The whole mass of books on faith and piety, down to the beginning of this century and beyond, have passed from England to Ireland and the United States. In several of them a negative decision is given. In none of them is the doctrine treated as *de fide*. . . .

We did indeed know that a school of theologians, whom we were in the habit of calling "ultramontanes," defended Papal Infallibility in a sense different from that of other theologians, and more favourable to the pontifical privileges; and this opinion, after the book *Du Pape,* by the eminent De Maistre,[32] had been translated into English, has had a great deal of success amongst clergy and laity, and still has; yet not as a doctrine of faith but as a free opinion. . . .

It is worth while, however, to glance at one of the six appendices

[32] See Bibliography.

which, vital as they are to Kenrick's general argument, are omitted from the official edition of Mansi that prints the speech itself.[33] His Appendix B gives quotations from the principal Irish bishops of the early decades of the nineteenth century to illustrate the kind of answer these conscientiously gave before a British government commission in 1825. During the eighteenth century, Roman Catholics in Britain and Ireland had suffered extreme political disabilities, and while some of these had been removed by the beginning of the nineteenth century, Roman Catholics were still excluded from Parliament, chiefly because of the declaration against transubstantiation which no Roman Catholic could make. One of the characteristic fears of many who felt Roman Catholicism to be fundamentally alien to the British spirit and quite irreconcilable with the "happy constitution in Church and State" which they believed they enjoyed, was that Roman Catholics owed allegiance to an alien *autocrat*. Some said the Romanists actually deified the Pope; others that they regarded him as infallible. Were these weird stores but the tales of popular religious prejudice, or was there sufficient substance in them to make it politically dangerous to grant Roman Catholics the emancipation these claimed through the very eloquent lips of the Irish lawyer, Daniel O'Connell? Plainly, it was a matter for serious inquiry, and a government commission made formal inquiries of Irish[34] Roman Catholic bishops and theologians concerning the question of infallibility. It was in face of the reassuring answers received from these bishops and theologians that the Roman Catholic Relief Act, 1829, was passed,

[33] See Bibliography, note on Kenrick.

[34] There were as yet no English or Scottish Roman Catholic bishops to whom such inquiries might have been addressed. It was not till 1850 that the Roman hierarchy was restored in England, by Pius IX, in face of strong British sentiment against its restoration. Till then Roman Catholics had been under Vicars Apostolic. It was restored in Scotland in 1878.

In 1788, the British Prime Minister Pitt had sought learned opinion on whether the doctrine of the Temporal Power of the Papacy (historically linked with infallibility) was an official doctrine of the Roman Church. Five great seats of learning, traditionally Roman Catholic, assured the British statesman that it was not, and maintained the contrary of the doctrine: Alcalá, Douay, Louvain, Salamanca, and the Sorbonne.

abolishing the declaration against transubstantiation, providing a form of oath to be used by Roman Catholics, and so enabling these to be eligible for membership of Parliament on the same terms as other persons.[35]

The commissioners had asked, in 1825, whether the authority of the Pope in spiritual matters was absolute or limited. Bishop Doyle had answered that it was limited. They asked whether papal authority was under the control of General Councils. Bishop Murray replied:

> That authority is limited by the councils and canons of the Church; he [the Pope] is the executive power of the Church, appointed to preside over it, and enforce its canons or laws. Those canons vest in individuals, for instance in Bishops, certain rights which of course it is the duty of the Pope to protect, and not to violate; his authority is thus limited by those canons.

The commissioners also asked whether the Roman clergy insisted that all the bulls of the Pope were entitled to obedience. From Dr. Oliver Kelly they were assured as follows:

> The Roman Catholic doctrine in respect to Bulls from the Pope is that they are always to be treated with respect; but if those Bulls or Rescripts proceeding from the Pope do contain doctrines or matters which are not compatible with the discipline of the particular Church to which they may be directed, they feel it their duty then to remonstrate respectfully, and not to receive the regulations that may emanate from the Pope.

Bishop Doyle was also asked in what respect the national canons received in Ireland, or any particular construction put upon the general canons, differed from those which are received in other countries. He explained that it might be received in France or Ireland, for instance, that the authority of a General Council was superior to that of the Pope, while in Italy or Spain such a canon might not be received. The crucial question, perhaps, was whether a decree of the Pope in matters of doctrine was valid without the consent of a Council, and to this Bishop Murray answered with admirable plainness: "A decree of the Pope in matters of doctrine

[35] Similar relief for Jews was not provided till 1866.

is not considered binding on Catholics, if it have not the consent of the whole Church, either dispersed or assembled, by its bishops in Council."

One of the Italian prelates who spoke during the special debate that began on June 6 was Cardinal Guidi, Archbishop of Bologna. He was a learned Dominican who had been professor at the Roman University, and knew that Papal Infallibility as it was to be defined was an innovation. His opposition seems to have been peculiarly resented by Pius. Perhaps the latter felt that while a prelate from a distant land might be pardoned for not feeling the beat of the papal pulse, an archbishop of Bologna was without excuse. A remarkable story was spread concerning Cardinal Guidi's interview with Pius on the afternoon of his speech. Dom Butler admits that it is substantially true.[36] "You are my enemy!" said the Pontiff when the Cardinal had been brought into the papal presence. "You are the coryphaeus of the Opposition, and ungrateful! You have taught doctrines that are heretical!" It was when the Cardinal then defended himself by an attempt to appeal to tradition that Pius uttered the now famous words: *La tradizione son' io*. Pius is said to have also rebuked Guidi for having allowed himself to be embraced by Strossmayer. Finally the Cardinal left the papal presence with a request. The irony of its politeness can scarcely be said to be much disguised: "Holy Father, have the goodness to read my speech."

What had the Cardinal Archbishop of Bologna said? He had begun by making the obvious and elementary historical observation that the infallibility of the Pope apart from the rest of the episcopate is a notion that was unknown in the Church till as late as the fourteenth century. He even found passages in Bellarmine and Perrone, the classic late medieval exponents of the doctrine, that were not favorable to it. This evoked rumbles of protest from the Majority and it is said that epithets hurled at him included *birbante* (scoundrel) and *brigantino* (brigand). But, undaunted, he went on to quote St. Thomas Aquinas against the doctrine of

[36] *The Vatican Council*, Vol. II, p. 98.

Papal Infallibility that was proposed. It is little wonder that Pius was displeased; but the papal displeasure against him that afternoon was such as to make credible even another story which would otherwise sound quite apocryphal. When the summer heat of Rome proved too much for some of the prelates unaccustomed to such a climate, requests were made that the sessions should be postponed till some of the members from northern climates (much less friendly, on the whole, to the infallibilist cause), who had taken ill, should recover and be able to take part again. It is said that Pius exclaimed, *Che crepino pure* ("Just let them die").[37] After all, Cardinal Antonelli had pointed out, they would not have stayed long enough to have been taken ill, had they not wasted so much time talking against Papal Infallibility.

When the vote was taken on July 13, on the whole of the Constitution *De Ecclesia*, including the proposed Decree on the infallibility of the Pope, 451 prelates voted *placet* (aye) and 88 *non placet* (no). Of the remainder of the prelates present in Rome or the neighborhood on that day, 62 voted *placet juxta modum* (amendment), while a large number abstained.

On July 15, Darboy, Archbishop of Paris, led a deputation to the Pope, accompanied by Bishop Ketteler of Mainz, another member of the Opposition who is said to have fallen on his knees at the Pope's feet to beg him to prevent the Decree from being promulgated. Pius replied, according to his policy, that the matter was one for the Council, not for him.[38] The following day, at the Pope's request, Darboy gave a written statement to the effect that (a) if a clause such as "the bishops not being excluded" were to be introduced after the words "when exercising the office of pastor and teacher of all nations"; (b) if the clause be removed that had been added at the eleventh hour to the chapter that attributed to the Pope the plenitude of his power; and, (c) if another deletion should be made to a similar effect; then the Opposition would not

[37] Fredrik Nielsen, *The History of the Papacy in the XIXth Century* (tr. A. J. Mason, John Murray, 1906) Vol. II, p. 361.
[38] E. C. Butler, *The Vatican Council*, Vol. II, p. 157.

vote against the Decree at the final session. In the meantime, on the same day, July 16, there were added to the text of the Decree, at the suggestion of some Spanish bishops, certain words especially abhorrent to the Minority.[39]

On Sunday morning, July 17, the Fathers were notified that the fourth public session would be held the following day, Monday, July 18, at nine o'clock in the morning. The Opposition was now plainly vanquished, and its leader, Dupanloup, persuaded those who had not already left Rome to leave in a body, before Monday, so as to avoid voting. In a conventionally polite letter to the Pope, dated July 17, they explained that their departure was due both to their desire not to have to say *non placet* to his face, and to their need to return to their long-unshepherded sheep.[40]

Haynald, Archbishop of Kalocsa, Hungary, traveled by train with Dupanloup from Rome on July 17, the eve of the final session. They were among the fleeing prelates. Dupanloup, just before leaving, had made a last desperate attempt to persuade the Pope to exercise prudence and apostolic moderation when the Council voted for infallibility and to postpone confirmation of the Council's findings till some future date. It is said that when Pius received Dupanloup's letter, he said, "The Bishop of Orleans is mad!"

In a railway compartment the two prelates, Haynald and Dupanloup, looked out on the plains of Lombardy on which the dawn of an historic day was breaking. As he woke in the refreshing cool morning air after the night's journey away from the heavy heat of Rome, the Opposition leader opened his breviary in silence. Haynald leant towards him. "Monseigneur," he said, "we have made a great mistake."

But Dupanloup made a gesture to indicate that he did not wish to discuss the subject.

"We have made a great mistake." The two prelates knew that the final voting would take place in Rome that morning. They knew, too, how great had been their efforts and those of the rest

[39] Appendix I, n. 52.
[40] Mansi, LII, 1325-1326.

of the Minority to avoid what they believed to be calamitous for Christendom. They could not but have felt bitterly unhappy in the choice which, for whatever reasons, they had made in leaving the battle on the eve of the final day.[41]

[41] Maynard, in his biography of Dupanloup, would have us believe that what Haynald was asking the Bishop of Orleans to regret with him was that they had ever opposed the victorious party at all. On this view, Haynald was inviting Dupanloup to join with him in an act of contrition for having been guilty of theological error. Lagrange, on the other hand, thinks that Haynald was expressing his feeling of shame that they had not stayed to the bitter end and boldly voted against the Majority, however overwhelming this might be, and however personally unpleasant for them might be the results of such courageous action. Readers must judge for themselves what the prelate from Hungary is likely, in the circumstances, to have meant when he said to his party's leader, on awakening at dawn in a railway compartment: *Monseigneur, nous avons fait une grande faute.*

4

THE INOPPORTUNIST LEGEND

ON JULY 18, 1870, at the final session of the Vatican Council, there were, out of 535 bishops, two still on the Minority side. These two were Mgr. Riccio, Bishop of Cajazzo, Sicily, and Mgr. Fitzgerald, Bishop of Little Rock, Arkansas. An odd combination of two undistinguished prelates. In the year 325, at the Council of Nicaea, by common consent the most important in the history of Christendom, there had been two bishops who had refused to vote with the majority. Roman Catholics have found in this comparison a token of historical continuity. But in view of our knowledge of the events, the coincidence, far from being provocative of such pious feelings, is uncommonly sinister.

Working at the University of Heidelberg in the spring of 1938, I can well remember the impression created on the politically ill-educated, democracy-spurning crowds in bars and taverns on the banks of the Neckar, when the figures of the Austrian "election" kept coming hourly over the radio. The issue was the absorption of Austria into the German Reich. The results of the election in every locality were remarkably alike. Within Germany the numbers in favor seemed to be always in the neighborhood of 99.5 per cent, while in Austria they were a mere 98.5 per cent. To anyone coming from outside the sphere of Hitler's control, the consistency in the figures suggested something very different from what it provoked in the minds of the German crowds in the taverns of Heidelberg. No doubt they would have seemed still more macabre

54

from inside the precincts of Belsen. The less one knew the more impressive they sounded.

I am not making the absurd suggestion that Pius was in the least like Hitler in his attitudes or actions. His whole outlook was radically different from that of any of the godless dictators of the twentieth century. But though the motives of the papalist party are not comparable to those of secular tyrants, their tactics have this in common: they depend for their efficacy on widespread ignorance of facts.

The result of the final voting bears almost no relation to the history of the debate. It succeeds, on the contrary, in effectively disguising this from those who do not adequately inquire into the story behind it, and to such it supports the legend that has since been discreetly, sometimes even timidly, created by apologists for the papalist cause. This legend is that everyone at the Council, with perhaps the exception of a very few eccentric theorists, really believed in Papal Infallibility; they questioned only the opportuneness of making this, in the particular circumstances that happened to prevail in Europe in 1870, the *official* doctrine of the Roman Church.

Ecclesiastics are, as a class, notoriously inclined, when any course of action is proposed, to question the ripeness of the time for taking it. The story, therefore, that has been increasingly affirmed or insinuated by modern Roman Catholic writers, that the Opposition at the Vatican Council was an opposition of this kind rings true; but it is not true.

Thus, Abbot B. C. Butler writes:

> The word which probably covers best the important part of the elements at the Council is not "Gallican" but "Inopportunist": for reasons differing no doubt to some extent from man to man, they thought it *inexpedient*[1] that the doctrine should be defined, yet, as in Dupanloup's case, this did not necessarily mean, even before the definition, that they rejected the doctrine.[2]

He goes on to quote a letter written by Dupanloup to the Pope,

[1] Abbot Butler italicizes.
[2] *The Church and Infallibility*, p. 94.

in which the leader of the Opposition expresses his views on the
inopportuneness of the proposed Decree.

Dupanloup's personal opinions on the subject are not in fact
clear. He did not fancy himself *persona grata* with Pius, and said
so in another letter in which he implored the Pope to be warned
of the danger of any such move. But Dupanloup was a special
case. He was certainly convinced of the extreme danger of any
action such as was in the Pope's mind, and yet it may well be, as
his language often suggests, that he did personally hold *some* doctrine of Papal Infallibility. If so, what it was he never really made
quite clear.[3] There are many possible doctrines one might hold
about the infallibility of the Church of which the Pope is (according to Roman teaching) the undisputed Head. But it is one thing
to believe, for instance, that as the Head of the Church the Pope
shares in a special measure the infallibility of the Church; another
to believe what Dupanloup and everyone else knew was in the
mind of the Pope and the papalist party, and what they intended
to proclaim. One of the best reasons for thinking a proposed
Decree inopportune is the belief that its terms have not been
carefully or even properly formulated. When we say that a speech
is "unwise," we commonly do not mean merely that it is a good
speech but not a discreet one to make at the time; we more often
mean that it is a speech that is in itself in need of being more
carefully thought out.

But let us suppose, even, that Dupanloup's view is better described as inopportunist. He was the undoubted leader of the
Opposition; but everyone knows that the personal views of the
leader of an Opposition are not necessarily those of the Opposition he leads. His function is to lead a party the members of
which may have many different reasons for opposing the Majority,

[3] Some twenty-five years before the Council, Dupanloup wrote: "The mind
of the Church is implied in a definition *ex cathedra* which is always in
conformity with it. The Pope recognizes it and defines it. He is *caput
ecclesiae*." (Quoted by E. C. Butler, *op. cit.*, Vol. II, p. 116.) This is very
different from what was proclaimed at the Council.

but are united simply by the fact that they wish to hinder or restrain an action that is proposed. Dupanloup, who had indefatigably written an enormous number of letters on the subject, and was in every way an outstanding figure in Europe, was the obvious man for the job; but from his own personal reasons for opposing the papalists on this question, nothing can be inferred concerning the reasons of the members of his party. A party leader might even be known to have quite an unworthy reason, a private interest, say, in the cause of his party; yet he might very well be the inevitable leader. So, even if Dupanloup had been merely a papalist who thought the year 1870 too early in human history for the Roman Church to declare her faith in the doctrine of Papal Infallibility committed by Christ to Peter and now to be set forth in the Dogmatic Constitution *De Ecclesia,* the Opposition might have been mainly composed of men of a very different cast of thought.

It is impossible to be certain about the inward motivations of men. One can only infer these from their words, and, even more, from their actions. The motives of the Opposition as a whole were no doubt mixed. Some did express themselves more in terms of their apprehension about the practical consequences of the proclamation of the doctrine than in terms of their positive disbelief in this. But here the Majority set the example. Manning and the Jesuits were reiterating with baneful monotony their plea that the circumstances, in their opinion, demanded the Decree. In such days as theirs, they contended, when wars and revolutions were in the air, the old conciliar procedure was too slow. It was as out of date in the warfare with the Devil as were bows and arrows in the battles of the world. A General Council might meet and the bishops be cut off by war from returning to their flocks; or they might even be prevented from assembling at all. What the Church needed was a Pope who could act for her absolutely. From the point of view of expediency, there was something to be said for their contentions. They had a good case, though not an incontestable one,[4] so long as only expediency was in question. And expediency is a powerful argument in any assembly. When it is used, the Opposition must take account of it and argue, if it can, inexpediency. But to call the Opposition at the Vatican Council "inopportunists" is, to say the least, no less unfair than it would be to dub the Majority "opportunists."

It is quite true that some of the Minority members of the Council did express their views cautiously. This is hardly surprising. After all, they *were* a minority, and they were a minority in a situation in which, we have abundantly seen, a minority had to be courageous to express itself at all. Some may have seemed very imprudent; others were more prudent in what they said. No one who is accustomed to the ways of ecclesiastical assemblies, Roman or otherwise, will be surprised at finding prudence among prelates. One does not burst into a bishop's room, even if one is oneself a bishop, and speak in the forthright language of one colonel to another. Ecclesiastics are less direct than other men, as a rule, in their way of saying important things. It would not be entirely surprising, therefore, even if it could be shown that there was not a single member of the Opposition who actually gave as his reason for being in that group the reason that was in his mind. The more cautious, the more prudent way was the conventional plea of inexpediency, especially when it provided the natural answer to the plea of expediency. Nor would there be any grave dishonesty in so doing, for if the doctrine was objectionable on the ground that it was unscriptural and unconstitutional it might certainly be said to be inexpedient for the Church of God to proclaim it. Such politeness would surely be, to say the least, pardonable.

On the other hand, there are in all assemblies men who are courageously outspoken—blunt, if you like. Even in the Vatican Council there were enough men of this caliber to give us some

---

[4] Not incontestable, since, if the Pope derived his authority from the Church, as in the Gallican view, he could have been given power to act *for* the Church, in time of emergency, after the manner in which Congress has given certain special powers, in time of war, to the President of the United States.

notion of the temper of the Opposition. They were loyal to the Roman Communion, which evokes a loyalty whose delicacy and strength few outside it commonly understand. But more because of than despite that loyalty, they spoke in a way that anyone, including themselves, must have seen from the first to be imprudent. Let us very briefly recall to mind some of these incautious prelates.

Does Strossmayer, for instance, sound like a believer in Papal Infallibility who thought it inadvisable to have the doctrine proclaimed till the world became less turbulent? Was Vérot likewise contented with the doctrine, and doubtful only of the wisdom of defining it so soon? Is it reasonable to think of that remarkable American, Peter Kenrick, as having been really a firm believer in the doctrine though he did not care to have it made official in 1870? Is the speech of the English Bishop of Clifton the report of a man who believed in the infallibility of the Pope but felt that the time was not yet ripe for proclaiming it? When he spoke of the faith of his own flock, and of what his clergy had diligently taught them, did he mean that they had been too ill taught to be ready, yet, for the true doctrine of Papal Infallibility which he longed to see included with the rest of the Deposit of Faith, but feared ought to be withheld from the faithful till they could be better prepared to receive it? Was the Cardinal Archbishop of Bologna an "inopportunist"? Was all the elaborate erudition, all the alert pugnacity of the Opposition speeches mustered only to show that it was inopportune to proclaim officially a universally believed doctrine of the Roman Church? Does what we have heard of the speeches of such men suggest that their attitude was exceptional? [5]

Is it really conceivable that merely "inopportunist" views were held by the bishops who, after seven months of unrelenting opposition to the Majority (entailing their immense unpopularity in just those circles where they would naturally wish to be popular), left Rome the day before the final voting, pleading in excuse that they

[5] See Maret, *Du Concile général.* Maret, Dean of the Faculty of Theology, Paris, had affirmed that Papal Infallibility was "a novel opinion in the Church" and involved "a radical and essential revolution in the constitution of the Church." (Coll. Lac. Vol. VII, 956.)

must be getting back to their long neglected flocks? Are we to suppose, moreover, that the Irish Roman Catholic hierarchy who gave evidence to the British government commission in 1825 (and who, if they had been still alive in 1870, would certainly have been numbered among the Opposition) would have nevertheless been properly dubbed "inopportunist" rather than "anti-infallibilist"? It would be indeed a most grave indictment of the Irish hierarchy to affirm anything of the sort, for it would imply either, (a) that the leaders of Irish Roman Catholicism conspicuously lacked the Mind of the Church, being ignorant of a matter which was, *ex hypothesi*, part of the deposit of faith given by Jesus Christ himself to the Apostles, or else, (b) that, having the Mind of the Church, they deliberately lied, giving false testimony to a royal commission with a view to obtaining political advantages in the British Parliament that should otherwise have been withheld to Roman Catholics in Britain. This second alternative would be a grave indictment of the moral character of the Irish hierarchy in 1825. But the first would be also no less serious an indictment of their theological orthodoxy.

Bishop Hefele, the learned historian who probably knew more of the history of the Councils than anyone else in the world, insisted most firmly that it was quite unknown in the ancient Church for controversies to be settled by an appeal to any one individual. Universality, antiquity, and consent: these were the criteria in all controversies, whether about faith or practice.[6] Yet promoters of the Inopportunist Legend would have us suppose that men who spoke like that really believed in Papal Infallibility but were demanding caution in promulgating it as official doctrine.

The Inopportunist Legend is comparatively recent in origin. It was certainly invented *ex post facto*. For it was known at the time, and talked about in every capital in the civilized world, that there was *doctrinal* discord among the Fathers on the infallibility question. Indeed, it was one of the arguments adduced by the

[6] The "Vincentian Rule," *infra*.

Majority that failure to promulgate the Decree would result in exhibiting to the world "disunity among Catholics."

If we look at the literature of the day we can find in it ample evidence that the Opposition was at the time, whatever might be its occasional essays in polite language, considered to be a very real Opposition indeed, though one whose effectiveness was gradually emasculated, and whose power was slowly whittled away as the Council proceeded. It was considered such an Opposition because it was recognized everywhere at the time that there was a real contradiction in the views that might be held about the infallibility doctrine, as this was envisaged by the Pope and his party.

This doctrine might be considered, as that party claimed it ought to be considered, a doctrine that was already implicit in what was being taught in the Church, the expression of what was already being unofficially expressed, and had been always taught from the time of the Apostles. But it was no less fully recognized that there was another and contradictory view, namely, that the doctrine proposed was an innovation and that, though there had been for some centuries a party that favored it, it was quite alien from the general teaching of the Church and repugnant to many of the authorities commonly held in greatest reverence by the Church. It was also known by everyone to be a doctrine which in any case, rightly or wrongly, would, if it became official, result in great changes in practice. Manning's biographer recognized this:

> I do not for a moment deny or wish to conceal the fact that the Vatican Decree introduced a far-reaching change if not in doctrine, in practice. It was not without reason that the opponents of the Papacy—the Civil Powers, the anti-Christian Party, the Revolution—took alarm. For the Definition of Papal Infallibility placed a powerful and ready weapon of defence, or, if needs be of offence, in the hands of the Church. In these days of quick action or quicker thought, the assembling of an Œcumenical Council is a slow process, a clumsy movement or method of defence in the face of an active enemy. Wars or the rumours of wars, revolutions or the fears of revolution, which

to-day is the normal state of European society, might retard or prevent altogether the meeting of a General Council; or, if assembled, it might be broken up by the action of a hostile State or by the outbreaks of an irreligious Revolution. By such methods, either arising from the natural course of events, as international wars must be accounted to-day, or designedly contrived by the subterranean action of its enemies, the Church, deprived of its spiritual weapons, would be paralysed in its action in the hour perhaps of gravest danger to Christian society. In a day of prolific error, new heresies might arise; a new code of morals be introduced subversive of Christian ethics, calling for rapid and formal condemnation by the Church. In these days of complicated action and rapid development and quick decision, the authority of a General Council, compared to that of an infallible Pope, is as unwieldy and as slow in its movements as the wooden ship of Nelson's day to an ironclad in our own. A strong factor in promoting the Vatican Decree was a common fear that the principle of authority, assailed on every side, was so weakened and whittled down as to endanger the existence of Christian society in Europe. The most efficacious remedy for this growing evil was, it seemed to the Vatican Council, to concentrate the supreme authority of the Church in the person of the Pope—the highest representative of moral power in the Christian world.[7]

This is the sort of language that many observers used at the time. It may be taken as typical. After the *fait accompli,* such language gradually died out. With secular circles increasingly uninterested, the Anglicans grieved, the Reformed Churches more than ever alienated, and Eastern Orthodoxy further outraged, it was possible for, and obviously advantageous to, Roman controversialists to soft-pedal the fact that there had ever been a real Opposition worth talking about. London's *Daily Telegraph* was expressing the view of the majority of Englishmen and Americans when it said:

What will be the result within the several Christian Churches? The answer must be that for the most part they will view the decree with profound indifference.

In the Synods and General Assemblies of Protestantism it will provoke no discussion. The Upper House of Convocation [Church of England] has indeed appointed a committee to watch the proceedings of the Vatican; but the step was taken in opposition to the

[7] Purcell, *Life of Cardinal Manning,* Vol. II, p. 415 f.

counsel of prelates who carry such weight as the Bishop of Glouces-
ter and the Bishop of London; and it has scarcely been noticed
by the mass of the nation.

Only one section of the English Church regards the dogmatic
verdict with interest or apprehension, and that is the ultra-High
Church section, which is separated from Rome by almost inappreci-
able distinctions of doctrine. . . .[8]

It was just such widespread indifference, however, that helped
to make it possible for the triumphant papalist party to foster the
Inopportunist Legend. Though the voices of Döllinger and his
associates continued to command the respectful attention of historians and the like, and to affect in one way or another Roman
Catholic Modernists such as Loisy, Dimnet, Von Hügel,[9] and Tyrrell, their message became increasingly remote to the ordinary man.

Some of the recalcitrant bishops were exceedingly dilatory in
sending in their submissions. But they all did, and the papalists
have ever since made a great deal of this fact. The alternative to
submission was excommunication. This extreme penalty is terrible
enough for a devout layman, since it deprives him of the sacraments, the greatest solace in a Catholic life. It is even worse for
a priest for it also cuts him off absolutely from every friend he is
likely to have, not to mention his livelihood, making him at worst
an object of contempt, at best an object of pity. But for a bishop
excommunication is a sentence almost past human endurance. Even
the most heroic could hardly be expected to face it. The last bishop
to submit was Strossmayer. In a pastoral letter of December 26,
1872, issued under his name, the Decree was published. But this
was done by his Vicar-General, and it is doubtful whether it had
his consent. Not till 1881 did he personally affirm his acceptance,
and then only for the sake of the Croat national cause.

On April 10, 1871, Hefele published the Decree, thus signifying
his belated submission. Almost all modern Roman Catholic con-

---

[8] *Daily Telegraph*, July 20, 1870.

[9] Maurice Nédoncelle holds that Von Hügel should not be classed as a
Modernist. While this is arguable, the arguments are not, I think, con-
vincing; but the question is too complex to be treated here. Cf. also Michael
de la Bedoyère, *The Life of Baron Von Hügel* (Dent, 1951), esp. pp. 117 ff.

troversialists are in the habit of interpreting this and the similar acts of the other Minority bishops as a final decision of faith after a period of gradually diminishing doubt. Whether such an interpretation is possible may be judged from what Hefele wrote to Döllinger on January 25, 1871, two and a half months before what Roman Catholics commonly take to be a genuinely interior submission and public acknowledgement of his slow-won faith in the infallibility of the Pope. Hefele wrote:

> Alas! I have to say with Schulte: "I have for many years lived in profound deception." I thought I was serving the Catholic Church; and I was serving the caricature that Romanism and Jesuitism have made of her. . . . At present the Romans are mishandling me by withholding my faculties of dispensation for forbidden degrees of affinity. They are using this as a means of molesting my flock, and the result is that some are living in concubinage or fall back on civil marriages; but what do they care at Rome about men's consciences, so long as they can satisfy their own lust for power?

This is strong language from a scholar of international reputation, an accomplished historian accustomed to write temperately and cautiously, and the acknowledged expert in that field of history more relevant than any other to the debates of the Vatican Council.

One can but guess at Hefele's inward thoughts in the years that followed. He was compelled, after submission, to falsify his story in a new editon of his *History of the Councils*.[10] Neither he nor any of the other bishops who were eventually forced into submission could openly avow even the shadow of a doubt on the subject of the Pope's infallibility. To some it was probably easier than it was to others to keep this macabre silence. From what we have seen of the character and temperament of Strossmayer, however, it is perhaps not too much to detect signs of pleasantly mischievous sarcasm in the extravagant expressions of devotion to the papacy in some of his later speeches. From a man who, till late in 1871, at least, kept company openly with Döllinger, the chief villain in the story from the papalist standpoint, and even then for long de-

[10] See C. B. Moss, *The Old Catholic Movement* (S. P. C. K., 1948), pp. 219 and 223.

ferred submission, speeches couched in language of such extreme devotion cannot but suggest that they were delivered tongue in cheek. Young men often radically change their minds; old men sometimes; old bishops almost never, so far as human history can tell us. Strossmayer was, at the time of his submission, a man of fifty-seven years of age and a bishop of twenty-two years' standing who had recently fought tooth and nail in the highest assembly of his Church against the doctrine of the infallibility of the Pope. He died in 1905, having received the pallium[11] in 1898.

Döllinger, who was only in priest's orders, and had been for long a bitter pill to the papalists, was excommunicated on April 17, 1871, at the age of seventy-two. Born in Bamberg, Bavaria, on February 28, 1799, he was the son of Ignaz Döllinger, a famous physiologist in his day. He was ordained priest in 1822, and after some parish work and a short period of teaching in a seminary he was nominated Professor of Ecclesiastical History at the University of Munich, which chair he later resigned on taking another in Dogmatic Theology. It was Döllinger's lectures at the University of Munich that established his reputation as a first-rank historian of the Church. His first published work, a treatise on the early history of the Eucharist, appeared in 1826, and was followed in 1828 by a manual of Church history, which embodied the substance of his lectures at the University. Ten years later he published an expansion of this work.

For some time his writings showed an increasing interest in political questions, and in 1845 he entered the Bavarian Parliament as representative of the University of Munich. Through hostile influences, he lost both his seat in Parliament and his chair at the University. Afterwards, however, in 1851, he was a delegate to the National Parliament of Frankfort, and about this time he developed a Church-and-State theory in which, at first, he advocated virtual separation; later on, he urged complete severance. Gradually he came to a position which, though doctrinally orthodox, was

---

[11] The pallium, conferred by the Pope, is a vestment for archbishops, who apply for it within three months of their consecration.

hostile to the temporal sovereignty of the Pope. In 1861 he delivered a series of lectures in which he strongly advocated that the
Pope should entirely relinquish his temporal estates, and he supported his arguments for this in subsequent writings. In 1864 he
vehemently opposed the *Syllabus*. Many of his works were translated into English, so that his name was by no means unfamiliar
to English and American scholars long before the Vatican Council,
though it was not till then that he became internationally famous.
It was clear that the Roman Catholic bishops of Germany were
divided on the issues to be discussed at the Council, and Döllinger
became a highly controversial figure. In March 1869 he wrote five
articles on the doctrine of Papal Infallibility in the *Augsburg Gazette*, and later, with the help of some of his friends, he expanded
these into a book published under the name of "Janus." His work
throughout the Council revealed that, though not a member, he
was by far the most determined and weighty influence on the Minority side. Mgr. Scherr, Archbishop of Munich, supported him,
argued against the papalists, and was among the Minority bishops
who left with Dupanloup the day before the final voting. Yet
Scherr, a weak and unscholarly man, accepted the decision and
wrote to the Faculty of Theology of the University of Munich,
asking them to do likewise. Only Döllinger and Friedrich stood
out, declining the archbishop's invitation. Two months later he
appealed to Döllinger to submit. Döllinger rejoined by asking what
good it could possibly do anyone if he, having taught against the
doctrine all his life, were to accept it as an old man. Who could
believe him if he submitted, let alone respect such a decision even
if he were to make it? Other friends begged him to submit, so as
to avoid the pain of spending his last years as an excommunicate
priest. He explained to each of them in turn that while he fully
believed a priest ought to make the utmost sacrifice for the
Church, this was one it was not in his power to make lawfully,
since such a submission would be nothing but an impudent public
lie. The day the Archbishop of Munich formally excommunicated
him, Döllinger wrote to a friend to the effect that he had no regrets

and would do the same thing if he had to go through it all over again. He was not leaving the Church, he maintained, but was only protesting against a new and false doctrine that had been illegally foisted upon her. He would continue to regard himself as a member and priest of the Catholic Church,[12] and he would go on protesting against the falsehood. Nor did he propose to give up the disciplines (fasting and abstinence, for example), accepted by Roman Catholics.

Honors, political and academic, were showered on Döllinger as a result of the impression he had made in his work against the papalists at the Council. In 1871 Oxford made him an honorary Doctor of Civil Law. The following year he received the Order of Merit from the King of Bavaria, and became Rector of the University of Munich." [13] Edinburgh gave him an honorary LL.D. He was appointed President of the Royal Academy of Science at Munich. In 1874 the German Emperor conferred on him the Order of the Red Eagle. He counted among his friends and admirers innumerable men of the greatest fame, not only historians and statesmen, but Roman Catholic theologians. In France Montalembert had been among his most intimate friends, and Lacordaire, Dupanloup, and Falloux all revered him. From the age of ten, when he had been presented to Napoleon shortly before the Battle of Wagram, he had been accustomed to the society of great men, and in his old age there were many in most of the countries of Europe who looked up to him with immense admiration and respect. That the action of the Archbishop of Munich was accounted precipitate even by the papalists themselves may be judged by the fact that when Mgr. Fessler, the Secretary at the Vatican Council, heard that it was intended, he went personally to Munich to try to arrange some way out, but arrived after the excommunication had taken place. The question at issue was really beyond Scherr, who acted under the influence of the Papal nuncio without

---

[12] I am informed that, according to a bishop of the Old Catholic Church (*infra*) who had all the archives of that Church in his possession, Döllinger continued to regard himself as a priest till his death.

[13] He was elected by 54 votes to 6.

taking into account the repercussions his action was bound to have on public opinion throughout Europe.

Döllinger is vulgarly credited with having "founded" the "Old Catholic" Church. What actually happened was that a meeting of ecclesiastics sympathetic to the anti-infallibilist position took place in Munich in September 1871, and was followed by a congress held the following year at Cologne. This congress included many distinguished foreign delegates, such as the Anglican Bishops of Ely and Lincoln, and the "Jansenist" Archbishop of Utrecht. Von Schulte took the chair. Döllinger, the real focus of interest, sat in a corner of the hall almost out of view and took very little part in the proceedings. On later occasions of this kind, however, he sometimes presided, as at Bonn in 1874-75, and he was always ready to give advice when asked. But he avoided any prominent position in the movement, beyond that which he could not fail to have accorded him by virtue of his personal prestige. Reinkens, one of the German professors who supported him, was consecrated to the episcopate by a Dutch bishop. The Old Catholic Church continues to exist to this day, though too little known. It remains, however, a salutary and inconvenient reminder to modern Roman Catholic scholars of the outrage perpetrated in 1871 on the leading German theologian of the Roman Catholic Church.

Döllinger never departed from the position to which he had always adhered. He refused ever to regard himself as cut off from the Catholic Church. In view of this, the coaxings and pleadings of the papalists for a "recantation" were beside the point. Leo XIII, successor of Pius, made no secret of his regret for the hasty excommunication. In 1886, Döllinger once again received a letter from his archbishop, pointing out that his submission would be a cause of rejoicing to millions of believing souls, and a token of his eternal salvation. Döllinger gave this letter long consideration before replying, on March 1, 1887. In the heat of controversy, he had sometimes used exaggerated language, as had almost everyone else, for controversy engenders this. Now in his eighty-ninth year, he replied with the utmost calm, dignity, and firmness, that he could not do what was asked of him. He pointed out that he had been publicly teaching the contrary of the doctrine for nearly half a century, until, without even a hearing, he had been, as the ancient formula puts it, "handed over to Satan." He reminded the archbishop that the ancient authority in Canon Law, Gratian, had held that excommunication was so terrible a penalty that if anyone should, out of true zeal, put an excommunicated person to death, he deserved no penance. He therefore did not underestimate the gravity of the sentence that had been passed on him by his archbishop at the instigation of ecclesiastical dignitaries, some of whom had been his own pupils. He went on: "I say to myself daily that I am a frail man, constantly prone to err in many ways. Fundamentally, the whole of my mental life has been a continual revision and laying aside of opinions and views formed earlier. I am conscious that I have never obdurately shut my eyes to a better judgment; at any rate I cannot remember such a case. . . . You counsel me to think of the salvation of my soul, and I meet this earnest admonition with reverent gratitude. In a mild and gentle fashion you are saying to me, 'If you die without having made a recantation, you will certainly go to eternal damnation in hell. . . .'" Nevertheless, he continued, he solemnly undertook to submit if anyone among the learned theologians of the archdiocese should be able publicly to refute him.

Far from any such public refutation of Döllinger being attempted, the aged scholar received a letter from the Papal nuncio on October 1 of the same year saying that "if the Jubilee of our Holy Father, the most blessed Virgin of the Rosary, and your good guardian angel, should put it into your heart to offer the Church a great consolation, I am at your disposal." Again Döllinger replied that he had for long taught the doctrine for which he had been excommunicated, and no Papal nuncio had ever remonstrated with him. He had persistently said what a Roman Catholic Catechism in use in England said, namely, that the doctrine of Papal Infallibility was a Protestant calumny. But since his excommunication sixteen years previously he had done a great deal of further study, and he now found that the doctrine was, to an even greater extent than he had supposed at the time of the Council, based on a mass of fictions and forgeries, many of which had already been recognized as such as early as the seventeenth century. Excommunicated, yet without a lie on his conscience, he felt able to face his impending death in a state of inward peace, and to look forward with tranquillity to what awaited him on the other shore. Were he to submit, his submission would involve such a deliberate lie that he could not with any such equanimity face the prospect of death.

Such was the man whom Dom Chapman, in a reply to the Anglican Bishop Gore, called "unscrupulous, unfair, untruthful" in controversy. His was the leading brain behind the arguments of the Minority at the Council, which Minority, we are now repeatedly assured by modern Roman Catholic writers, did not generally oppose the doctrine of Papal Infallibility, but only the expediency of defining it at that particular time. Döllinger died on January 10, 1890, a few weeks before his ninety-first birthday.

One of Döllinger's closest collaborators against the Majority bishops was an old English pupil of his, John Emerich Edward Dalberg Acton, the only son of Sir Richard Acton, seventh baronet. Born in Naples on January 10, 1834, of a traditionally Roman Catholic family, he was prevented by the statutes then in force at the University of Cambridge from going there as he would have wished. He studied at various seats of learning, including Edinburgh and Munich, and it was at the latter that he became the pupil and lifelong friend of Döllinger, who inspired him with a passionate zest for historical research. An ardent liberal in politics, he spent much of his time in the centers of liberalism in Europe and the United States. After some years as a Member of Parliament, he left political life and devoted himself more wholly to the editorship of a Roman Catholic periodical which, after it had been censured by the hierarchy, he eventually discontinued. After the Vatican Council he continued to hold with impunity the same views for which Döllinger was "handed over to Satan" by the

ecclesiastical authorities. Acton's lay status no doubt partly protected him; but had he been a nonentity it is unlikely that it
would have been of any such avail. In the Middle Ages, such
contumacy generally led to the stake, unless one were protected, as
was Luther, by a powerful prince. In the nineteenth century there
was no question of burning; but the authorities still could and did
enforce the ultimate sanction available to them against Döllinger,
while not touching his illustrious pupil whom Queen Victoria had,
on Gladstone's advice, raised to the Peerage in 1869. A few years
before his death in 1902, he was appointed, to his great joy, Regius
Professor of Modern History at Cambridge, and it was he who
planned, though he did not live to see, the now famous *Cambridge
Modern History*. He died openly and avowedly unrepentant of his
doctrine, and in good standing with the Roman Church.

The temper of the Opposition, before, at, and after the Council,
was beyond all question widely known to the papalist party. That
modern Roman Catholic writers have since dared to try to foist the
Inopportunist Legend on the world, is one of their gravest self-
indictments. One is tempted to wonder whether it might not be a
psychological projection. May it not be that the Majority believed
the doctrine to be expedient, though they did not entirely believe
what it taught? Of course some believed it fanatically; but motives are always mixed, and the motives behind a belief that is
held fanatically are always to be suspected.

There can be no doubt that to the extent that the Majority wanted
the promulgation of the Decree because they deemed it expedient,
they wanted it because they were afraid. They saw, and the
leaders of the party were not slow to encourage them to see that
the position of the Roman Church in the nineteenth century was
extremely perilous. In face of the growing liberalism of Europe
and the world, and particularly in face of events in Italy itself, the
Church was in a very awkward situation. She could be reformed,
but the faithful were not, intellectually or otherwise, prepared for
the extensive reforms that were needed. In any case, reform is
always the more arduous, the more demanding course to take.

Events in Italy made it, as Pius had discovered early in his pontificate, exceptionally difficult. Yet, as matters stood, the Roman Church could see no rosy future for herself. She had moved too slowly. The storms of the world seemed to be closing in on her. She had the promise of divine guidance; but, humanly speaking, her days seemed to be numbered. There were too many forces against her. Deprived of her old weapons, she felt ill equipped for her mission in the world. More troubles were likely to be ahead of her; troubles whose terrors none might foresee.

It is easy to believe in one's cause and in God's interest in and care for it, when things are going well; much more difficult when they are going badly. Had the Jesuits and the Majority bishops really been thoroughly convinced at heart of the infallibility of the Church, they could hardly have been so fanatically determined to secure the promulgation of the doctrine of the infallibility of the Pope. Yet they were plainly so set on this that they were willing to achieve it even if it meant employing the desperate tactics that were in fact employed in putting down and discrediting the Opposition. If the papalist party had believed at heart, serenely and without fear, that the Holy Ghost was with the Church, they could not have been so seriously troubled by the prospect of their views not being made official at the Vatican Council. Secure in their confidence in the divine guidance of the Church, they need not have gone to such extremes to obtain the expression of what they professed to believe was actually the Church's Mind. They could have hoped that at some future Council, God willing, there would be real moral unanimity, without contrivance. Why hurry? No one in the world ever expects haste of an ecclesiastical body. It was not as if they were to be reproached by anyone for being too slow.

But the mind of the papalists was, in fact, very different. Behind their show of fanatical zeal for a theological doctrine was a large measure of nervous skepticism about the infallibility of the Church herself. If, in so perilous a situation, the Church's infallibility were in question, the best way to nip the danger in the bud was to affirm the infallibility of the Pope so that the fears that were rising out of the growing doubts might not come to the surface. The faithful were already, chiefly through Jesuit activities, so trained as to make them psychologically prepared for the papalist remedy.

Legends as such may be not only beautiful but instructive. They may express ideas which cannot satisfactorily be expressed in any other way. One of the most famous legends is associated with the fourth-century Council of Nicaea. When the assembled bishops took their places on their thrones there were 318 of them, and yet as soon as they rose up there were 319. No amount of counting could square the discrepancy. Whenever the tellers approached the last of the series, this bishop immediately turned into the likeness of him who had appeared to be only the penultimate one. As the modern philosopher and mathematician Whitehead pointed out, such a story cannot be "disproved" logically or mathematically. All that can be said is that if such occurrences were frequent the application of the mathematical theory of cardinal numbers would be rendered impracticable. For "it is quite possible," said White-head, "to imagine a universe in which any act of counting by a being in it annihilates some members of the class counted during the time and only during the time of its continuance."

The didactic value of *such* a legend is immense. How else could one so vividly get over to the ordinary man the notion that in addition to 318 bishops there was an all-important three hundred and nineteenth member of the Council—to wit, the Spirit of God? The common man, hearing the principles of Christian democracy expounded to him, is notoriously prone to imagine that you have got a Christian democracy as soon as you have got all the people expressing their will. What he is likely to forget is that "the voice of the people is the voice of God" only if the people have first sought the presence of God in their midst, so that, hearing him in their hearts, they may voice his utterances from their lips. Moreover, despite the pretensions of some of us to being very uncommon men, there is none of us who is uncommon enough not to be in danger of slipping into such facile misconceptions of Christian democracy. So we can all most profitably listen to legends. They may be very wholesome. After all, the story of the Good Samaritan is a legend. No one ever supposed it to be anything else.

The Inopportunist Legend, however, can teach no religious truth to anyone. Its development exhibits, rather, the spiritual disquietude, the psychological fears, of the party which, having promulgated the Decree, had afterwards endeavored to disguise its own state of mind by attributing such a state of mind to the Opposition. This attitude was present in the very act of calling the Vatican Council. From the papalist standpoint the Council need not have been called at all; that is, there was no fundamental, theological necessity for it. The Pope had already done without it earlier in his remarkable pontificate when he had ended an ancient theological controversy by defining, on his own authority, the doctrine of the Immaculate Conception. Likewise, he could simply have intimated to the world, in his role of pastor and doctor of all Christians, that he was personally infallible in the sense actually defined in 1870. From the papalist point of view, therefore, there could be but one reason for calling the Vatican Council: to determine whether the infallible Pope's infallibility would be accepted by at least a workable majority in the Church. But if the Pope knew exactly what the Holy Ghost wanted, why did he need to secure the support of the faithful?

From the point of view of the conciliar party, however, about which controversialists from the other side naturally tell us less and less as the decades pass, the situation was very different. From the standpoint of those who had come to Rome to deliberate on a question that had vexed the Church for centuries and who hoped by the tried and trusted means of procedure in the Church to arrive at last at a satisfactory conclusion, or else, should such be the will of God, to return home in the knowledge that they had at any rate done their duty, it was naturally of the greatest possible concern that all should be constitutional. So, when at one point the Majority at the Vatican Council were so alarmed that they petitioned the Pope to decree his own infallibility, the Minority can hardly be blamed for framing a petition which, discreetly avoiding the whole question of whether the Pope was infallible or not, suggested to the agitated Majority that any statement that he was infallible might be "inopportune."

5

THE MEANING OF INFALLIBILITY

EVERYONE at the Vatican Council believed in some sense in the infallibility of the Church. But what exactly does this mean? It must be remembered here and in all matters concerning the teaching of the Roman Church that not only is Latin the official language of this Church: she *thinks* in it. So much so that almost any well-trained priest will testify that it is easier for him to discuss theology in Latin than in English or any other language. English is especially misleading when, as often, it uses words that are derived from Latin, because in spite of the derivation the meaning of the word changes throughout the centuries, and the change is perceptible only to those who know something of the history of English words. A well-known example is the English word "prevent." This comes from the Latin word *praevenire*, which means "to come before," that is, "to precede." The word occurs in the English Bible; for instance, when the Psalmist cries, "Let thy tender mercies speedily prevent us." [1] In the Communion Service of the Church of England the word is still used in this old sense: "Prevent us, O Lord, in all our doings with thy most gracious favour." To the modern ear, such a prayer sounds as if God were being asked to impede us in some way. To avoid such a misunderstanding, the American Episcopal Church uses the words "Direct us," as less susceptible to misunderstanding by a modern worshiper. But this is only a striking case of what happens wherever Latin ideas are expressed in English: in reading the anglicized word we read into it the modern English idea that it suggests to us rather

---

[1] Psalms lxxix. 8.

than the Latin idea it is meant to translate. So in trying to understand such translated ideas we must always be on our guard against this sort of thing. The word "infallible" is one that must be so investigated if we are to understand what is meant by the alleged infallibility of the Pope.

The Latin word *infallibilis* is itself derived from the Latin verb *fallere,* which means literally "to fall," or "to make a slip." Fundamentally, therefore, to say that something is *infallibilis* is to say that it is non-slipping. Had there been non-slip flooring in Justinian's time, it might conceivably have been advertised by the Roman merchants as *infallibilis.*[2] But *fallere* had also a metaphorical sense: "to deceive" or "to disappoint." Hence, a man who is so dependable that we should say of him, "he never lets you down," might very well come to be called *infallibilis.* We should never in modern speech call him infallible; not because we could be any more skeptical of human dependability than were the ancients, but because the significance of the word has changed. We should never call any man infallible in the modern sense, because the word too strikingly suggests to us nowadays something quite superhuman. Yet we often call a man indefatigable (incapable of being tired out), not because we really believe any human being is, strictly speaking, insusceptible to fatigue, but rather because "indefatigability" does not suggest to us a superhuman quality to such an extent as to make it impossible for us to use the word when we allow ourselves a little literary exaggeration in

[2] I mean only to suggest that the word *could* have been used in a sense such as is suggested by Horace's use of *fallax* in reference to a farm; not to assert that it actually was so used, for of this there is no evidence. The *Thesaurus Linguae Latinae* (vol. vii, fasc. ix, col. 1336) gives only one instance of the use of the word: *Opus imperfectum in Matt., Homilia 22.* This is the work of an unidentified Arian writer. Migne (P.G. 56, col. 751) gives the form *infalsabilis,* with *infallibilis* and *ineffabilis* as *var. lect.* (Haec [*infalsabilis*] est vera lectio: nam hic scriptor verba multa efformat, quae non sunt in usu.) The passage reads: "Magistra enim omnis justitiae ipsa natura est hominum, et scriptura infalsabilis [infallibilis] de Deo creaturae sunt omnium rerum: quia nihil est creatum in mundo, per quod non manifestissime Deus ostendatur." Professor Manu Leumann of Zürich, an international authority in philology, assures me that no earlier, pre-theological use of the word is known.

our speech. In Latin, however, a less fluid language, the word *infallibilis* has continued to connote simply "incapable of failing," that is, entirely reliable for the purpose one has in mind. If we spoke Latin in modern America, not only might our non-slip floors be advertised as *infallibiles;* we might very well tell a washing-machine salesman in New York that we would not buy unless he gave us a five-year guarantee of infallibility. If we then returned later to complain that it did not thoroughly dry the clothes, he would probably reply that it was not intended to do so: it was guaranteed *infallibilis* only for the purpose for which it was intended.

There is a sense in which the British and American peoples believed, during World War II, for instance, in the infallibility of the Allies' cause. This, their leaders very properly assured them, *could not fail,* so long as men and women in the democratic lands cherished their freedom as a priceless treasure. Even if the Nazis were to invade Britain, said Churchill, and that island were to be trampled under the heel of an arrogant and victorious German army, still the indomitable spirit of Britain would fight on till it shook off the yoke of the tyrant. The integrity of Britain would remain. Even if temporarily defeated on her own ground, the might of British courage and persistence would never die and would in the long run restore that freedom and independence that Britons account more precious than life itself.

But is not this a belief in infallibility? [3] Britain cannot fail. In some form it must go on, and whatever be the form of its survival it must remain essentially the same. This is perhaps not necessarily, though it is in fact sometimes closely associated with, a supernatural theory of infallibility. It is not a jingoistic, my-country-right-or-wrong notion. To say "My country, right or wrong" is, Chesterton used to remark, like saying, "My mother drunk or sober." As a matter of fact, Stephen Decatur when he said "My country, right

---

[3] Some would distinguish infallibility from indefectibility. In view of the etymology of the former term I think the value of the distinction is overrated. Others would object that even indefectibility cannot be predicated of a nation *in any sense.*

or wrong" at a dinner given in his honor in 1816, added an aspiration that it might always be in the right. However, one should say, rather, as did Carl Schurz in a speech in the American Senate in 1872: "When right, to be kept right; when wrong to be put right." A Christian patriot may believe that so long as his country behaves itself on the whole, so long as it is in the right before God, God himself will defend it, in the sense that God will defend the right. The inscription, "In God we trust," which caused much controversy when it was put on American postage stamps, can be so interpreted. It is not an entirely impious faith. America cannot fail. . . . America is infallible, *if she trusts in God.*

There is, therefore, nothing at all unusual or remarkable in the mere notion that the Church is infallible. If a nation can be believed to be infallible, how much more the company of Christ's faithful on earth? It would indeed be exceedingly astonishing if Christians did not in some sense believe in the infallibility of the Church. It would be certainly surprising if such belief had no pretensions to a supernatural basis that would give it a vigor and vivacity such as one would hardly expect of a merely political unit of human society.

As a matter of fact, not only the Roman Church, but every Christian society believes in some sense in its own infallibility. Far from repudiating infallibility as a Roman corruption, or Anglican notion, or Orthodox decrepitude, Christian societies commonly lean very heavily on the idea of it, sometimes even to the detriment of Christian action. If, as St. Paul says in his letter to the Romans, "neither death, nor life, nor angels, nor principalities, nor powers, nor things present, nor things to come, nor height, nor depth, nor any other creature," be able to separate us from "the love of God, which is in Christ Jesus our Lord," are we not *all* in some sense infallible?

There is, however, historically, a special sense in which the Church was accounted infallible. For when the first Christians felt that Pentecost was the fulfilment of Christ's promise that he would be with them "alway, even unto the end of the world," they believed that God was actually present among them as they assembled for worship as his Church on earth. Believing also that a saving doctrine had been committed to that Church, they were convinced that the Church was safeguarded from all evil, including, of course, all radical error about the things that pertain to salvation. How could the Church fail with God actually present in her midst?

It is well known that the first Christians anticipated the speedy end of the world, and that this expectation faded slowly. It affected their whole outlook, discouraging at first even the setting down of records: the earliest Gospel (Mark) was not written till about forty years after the Crucifixion. Only with the waning of this anticipation of Christ's speedy return to earth, combined with alarm at the embarrassing eccentricities of belief that were being spread in the Church, did the Christians begin to address themselves seriously to discovering the criteria of orthodoxy. Having no written constitution or articles of association, they had to consider how to distinguish the essential faith of Christians from the vagaries of eccentrics who poured into the Church from a pagan world teeming with eclectic ideas. It was the life of the Church that seemed to be at stake. They had to determine more clearly for themselves the nature of the teaching that was, they believed, implicit in and inseparable from that life.

In the second century, when a Marcionite, for example, confronted Christians with views that seemed to endanger the Church's very life, these could not fail to contrast such novel views with the teaching of the Apostles. This was plainly a surer guide to the truth than something excogitated by some convert of yesterday with ill-considered, half-pagan notions buzzing inside his excited brain. So the most obvious criterion, perhaps, was apostolicity. And as the organization of the Church developed, the bishops or other recognized leaders of the Church were, no less plainly, the custodians of that apostolic truth. For who else should guard the Church's treasure? Moreover, in view of Rome's prestige and the association of it with St. Peter, the Bishop of Rome could not fail to be accounted in some sense a special guardian of the deposit of the Church's faith. But there is no clear evidence at all, in the documents of the first few centuries, that this special responsibility of the Bishop of Rome was in the least like the sort of thing asserted by the Vatican Decree, and there is a great deal of evidence that it was not.[4]

Since there was no written constitution, apart from the Scriptures, to set forth the exact authority invested in any person or persons, there is, of course, no definitive document to which an historian may turn. One can only use the information and the historical sense one has. But one thing is certain: the earliest Christians had, implicitly, a constitutional theory about their society. For every society on earth has a constitution; some a written one, such as the American, others an unwritten one, after the British fashion. Religious societies are no exception. Islam, for instance, has its Koran, or holy book, which all orthodox Muslims accept as their absolute standard in faith and morals. No Muslim, however much he may deviate from the orthodox pattern, would allow that the Sunna, or "traditions," might supplant the Koran, which, in Muslim countries, may be quoted in the law courts as the final authority. Nor would orthodox Jews, for all their reverence for the Talmud, ever think of exalting it, or any other literature, above the Torah, or "Law of Moses," as the supreme authority. In such religions the final authority is written and unchangeable.

The more extremely bibliolatrous sects have in the past approached the Scriptures of the Old and New Testaments in a manner akin to that of Jews and Muslims towards their respective Scriptures. Modern Biblical scholarship, however, has made such an attitude untenable, since it is now much plainer than it was in the nineteenth century that the New Testament was the product of an already very lively Church which had evidently got along without a New Testament better than many societies of Christians seem to have got along *with* one. Since even the earliest epistle in the New Testament was not written till nearly twenty years after the Crucifixion, and since all the Apostles were dead before the New Testament was compiled in its present form, it can hardly be said

[4] See Giles, *Documents Illustrating Papal Authority;* also *infra.*

that the New Testament has always been the indispensable rule of faith for every Christian. It was not for St. Paul. Nor, when it was compiled and set apart as on a par with the Old Testament that was the staple reading of the earliest Christians, could it have been intended by anyone to be more than a treasury for the living communities that were the Church. It was, therefore, a guide-book to the City of God rather than the City itself. It was, however, a very important guide-book. It contained the documents generally accounted reliable, contradistinguished from others that were considered "doubtful"—eccentric in their interpretations. Nothing is more embarrassing to a new organization than the activities of those of its new members who insist on interpreting its value in terms of their own necessarily limited, individual appreciation.

How, then, did these primitive Christians think of their society? A society, for example a family, that goes back for several generations, extends beyond its present, living members. In any matter of controversy, in any sort of meeting, the will of the meeting is to be ascertained. But before the will is ascertained there is of course discussion, to enable the meeting to make up its mind and *have* a will. Uppermost in the minds of conscientious members of long standing will always be the thought of what other members, living or dead, would have said. In such a society, conscious of roots far deeper than the present, there is no question of consulting only "the meeting," of deciding questions by a mere counting of noses. What really is consulted, strictly speaking, is the will not only of the members present, but also of the absent members. Most especially was this true of a society such as that of the earliest Christians who reckoned those who were "asleep in the Lord" very definitely on the membership roll. The grave could never diminish this. Had not Christ "triumphed over the grave"?

So, the Christian Church of the first few centuries was certainly not a democracy in the modern sense of the term. But on the other hand it was anything other than an autocracy. It had in it the spiritual source of modern democratic forms of government, free from the self-regarding characteristics of the modern democratic

State. Later on, there are plainly democratic principles in the notion of a Christian *respublica*. What certainly most impressed the
first-century Christians about themselves and their society was that
this was a living unity, whose life-principle was the risen Christ,
always deemed to be present in their midst. When disputes arose
they were without any written constitution to guide them in deciding these disputes, and so they had to settle them with reference
to the Infallible Guide—Christ who lived in their hearts. Had
there been a single recognized authority in the first century, the
tone of Paul's letters to the Corinthians could not but have been
very different. What is evident in the literature of the apostolic and
sub-apostolic ages is that apostleship carries immense prestige and
influence in the Christian community. To the Apostles a commission has been given, a commission to teach, to speak the truth in
love. Local communities of Christians that were specially associated with the Apostles inherited much of the prestige these had
enjoyed and the influence they had exercised. Conspicuous, pre-
eminent even, among these communities, was that of Rome, which
Ignatius, Bishop of Antioch, writing early in the second century,
addresses with much respect as being that community which,
among the scattered communities of Christians in Italy, "presides in
love."

The testimony of Ignatius is important. He certainly was a champion of order and unity in the Church. Not a Roman citizen, and
having, in common with Christians generally, no reason to have any
love for the imperial city itself, he looks to the Roman community
of Christians as the main branch of the Christian family. But
churches addressed each other as brothers; sometimes one spoke as
a big brother, never as a lord. It is a principle of modern democracies that they should govern themselves and that government
should be, in the words of Lincoln's Gettysburg address, "of the
people, by the people, for the people." The will of the people is
the ultimate arbiter. In the Christian Church, on the other hand,
the ultimate arbiter has always been God. But God, in the risen
Christ, was, they believed, present with them. Christ had prom-

ised that he would be with them "alway, even unto the end of the world." It was indeed, in a sense, government "of the people, by the people, for the people," but divinely guaranteed.[5] God himself was infinitely active among them: how could they go wrong? The Church was infallible because she was God's Church.

It is such a belief and trust that the Christian Church is so safe-guarded that gave the Christians the confidence that made possible their spectacular spiritual triumph in the world. Their doctrine of the infallibility of the Church was, of course, a "supernatural" doctrine. It was in some measure an inheritance from Judaism. *Dominus illuminatio mea,* sings the Psalmist:

> The Lord is my light and my salvation; whom then shall I fear: the Lord is the strength of my life; of whom then shall I be afraid? When the wicked, even mine enemies and my foes, came upon me to eat up my flesh: they stumbled and fell. Though an host of men were laid against me, yet shall not my heart be afraid: and though there rose up war against me, yet I will put my trust in him. . . . For in the time of trouble he shall hide me in his tabernacle: yea, in the secret place of his dwelling shall he hide me, and set me upon a rock of stone.

If an individual Hebrew could feel such security, such peace of mind, such infallible protection from error, how much more the whole body of Christians assured of the presence in their midst of their risen Lord and Savior? Christ was among them, how could they go astray?

They were well aware that trouble might come. Trouble was indigenous to Christendom. But internal strife did not shock them as it tends to shock us today. For they had no illusions about human frailty, any more than they had illusions about the terror and certainty of death. Nevertheless, they enjoyed a peculiar confidence that they could never really go off the rails. Since Christ was risen, triumphant over the *power* of death, and reigning in their midst, they could sing with greater confidence than even that which inspired the author of the psalm:

[5] Of course I am not suggesting that the nature and purpose of the Church are such that Lincoln's words should apply to the Church in the sense in which they apply to the State.

Therefore will we not fear, though the earth be moved: and though the hills be carried into the midst of the sea; though the waters thereof rage and swell: and though the mountains shake at the tempest of the same. The rivers of the flood thereof shall make glad the city of God: the holy place of the tabernacle of the most Highest. God is in the midst of her, therefore shall she not be removed.

Without such a confidence, the Church of the first centuries could not possibly have withstood the forces ranged against her. Only because she believed that Christ's ship, however much she might toss on the seas, could never be wrecked, could she have carried on. Christians might err; they did err most grievously; but their mistakes could never wreck the precious ship of God. This vessel was unsinkable. This Church was infallible.

In face of the troubles of the first few hundred years, therefore, Christians enjoyed this sort of assurance. Innovators and others often came along with ideas that seemed questionable, and the Christians who wanted to test for themselves whether such strange-sounding doctrines really "belonged" to Christ's Church, did not depend on their own feelings in the matter or on their own mental judgments. They sought the opinion of others whom they deemed holier or wiser or more learned than themselves. It seems plain that they recognized that even the holiest Christian on earth, and certainly the most learned, might err in his judgments on such matters. While they certainly did not just count heads, they always felt that two heads were likely to be better than one. While they were impressed by the individual authority of certain men, the official custodians of the apostolic tradition, they always preferred to hear more than one custodian.

That such was the attitude of Catholic Christians in ancient times is borne out by many documents, not least the famous fifth-century passage in which is set forth what has come to be known to scholars as the Vincentian Rule. In this passage Vincent of Lérins proposes three criteria in deciding the orthodoxy of any doctrine: "universality, antiquity, and consent." While Vincent, in common with the Fathers of the Church generally, fully recognizes that the Bishop of Rome has a special place as the custodian of the apostolic faith, and ought therefore always to be listened to with the utmost respect, he directs his readers to the authority of councils, and his final test is that a doctrine should not command a Christian's assent unless it has been believed by the faithful generally in all places and at all times. Here is what he says:

> In the Catholic Church itself we must be very careful to hold that which has been believed everywhere, always, by all. . . . And we shall observe this rule if we follow universality, antiquity, consent. We shall follow (the rule of) universality if we confess that faith to be true which the entire Church throughout the world confesses; (we shall follow the rule of) antiquity if we in no way depart from those interpretations that plainly our holy ancestors and fathers proclaimed; (and we shall follow the rule of) consent if in antiquity itself we follow with eagerness the interpretations and decisions of all, or practically all, priests and teachers alike.
>
> What, then, will the Catholic Christian do if any part of the Church has cut itself off . . . ? What if some novel contagion should try to poison the entire Church . . . ? Then he will take care to adhere to antiquity. . . . What if in antiquity itself an error should be detected on the part of two or three persons, or perhaps a city or even a province? Then he will take care to prefer the decrees of an ancient general council, if there be one, to the temerity and ignorance of a few men. But what if some error should arise about which nothing of this kind should be found? Then he must take pains to discover and compare the opinions of the ancients . . . , conspicuous and approved teachers; and whatever he shall find has been held, written and taught, not by one or two only, but by all equally and with one accord, openly, often and persistently, that is what he must understand should be believed also by himself, quite unhesitatingly.[6]

When a bishop, notably the Bishop of Rome, voiced his judgment on questions of doctrine, Christians listened with the utmost respect; but they applied tests such as Vincent's. Moreover, there is not a shred of evidence that they would have been in the least surprised to find that even the Bishop of Rome was wrong. The more serious trouble arose when he was right. That is to say, when a pope's judgment was corroborated by the judgment of the

---

[6] *Commonitorium*, Migne, *Patres Latini*, L, 640 ff.

Church, he was inclined to interpret the situation thus: God had in the first instance guided his judgment and then in the second instance given him an eloquent testimony that this was so. Not only was this a natural feeling for him to have; the more pious a man he was the more he would be inclined to have it. The Church would respect him for having it; but that is not to say she was willing to depend wholly upon it.

Many instances might be cited from the documents to show how this worked out in practice. At the Council of Chalcedon, for example, which has always been regarded as of first-rate importance in the history of the Christian Church, a letter of Pope Leo to Flavian, which had been suppressed at an earlier council, was read at the second session, held October 10, 451. This letter was evidently pleasing to most of the Fathers. A few, however, asked and received some days to consider it. At the fourth session, held a week later, the question was put to the Council once again, whether the letter expressed the Christian Faith. The Judges (a sort of committee on procedure) put the question thus:

> Let every one of the bishops here assembled declare whether the Epistle of Archbishop Leo is in accordance with the exposition of the 318 Fathers of Nicaea, and with the decrees of the 150 Fathers who were later assembled in the royal city.

Anatolius, Bishop of Constantinople, then spoke as follows:

> The letter of the most holy Archbishop Leo agrees with the creed of the 318 holy Fathers of Nicaea, and of the 150 who afterwards assembled at Constantinople and confirmed the same faith; also with the proceedings of the ecumenical synod at Ephesus held under blessed Cyril, who is among the saints, which synod condemned Nestorius. I therefore agree to it and have signed willingly.[7]

Numerous other bishops spoke to the same effect, and the remainder, asked for their views, shouted together that they were of the same mind. The Council later wrote felicitating Leo on the excellent guidance he had given them at the Council; but while they

[7] Hefele III, 315.

spoke of him as having supplied them with heavenly food, even as being their chief, "as head to members," they said nothing that can be taken as clear evidence of their recognizing him to be possessed of anything such as the infallibility later claimed by the papacy. That they thought him extraordinarily dependable as an interpreter of their own beliefs is beyond dispute. But it proves nothing. The American people might well think this of their president without implying for a moment that they considered him to be infallible.

Leo, on the other hand, in a letter written two years after the Council, uses language that exhibits papal pretensions in embryonic form:

> Wherefore we glory in the Lord. . . . who has permitted us to sustain no harm in our brethren, but has corroborated, by the irrevocable assent of the entire brotherhood, what He had before defined by our ministry, to show that what has already been enacted by the primatial See and received by the judgment of all the Christian world, had proceeded truly from Himself, that in this too the members may agree with the Head.[8]

Later in the history of the Church, those who held conciliarist views, against papalist pretensions, saw much in passages such as this to support their position.[9] For the obvious implication is that a pope's judgments had to be *corroborated*. Even a pope whose views received such corroboration and was feeling that this fact demonstrated that God had indeed guided his judgments when he gave these, implied in his own letter that the judgments called for such corroboration. In other words, Leo was naturally glad that he did have the Mind of the Church. He felt that this was as it should be. He even felt that had there been no corroboration of his views by the Church, he would have been able, by God's guidance of him personally, to keep the Church from error. But there is no clear evidence that he went so far as to hold that the Church need not make the final decision in council. And if even Leo did not feel this, certainly the other bishops did not. On the contrary

---

[8] Migne LIV, 1046 (Leo to Theodoret of Cyrus, Ep. 120, *Remeantibus*)
[9] See, for example, Bossuet, Œuvres IX, p. 40 A (Paris 1836).

they took it for granted that it was their most solemn responsibility to test everything by the accustomed methods, not accepting any single authority, however weighty, but sifting all the evidence in a fashion such as is indicated in the Vincentian Rule.

It cannot but seem a far cry from that Church of the fifth century to the world-wide organization whose leaders met in 1870 in a transept of St. Peter's Church in Rome to hear proclaimed the personal infallibility of the Pope. The notion that any human being is, in any sense, and in any circumstances, personally infallible, does not commend itself to the modern mind.[10] It commended itself no more when the personal infallibility was claimed by a pontiff who had, only six years previously, publicly condemned in the harshest language practically every movement that the conscience of the nineteenth-century world held dear. That the document in which he did so, the *Syllabus of Errors*, was directed primarily at his political enemies hardly increased its palatability.[11] To many, the notion of anyone having personal infallibility of any kind was too repugnant to make it seem even worthy of serious consideration at all. Monsignor Ronald Knox once said of Protestants: "They seem to think that the Pope, like the High Priest in the Old Testament, keeps a kind of Urim and Thummim somewhere in the Vatican and that if he wants to know the answer to a vexed question he just applies to the oracle and the answer is miraculously given him." Nor does Monsignor Knox overdraw the typical Protestant attitude to the doctrine of Papal Infallibility. It may, however, be less far removed from the popular Roman attitude than he would readily admit. And, as we shall see, even such a crude notion as this is less loaded with difficulties than the more learned explanations offered by Roman Catholic exponents of the doctrine.[12]

The doctrine of the personal infallibility of the Roman Pontiff was at variance with at least a great deal of learned opinion in

[10] I do not mean, of course, that "the modern mind" itself is infallible.
[11] See, however, Hales, *Pio Nono,* pp. 258 ff.
[12] See Chapter 8.

the Roman Communion itself, before 1870, as well as thoroughly distasteful to all Protestants and the entire Eastern Orthodox Communion. The only persons who were not puzzled by it were extreme papalists and extreme atheists. Papalists were not puzzled by it for obvious reasons: they would have wished indeed that the Vatican pronouncement of 1870 had gone further, even, than it did. Atheists were not puzzled by it because they thought Christianity so radically absurd that the more ridiculous its beliefs became the better these beliefs seemed to them to exhibit the general absurdity of the Christian religion.

To describe the Pope as *personally* infallible is, however, not strictly a fair representation of the Vatican pronouncement. Rather is he said to be infallible in the personal performance of certain duties in his unique position as Head of the Church. That the Pope shares somehow in the infallibility of the Church is self-evident to all who admit that Christ's Church is in any way divinely guarded from error. But the question is: what precisely is his share?

The notion that the infallibility of the Church can be invested in its officers is an ancient one, whence springs the great authority that General Councils have enjoyed from the earliest times. If the early Christians were instinctively as democratic as I have suggested (and it will be seen later that medieval political theory helps to confirm that such was their instinct), these councils would have been, even apart from the question of apostolicity, a natural and inevitable development. As soon as the number of Christians increased as it did within a generation, and as soon as Christianity spread as far as it did within that time, the possibility of Christians meeting in one great conclave was plainly out of the question. To the appointed officers of the Church, therefore, authority *had* to be delegated. If it was God's will that his Church should spread as it did, it was surely his will that some such delegation of authority should take place.

The development of the papacy is a highly controversial question; but it did at any rate come into prominence at a fairly early date, and it soon became plain that the Pope's position in such councils was a peculiar one. But what was it? Naturally there were parties in the Church on such an unsettled question, which by the fifteenth century was still much disputed. The Council of Constance maintained that a general or ecumenical council, *as representing* the whole Church, held its power immediately from Christ, and that even the Pope himself was bound to obey such a council. This view was not agreeable to the popes. These had their own theological party whose views are expressed by Bellarmine late in the sixteenth century. According to this viewpoint, the supreme judge in controversies about faith and morals is the Pope, who is inerrant when he instructs the whole Church on such matters. In the seventeenth and eighteenth centuries, the view prevailed in France ("eldest daughter of the Roman Church") that a General Council is superior to the Pope.

The question was never settled till the time of the Vatican Council in 1870. There was certainly a strongly papalist party in the Roman Church, and the Jesuits were champions of it; but there was, no less, a considerable party against it. The latter, the conciliar party, was supported by most able and learned men. Its exponents, however, were on the whole thinkers rather than men of action. Thinkers are commonly liberals in one sense or another and perhaps they are seldom as vociferous in promoting their views as are men who look more to expediency and immediate practical success. The victory of the latter over the former is, at any rate, a commonplace in history, not least in ecclesiastical history. But the thinkers are often right, and the others wrong. This phenomenon is by no means peculiar to the Roman Church.

In the seventeenth century, the English Roman Catholic poet Dryden could write lines that express the vague opinion of the average Roman Catholic of his day:

> I then affirm, that this unfailing guide
> In Pope and general councils must reside,

> Both lawful, both combined; what one decrees
> By numerous votes, the other ratifies:
> On this undoubted sense the Church relies.[13]

This is a reasonable, facing-both-ways position, suited to the man-in-the-street who could not be expected either to follow the historical expositions of the learned or to swallow whole the contentions of those who pressed for the autocratic interpretation that eventually triumphed. Whether the victory was a legal one within the constitution of the Roman Church itself is highly questionable. No effort was spared to make it *appear* legal. Pius IX omitted nothing that might conduce to that end, hoping that the *fait accompli* would be the final and best justification of what happened. Success may be, like possession, nine-tenths of the law; but it is not even one-tenth of the moral law. Technically, the Vatican Council was never completed. It was prorogued. On the conciliar view, could a future session of the Council review the Decree of 1870 and repudiate papalism in favor of a conciliar and more liberal doctrine of the Church? The notion that this is unlikely ever to happen is one that it is naturally in the interests of the papalist party to foster.

[13] *The Hind and the Panther*. Richard Baxter expresses the difficulties of such a position:
> "When Popes damn Popes, and Councils damn them all,
>   And Popes damn Councils, what must Christians do?
> When they each other's laws damn and recall,
>   How shall we know whose power then was true?"

6

THE DEMOCRATIC TRADITION
IN THE MIDDLE AGES

THE Middle Ages recognized two legal systems—that of the Civil Law and that of the Canon Law. The former had great antiquity; but it seemed remote, for the conditions to which it belonged were very different from those that prevailed in the Middle Ages. Its prestige was therefore academic rather than practical. The Canon Law, on the other hand, was new—the creation of medieval Christian civilization. But its greater applicability to actual conditions gave it a superior importance in the medieval life it touched at every point. Therefore, when the papalists, whose influence on the Canon Law was naturally great, invoked it against their adversaries, they could often do so with what was to the medieval mind a great show of argument. Some of the papalist champions proclaimed very extravagant views; for instance, that the Pope can do anything he pleases to do, and even that he can do whatever God can do.[1] They held, therefore, that he could dispense from all law, even, according to Pope Innocent IV, from the precepts of the Gospel, though not from its spirit.[2] On such views, the papal powers were for all practical purposes limitless. The restrictions on these powers were so academic and technical that we need not consider them here. The Pope could, for example, depose kings

[1] Panormitanus, *Commentaria in Decretales* (Lyons, 1512) I. vi. 34, fol. 115 verso, no. 18: "papa potest facere quicquid Deus potest."
[2] Innocent IV, *Commentaria in Quinque Libros Decretalium* (Venice, 1578), I. ix. 11, fol. 95: "Dispensat contra verba evangelii, licet non contra mentem." Maitland calls him the greatest lawyer of all popes.

and commit individuals to slavery for life. He could declare any political action null and void, as Innocent III declared Magna Carta, on the pretext that the English King had consented to it under pressure. Moreover, while in fact only Christendom was under the Pope's power, by right he was Lord of all men. And when the Pope exceeded even the almost boundless powers he claimed, the papalist lawyers could, often by the wildest and flimsiest of arguments, interpret his action so as to legitimize it.

From the standpoint of such jurists, there could hardly be any question of papal fallibility in matters of doctrine. The Pope was not only personally infallible in such matters; he was almost impeccable. But alongside this interpretation of the papal power as quite despotic, there was the fundamental principle of popular sovereignty. This principle had most ancient roots in Christian thought. In the earlier Middle Ages, however, when European society was primitive and insecure, it was very difficult for the ordinary man to envisage it in practical politics, while autocracy was something everyone could understand. Naturally, the champions of papalism made the most of the political inexperience of the society with which they had to deal. Nevertheless, the essentially democratic tradition in Christianity was sufficiently strong to remain not entirely crushed by even so mighty an adversary. It is in that early Christian and medieval tradition that the roots of modern democracy are to be found. Lord Acton puts this case strongly. "[In the Middle Ages,] Representative government, which was unknown to the ancients, was almost universal. The methods of election were crude; but the principle that no tax was lawful that was not granted by the class that paid it—that is, that taxation was inseparable from representation—was recognized, not as the privilege of certain countries, but as the right of all. . . . Slavery was almost everywhere extinct; and absolute power was deemed more intolerable and more criminal than slavery." [3]

Totalitarianism is pre- and post-Christian. There are, it is true, obvious differences between ancient and modern totalitarian States

[3] *History of Freedom* (Macmillan, 1909), p. 39.

and between ancient and modern totalitarian ideals. The idea of the *non*-totalitarian State is clearly present in first-century Christian writers, among whom it is an innovation, though by no means always a conscious one. "Render to Caesar the things that are Caesar's, and to God the things that are God's," enjoined Jesus. "Fear God, honor the King," is the similar doctrine we find in the First Epistle of Peter. Such utterances were conditioned by the very peculiar attitude of the Roman government. They did not represent the common Jewish attitude; certainly not the Gentile one.

In describing the ways of Christians and their relation to the political society to which they belonged, the anonymous writer of the mid-second-century letter to Diognetus says:

> While they dwell in cities of the Greeks and of the barbarians as the lot of each is cast, and follow the native customs in dress and food and the other arrangements of life, yet the constitution of their own citizenship, which they set forth, is marvellous, and admittedly contradicts expectation. They dwell in their own countries, but only as sojourners; they bear their share in all things as citizens, and they endure all hardships as strangers. Every foreign country is a fatherland to them, and every fatherland is foreign. . . . They obey the established laws, and they surpass the laws in their own lives.

It is plain that no class of Christians is envisaged as directing the State in the manner of Plato's philosopher-kings. Christians as such do not rule the State; they are loyal to it—at any rate to the extent, and it is a very large extent, to which the State does not go beyond certain limits. This is the principle from which, despite great changes, medieval political theory never radically departed. The area of the State's powers, functions, and duties had to be fully worked out; but already one thing was clear—Christianity excluded both theocracy on the one hand and absolute monarchy on the other. Stuart absolutism would have been as repugnant to it as was the Muslim theocracy that was to be the ideal of Islam.

St. Augustine's *City of God* was no innovation. Nor did he envisage any radical change till the end of human history. The two "cities," are "entangled together in this world, and intermixed until the last judgment effects their separation." The subsequent development of medieval political theory is such that this view is never entirely repudiated. For all Augustine's debt to Neoplatonism, he was in respect of his political theory neither Platonic nor Plotinian. He followed the New Testament injunctions. But he wrote quite naturally of a Christian *respublica*.[4] Institutions such as slavery were conventions inherited from the past; they did not belong to the *respublica*. While he did not think they were entirely repugnant to it, they could no more be said to belong to it than the persistence of aristocracies in modern France can be said to belong to the French Republic. As medieval civilization developed, the dual citizenship that the individual in the Latin west inevitably inherited greatly strengthened the notion of the *respublica*. As a member of the Church, the individual could, with all the power of the Church behind him, face up to a secular tyrant, while as a member of a State he could stand up in the strength of his citizenship against ecclesiastical tyranny. This ideal worked—not perfectly, for ideals never do; but well enough to keep totalitarianism out of fashion.

But there was another and in some ways even more fundamental principle in medieval political theory. Throughout the Middle Ages it was widely taught that political authority was vested in the people. It may have been very difficult for the people to exercise their authority in practice; but the principle was recognized, and the recognition of a principle is extremely important in political and constitutional affairs. No American would claim that the American ideal of political equality has been fully achieved in practice; but every loyal American would resist any contention that the idea of equality has failed. On the contrary, he would strongly affirm the immense importance of the fact that though political equality has been imperfectly achieved, its achievement is gradually coming into sight, and this has been made possible only through widespread acceptance of the principle, belief in which has never been dimmed by the great difficulties attending its translation into actual fact.

---

[4] It should be noted, however, that, historically "respublica" did not mean "republic" in the modern sense. It was applied to the Roman Empire at every stage.

The history of the notion of popular sovereignty, which is the essence of modern democratic theory, deserves, therefore, careful examination.

Three fundamental principles were stressed by the medieval canonists, not least by the masters of the great legal school of Bologna. Firstly, laws are the expression of the Natural Law (*ius naturale*) in the particular situation of a given society and age. They can never be simply the expression of a ruler's will. Secondly, the source of authority is unquestionably the people. Some jurists did contend that the people yielded their authority to the Emperor; but this was a minority view. The majority indubitably held that such a transference of popular authority was legally impossible. The people might *delegate* their authority to a ruler; they could never relinquish it permanently in his favor. This doctrine has immense importance. For it entails the corollary that if a ruler flagrantly abuses his position he may be deposed by the people, and the deposition, however great be the bloodshed attending it, will be constitutional. It will be not a rebellion on the part of the people, but rather a police action by them against an unjust tyrant usurping their place or illicitly acting as their appointee. Thirdly, there is the characteristically medieval doctrine of the coexistence and collaboration of two equally sacred legal systems, that of the Church and that of the State.

These formulations of medieval legal principle had further support from another quarter. In the feudal law that grew up with the development of the medieval system of land tenure, it was already recognized that the purpose of all laws is to maintain "justice," not to serve the caprice of a prince or noble. According to this theory, there is between a prince and his people a pact based on such principles of "justice." As partners to a contract, both have the right to expect benefits from it. In particular, it is the duty of the prince to protect his humblest subjects from the greed or cruelty of his stronger and richer ones. Such feudal notions harmonized in theory with the more academic view of the Bologna jurists.

In the *Policraticus,* the most comprehensive eleventh-century treatise on political theory, John of Salisbury sees no difficulty in distinguishing between a prince and a tyrant. The prince is subject to justice (*aequitas*), which John defines, in accordance with the lawyers' convention, as giving to each his own (*tribuens unicuique quod suum est*). It is the law's business to interpret this justice, and it is good or bad law according to the success of the interpretation. The prince is the servant of the law, though very distinguished moral qualities are demanded of him. John, in contradistinction to the commonly accepted principles of feudal law, though not radically out of harmony with these, does not envisage a pact between prince and thrall. The prince's authority, it seems, comes directly from God. But it is an authority much limited by the authority God gives his people, for it is *lawful* for these to rise against any prince who clearly abuses his divine commission. In such a case, becoming a tyrant he immediately becomes also an outlaw and may be, if necessary, killed. The only limitation of the people's right to destroy such a tyrant is that they must not poison him! Any other means may licitly be used. In some cases it may be the people's bounden duty so to rise against a tyrant. In all cases it is their right, regardless of whether they are able in practice to exercise their right.

Manegold, John's German contemporary, is more forthright, less academic; but the basic democratic principles are common to both of them. Manegold also takes it for granted that the prince must exercise his functions for the good of the society and according to *aequitatem*. Unlike John, however, and in conformity with feudal theory,[5] he regards the relationship between prince and people as based on a pact entered into when the latter appointed their prince and placed him in his exalted position. Manegold says bluntly that a prince who dishonors this contract may be "fired" just as may a

[5] Manegold's theory owes little, however, to any tradition, and merits closer inspection than most scholars have given it. Manegold was an exceptional, independent thinker. For him, *justitia* is the end of the kingly office, not merely the limitation of the power that springs from anointing. (See his *Liber ad Gebehardum*, cc. 30-48.) He flourished about 1080, and is not to be confused with the French Manegold who taught William of Champeaux a generation earlier.

swineherd who neglects the pigs committed to his care. The prince and the swineherd have indeed very different functions; but the terms of their appointment are essentially comparable.

The medieval political thinkers got the notion of Natural Law from the ancients. It came to them indirectly and they christianized it. The period of half a millennium from the middle of the sixth to the middle of the eleventh century was on the whole too turbulent to be progressive or reflective, so that when the political theorists of the eleventh century went to work they had to take every source they knew. It was natural that they should look to the principles of the Roman (Civil) law that linked the Christian society to its illustrious pagan past. The book to which we today owe most of our knowledge of the law of classical Rome is, of course, the *Institutes* of Gaius. This the eleventh-century writers knew mainly through Justinian, the compilers of whose *Institutes* imperfectly grasped the methods of Gaius, sometimes obscured his plan, and copiously used other works. Both Gaius and Justinian, however, begin their books with some observations on the origins of the law they propose to set forth. For Gaius the law is made up of two elements—the Civil Law (*ius civile*), supposed to be peculiar to Rome, and the Law of Nations (*ius gentium*), believed to be common to all peoples. From the universality that he attributes to the Law of Nations, Gaius infers that it must be somehow or other implanted in human nature. But he does not here use the term that was to become so important in the Middle Ages—"Natural Law." Justinian follows Gaius; but he prefixes certain phrases on the authority of Ulpian, the great Roman jurist who served under Septimius Severus and Caracalla, writing mainly between A.D. 211 and 222. It is on Ulpian's authority that he adds the term "Natural Law." He describes this as consisting in the animal instincts, and so, he says, the lower animals are acquainted with it. Ulpian had in fact distinguished the Law of Nations from the Natural Law by remarking that the essential difference lay in the fact that while the former belonged exclusively to mankind, the latter did not. This doctrine is peculiar to Ulpian, who, though he mentioned it, did not make a great deal of it. No doubt he had a somewhat confused notion of instincts that might be interpreted as moral or biological according to the view one might care to take of the nature of instincts.

When the ecclesiastical or Canon Law of the Middle Ages began to be formulated there was little of this jurisprudence in it. The early codifications were mainly practical in character. But as soon as the Canon Law came to have an important place alongside of Roman Law and Feudal Law, the term "Natural Law" was readily used by the canonists. It was used much in the sense of Plato's "law of nature" and Pindar's "natural justice." It is practically impossible, however, that the canonists who began so to use the term should have associated it with such Greek sources: they knew Plato little and Pindar less. It was rather that, having the authority of Justinian for the use of the term, they sanctified this by investing it as fully as possible with one of the meanings which, we have seen, it was capable of bearing. Man, in spite of the diseased state of mind that in fact commonly warps his judgment and curtails his imagination (a state which Christian writers had for long called "original sin"), retains some measure of the glory of his preternatural and healthier condition before the fall of Adam. It is thus that there is in him a vestigial consciousness of all human laws having their spring in that preter-natural righteousness he has all but lost. Certain texts in Cicero's *De Legibus* support this interpretation, in so far as it can be supported in Stoicism: the existence of Natural Law is revealed to man. It is revealed, Aristotle notwithstanding, in an interior *voice* that proclaims that men are by nature equal. It is known that these Ciceronian texts, and also similar ones in Seneca, were available to the eleventh-century political theorists.

Probably not even all this somewhat complicated process of thought could have made the political theory of the Middle Ages as democratic as it was, had not the medieval theorists inherited New Testament teaching. According to this, whatever be the ranks of office in Christ's Church or in the State, Christians are members of a brotherhood under God, who puts it into their hearts to address him, as did the first, Aramaic-speaking disciples: Abba, Father. It is in this brotherhood that "there is neither Jew nor Greek, there is neither bond nor free, there is neither male nor female." But when everyone, practically speaking,[6] is a member of both Church and State, is not everyone equal? Then is not the will of the people in such a State an expression of the will of God?

At no time did all medieval thinkers cherish either the ideal or the hope that the papacy should dominate the world after the manner of a Byzantine despot. Nevertheless, by the time of the Greek Schism in the middle of the eleventh century, the schism that still separates Roman Christendom from that of the papacy-repudiating East,[7] it had for long been felt in the Latin West that the failure of the Church to realize the Augustinian ideal was due to the fact that the Church was in practice at the mercy of imperial politics. In the eyes of the political reformers of the eleventh century, it must have seemed almost a truism that if only the Church throughout the world could be better and more adequately represented at Rome, society would be more truly served and its good more vigorously promoted. For example, Leo IX, when he became Pope in 1049, found his immediate advisers, the cardinals, recruited exclusively from Roman families whose interests were far too deeply vested in local secular affairs to permit these men, even if they had been themselves conspicuously independent in mind, to perform their high function for the good of Christendom. Leo's appointment of advisers more representative of the whole Christian West reformed not only the cardinalate but the whole Church. This reforming action was in many ways the expression of Cluniac ideas. The tenth-century Cluniac reform of the Benedictine Order had aimed at the establishment of monastic lands that would be free of

[6] The fact that I do not here take into consideration the Jewish and Muslim elements does not mean that I ignore the problem of minorities in the medieval society, any more than it means that I ignore the great contributions of the thinkers of these minorities to medieval life and culture. To consider such matters here would, however, lead us far from our main topic.

[7] On the history of the thought and events leading to the repudiation of papal pretensions in the earlier half of Christendom, by far the best recent treatment is in Professor Runciman's *The Earlier Schism*. (See Bibliography.)

both episcopal and worldly interference; free of the former because this had become too much entangled with the latter. The Cluniac abbeys were nevertheless to be under the protection of the Pope. This was to be the solution, *faute de mieux*. It was, or seemed to be, the most practical measure available. And perhaps the best way for a zealous Christian community to carry on its work with a minimum of interference and yet a maximum of wise counsel is to submit to a bishop as far away as possible from the scene of its labors.

The mother-house of Cluny had the good fortune to be served by a series of abbots of remarkable character and ability, and Cluny became, in the early eleventh century, under its fifth abbot, the headquarters of all the Cluniac houses, the superiors of which were appointed by and responsible to the abbot of Cluny. This was a radical departure from the monastic constitution to that date. The Cluniacs became the nearest approach then conceivable to what the Jesuits were to become several centuries later—an autocratically ruled society of men within the Church. Their constitution had an important effect on the lines on which the Church was reformed in the eleventh and twelfth centuries. But while it turned out that it helped to enhance the independence of the papacy and establish the Pope's plenitude of power as the Head of the Church, it did not eradicate the basic principle that in the *respublica* of Christian society, the ultimate political authority lies in that Natural Law of which the people are, under God, the bearers.

It had sometimes, rather, the opposite effect of reinforcing this principle. For example, when the notorious Roger Norreys had been imposed by royal influence as Lord Abbot of Evesham, in 1191, that great abbey quickly fell into such an evil state that the poor monks had to instigate a complaint to the papal legate that, far from being able to discharge their charitable obligations towards the poor, they had themselves been reduced to beggary, extreme cold, and a diet of bread and water. They had had to neglect their choir office and the Mass because their clothes were too indecent to permit them to appear in public, while at the same time the Lord Abbot was living fastidiously in his lodging, wearing secular clothes, entertaining young women, and entirely neglecting the administrative responsibilities of his position, which in that age were very considerable, except to the extent that his own unedifying manner of life seemed to be affected. Not only did the monks' complaint receive a sympathetic hearing: the Lord Abbot was deposed. It shocks the modern ear to hear that he got another executive position of inferior rank; but at any rate he was discharged from the one in which he had so badly served God and man. The papacy, in the very act of wielding its power, could not help perpetuating the principle of popular sovereignty.

What distinguished this older tradition, at its best and at its worst, from the spirit of the friars who appeared early in the thirteenth century, was not any radical difference in their interpretation of the principles of medieval political theory, but rather the much greater effectiveness of the friars' methods in putting these principles into practice. Naturally, the friars were from the first thoroughly odious to the less worthy representatives of the older system who did not *want* the basic principles to be put into practice. About 1220, St. Dominic provided a constitution for his new Order that reflects the fundamentally democratic principle that underpinned all medieval theory.

The constitution of the Dominicans is indeed so strikingly democratic that it might almost be that of a modern American or English organization. It combined a discreet provision for that executive authority necessary to the efficient working of any highly mobile, active society, with both a full measure of representative government, and that limitation of the power and tenure of the office-bearers that is familiar to us in the modern democratic organization. It was provided, for instance, that every Dominican house should elect its own superior, and that the latter should preside, not permanently (*ad vitam aut culpam*) as was the case in the established, ancient Orders, but for four years only. The whole territory, which was in principle the world, was divided into provinces, each under a provincial chapter consisting of all the priors of the individual houses. The general chapter sat as a supreme court above the provincial chapter. It consisted not only of the provincial priors, but also of a delegate from each province popularly elected for the purpose. It was to this general chapter that was confided the duty of electing a master-general, who alone was to be appointed for life.

The friars were in practice, moreover, in many ways the champions in the thirteenth century of the theoretically indisputable principle of popular sovereignty. From the point of view of their reactionary contemporaries they were the political liberals of their day, peculiarly dangerous because they really took the democratic principles seriously. They quickly became the intellectuals of the age. Of the Dominicans this is obviously the case; but it is no less true of the Franciscans, whose rule, at first, forbade them even the possession of a book. These turned into a company of impressively active thinkers and political leaders. A pious brother lamented, indeed, that Paris had destroyed Assisi. And later in the century, the Lord Abbot of Peterborough (Grosseteste's abbey), writing of the year 1224, involuntarily paid the Franciscans the compliment of exclaiming: "In that year, O misery! O more than misery! O cruel scourge! The Friars Minor came to England." There was, as is evident from Chaucer, a general objection to the Franciscans' freedom from episcopal control. This led to abuses. But the Lord Abbot seems to express a regret at the emergence of efficient machinery for the promotion of democratic ideals, against which he could really find little to say, however, in principle.

By what may seem a curious paradox, it was just these friars, however, who helped to foster papal autocracy. The friars thought they saw in the Pope the most effective means of checking tyrannical princes as well as worldly bishops, abbots, and the like, all in the interest of the people. Insisting on the historic Christian doctrine of popular sovereignty, and recognizing that, according to the accepted view, a tyrannical prince may be resisted (by force, if necessary), they asked: but what if the people are in fact powerless? Under an efficient tyrant they are indeed likely to be rendered so. And so, of course, they commonly were in fact. Whom, then, are they to invoke? The Emperor? But the Emperors were often unable to help even if they so wished. Imperial unity was an ideal too far removed from actuality to be the subject of any realistic theory in politics. When Thomas Aquinas and others of this period speak of "the State," they are usually thinking of one of the small feudal principalities or duchies or municipal republics that they knew. Mr. Christopher Dawson reminds us that "the germs of decay were inherent in the Carolingian State from its origin," and if this cannot be said of Otto's more durable achievement, it is perhaps only because it was more fully decayed at the start. At any rate, what everyone saw, standing above these numerous little independencies, was, of course, the only international institution that existed—the Church—to which in theory, and to a great extent in practice, every citizen of every such little State belonged. In marked contrast to the relative insecurity of even the strongest of these States was the immense unity of the Church, believed to be divinely founded. Was it not, indeed, commonly said to be founded on a rock? Was not Peter that rock? The Bishop of Rome claimed to be Peter's successor. Why not then look to him? The Pope seemed not only the most reliable but the only available protector of all peoples, in the political insecurity of the Middle Ages.

The people had the undoubted authority but they lacked the power. To whom were they to delegate their authority, so that they might have at their command power to resist tyranny, perhaps in the form of an unworthy prince, which they might indeed be bound to do? To the Pope, of course, their protector. There was no guarantee, they well knew, that a pope should be a good man; but was it not, after all, more reasonable to expect goodness in a pope than to hope for it in a prince?

This political idealism of the thirteenth century sprang from a natural, healthy longing in the Christian *respublica*. It was sustained by the devotion, eloquence, and erudition of the friars, who could very honestly support it from the Christian political tradition. It seemed they were only endeavoring to apply venerable Christian principles to the situation in hand. But, in the process, many of them were easily won over to papalism. Unfortunately, history abounds with instances to show that the people are sometimes worse served by their own appointed champions than by their more obvious enemies. Despite some impressive medieval experiments in democracy, men had not yet learned to devise an efficient democratic machinery that would safeguard the historic Christian ideal and put the traditional jurisprudence into practice. We cannot well blame medieval civilization for this failure, or for its readiness to look to the Pope as an independent arbitrator who might be expected to safeguard its interests and defend its rights. After all, the theorists of much later ages who fostered the enthusiasms that spawned Cromwells and Napoleons, not to mention worse, had still not learned the lesson.

Furthermore, there is no doubt that the papacy did sometimes intervene in political affairs for the good not only of the Christian *respublica* but also of the minorities, the unhappy victims of shameful persecutions engendered by vulgar prejudice and superstition. Towards the end of the thirteenth century, for instance, Pope Gregory X issued a most firm injunction against the maltreatment of the Jews, in which he clearly delineated the ignorant and superstitious character of anti-Semitic hate. Gregory ordered the release of all Jews wrongfully imprisoned, and decreed that no Christians were to be obeyed who sought on frivolous pretexts to seize law-abiding Jews. Here indeed was protection for the people. It is no wonder that the most serious-minded people sought it for the whole world.

Papal interventions were not always, however, so felicitous. The Emperor Frederick I, who was probably as good a Christian emperor as any throughout the Middle Ages, had uttered a manifesto about the middle of the twelfth century, reproaching the papacy in language whose dignity, firmness, and temperance mark this document as a medieval classic. Speaking with great reverence for the Church, for the safety of which he accounted himself responsible to God, he records how, while he was holding court at Besançon, he honorably received the papal legates and, according to custom, assembled his princes together that all might listen reverently to the voice of the Church. Great was his astonishment, he says, to find that the message from the lord Pope (Adrian IV) consisted of an affirmation that the imperial crown was in the gift of the papacy and that it might please the Church to bestow even greater honor on the Emperor in time to come. So indignant were the assembled princes, continues the record, that but for the clemency enjoined by the Emperor, whose duty to God it is to protect his subjects even when they are the bearers of insults to the imperial majesty, they would have "condemned those two unhallowed priests to the punishment of death."

It is then that he enunciates what is indubitably a very tenable medieval theory: "And inasmuch as the kingdom, together with the empire, is *by the election of the princes* ours from God alone, who by the Passion of his Son Christ subjected the world to the rule of the two necessary swords; and since Peter the apostle instructed the world with this doctrine, 'Fear God, honour the King,' whosoever shall say that we received the imperial crown as a benefice from the lord Pope, goes against the institutions of God and the doctrine of Peter, and shall be guilty of lying." He appeals to Christendom to bear in mind how he has striven not only to preserve the Church from its foes but also to conserve to it all the immense prerogatives and dignity with which God has invested it, and to resist in every way what he calls an *"unheard-of innovation";* that is, the notion that the imperial crown is not the gift of God speaking through the people, but nothing more than a papal appointment.

It seems a very far cry from this twelfth-century atmosphere to that of the fifteenth-century chronicler who, describing an emperor's election and coronation, recounts how the emperor kneels at the feet of the Pope, "in token of his humility and to do honour to the holy Roman Church, whose vassal he is." Medieval constitutional theory had not changed. But thinkers such as St. Thomas, whose political doctrine was in some ways democratic according to medieval tradition, supported the claims of the now rapidly growing papalist party. Pope Boniface VIII, than whom there was no doughtier papalist, speaks of *both* swords, spiritual and temporal, as committed to Peter and his successors, and charges any who think otherwise with adhering to the dualistic, Manichaean heresy that the world is an arena of combat between a good and an evil deity. But many learned men were in this uncomfortable condemnation, including, for instance, Dante, who had no love for the reigning pontiff, Boniface VIII. In the eighth circle of hell, Dante finds himself mistaken for that Pope by one of Boniface's predecessors, Nicholas III, already, according to Dante, in hell. Nicholas might have been excused for the error, since he was at the disadvantage, while receiving his visitor, of having his head immersed in a hole and his feet extended upwards, aflame. Mistaking the poet for his own successor in the chair of St. Peter, he greets Dante with but little surprise: "Boniface, are you here already?" [8] Dante's satirical wit was his own, but he was not alone in combining a delicate medieval piety and religious fervor with a robust dislike of papal innovations in political theory. And innovation it certainly was for popes to claim, as did Boniface, that all princely opposition to the papacy was simply insurrection.

The disillusioned fourteenth-century theorists, on the other hand, were forced to devise more elaborate methods of protecting the people's rights. To them is commonly attributed a break from the older medieval political tradition and the beginning of a modern one. But there is really no radical break. They develop, along anti-papalist lines, principles that were already recognized. There is no fundamentally new doctrine even among the jurists of the French King Philip the Fair, in their championship of the rights of the King against the Pope—such jurists as John of Paris or even Peter du Bois. The theories of Ockham and Marsilius of Padua were naturally distasteful to the papalists who wished to paralyze the secular arm of the Christian *respublica* in order to give more power to the elbow of the Pope. But neither of them was a revolutionary in political theory. In the famous *Defensor Pacis* Mar-

[8] *Se' tu gia costi ritto, Bonifazio?*

silius distinguishes between two aspects of the legislative action of
the people in the exercise of their sovereign power, namely, (a)
the preparation of the laws—what modern lawyers would call
draftsmanship, and (b) the approbation of these laws. While the
mass of the people, and even the civically educated whom he calls
the *pars valentior,* are disqualified, for lack of technical skill, from
preparing the laws, they nevertheless retain the full legal right to
pass or reject the laws that have been prepared by their appointed
experts, the *sapientes.* Though they cannot frame laws themselves,
they are fully capable of grasping the general sense of the laws
that are drafted for their scrutiny. As Marsilius puts it: a man may
very well lack the technical skill to paint a picture; but this does
not prevent his being thoroughly able to appreciate it when
painted. The people need not only legal draftsmen, however; they
must have an executive. In some cases they may conceivably execute the laws themselves; but since this is generally impracticable
they elect a prince or other ruler. This ruler should really have no
more power over them against their will, however, than has a modern police force in a modern democratic State.

If popular sovereignty is the basis of the Christian State, is it
not also the basis of the Christian Church? This is the view of
some of the great fourteenth- and fifteenth-century theorists. Hence
the connection between the development of medieval political theory and the ill-fated conciliar movement that preceded but failed to
avert the Lutheran Reformation. But the application of medieval
political theory to the organization of the Church itself is much
thornier. For the kind of authority committed from early times to
the leaders of the Church was different from that vested in secular
rulers. According to the anti-papalists of the fifteenth century,
Church and State are but two faces of the same Christian *respublica.* God has given Peter to the Church, not the Church to Peter.
As the people need a prince, so the same people need a pope; the
first to execute their will as citizens of the earthly City, the second
to execute their will as citizens of the heavenly one. John Wyclif
and such extremists went so far as to insist that the temporal estate

of the Church belongs to the people, though it be administered by the Pope. The Church's spiritual estate is likewise theirs.

But one did not need to be a Wyclif to maintain the clear superiority of a General Council over the Pope. According to the fifteenth-century Nicholas of Cusa, a Cardinal of the Roman Church and one of the greatest minds of the Middle Ages, the General Council consists of the people's representatives. Such representation is limited, of course, by the divinely committed organization of the Church; yet this does not injure the doctrine that popular sovereignty is in the Church as well as in the State. For the members of the Council are required to express not merely their own views but the mind of that area of the Church that they represent. The importance of this aspect of the question is that since the Council derives its authority from the people, it is authoritative only to the extent that it truly expresses the mind of the Church, which is the whole body of the faithful. According to this view, a General Council can depose a pope not only for heresy but also for other reasons—reasons such as those for which a prince might be deposed by his people. Here was a more moderate position than that of Wyclif.

Such extreme views as Wyclif's were by no means unchallenged. It was at the opposite extreme that the papalist party was developed, and fostered by the exceedingly partisan Jesuits. Neither party represented the full round of the medieval tradition. The constitutional history of the Church throughout the Middle Ages was certainly more democratic than ever it has been since the advent of Jesuit influence. Yet it was also ill represented in Wyclif's position.

The ideal of the Middle Ages was that God should redeem the world through the ever-widening influence of the Church's ever-deepening life. That the divine life of Christ himself was *in* the Church was not doubted. Nor was it questioned that the guardianship of the teaching divinely committed to the Church was in a very special manner in the hands of those who inherited this spiritual treasure from the Apostles and their successors. But on the other hand the Church was also *for* the people. The strong emphasis on popular sovereignty in political theory could hardly fail to raise in men's minds the question of the manner in which and the extent to which the people were represented in the Church by those whom God had set over them there.

Historically, there was in fact an intimate association between the political doctrine of popular sovereignty and the conciliarist interpretation of the constitution of the Church. The affinity between the two notions made it often appear especially obvious to the secular princes, who wished to set forth their claims to the world at large, that they should support these by appeal to the conciliarist rather than the papalist elements in the Church. This was plain enough to anyone before the question of the constitution of the Church became, in the thirteenth and fourteenth centuries, a very technical one. When the conciliar idea was then developed into a theory to be set alongside the theory of papal absolutism, there were great difficulties in discussing it. In an age when men were less conscious than they now are of the need for linguistic analysis, the phrase *Romana ecclesia,* for example, was highly ambiguous. It could mean, on the one hand, the local church in Rome that from the earliest times had had a remarkable prestige and had retained this in the west, and, on the other hand, the entire company of Christ's faithful people, the *congregatio fidelium.* But the term *ecclesia* itself was laden with ambiguities. The late twelfth- and thirteenth-century canonists were by no means, however, entirely unaware of these ambiguities, and the greatest of them, Huguccio, Bishop of Pisa, drew the extremely important distinction between, on the one hand, the Roman Church which, consisting of the Pope and the cardinals, possessed a degree of authority not enjoyed by other corporations in Christ's Church, and, on the other hand, the Roman Church which, consisting of the whole body of the faithful, was divinely preserved from all radical error. This interpretation was very widely accepted indeed; so much so that before conciliarism became a definite constitutional theory in opposition to papal absolutism, the distinction between the Pope's restricted and relative authority in matters of faith and the inerrancy of the whole body of the faithful had for long been a commonplace among the canonists. In the later disputes the conciliarists developed the early canonists' doctrine along special lines and sometimes in a different spirit; but it was the distinction the latter had made that the conciliarists later took into account, while the papalists, on the contrary, sought to suppress such notions.

Gratian had not himself favored limitation of the Pope's authority; but he extensively discussed the whole question. His successors, however, insisted that there were certainly cases in which the authority of a General Council was greater than that of the Pope. It is the reasons for their insistence on this that specially concern us here. For the principle they applied was the principle of the old Roman Law that what affects all is to be judged by all; hence the Pope, though he might be accounted the supreme judge in matters of faith, was nevertheless no more than a judge. That is to say, he was bound to consider what a General Council said, and he most certainly could not arrogate to himself the functions of the latter. The Pope was, in accordance with the fundamental medieval principle, as much subject to the faith of the Church as a prince was subject to the "justice" written in the hearts of his people. It was not that a prince was "superior" or "inferior" to the people absolutely: both were, in theory, bound to God in their sacred relationship. Likewise, Pope and Council were in a sense equal; but this did not mean that the one could ordinarily act without the other, and as soon as a Pope transgressed the limits of his function it was the business of a General Council to put the Church into a better state of health. The Pope stood *in figura ecclesiae*; the decrees of a General Council were established "by universal consent." To such notions nothing could be more repugnant than the decrees of the Vatican Council, in the powers they conferred on the Pope, in the reasons adduced for the vesting of such powers in him, and in the manner in which the decrees themselves were promulgated —without precedent, as we have noted, in the history of the Church.

The immense intricacies in the development of conciliarism are beyond the scope of this study of the background of the Vatican Council. Yet it is important for us to be clear about the general principles of medieval thought on the subject, and wherever we turn in the Middle Ages we find evidence of a most widespread and lively antipathy to that absolutism that is implied in the Vatican decrees in 1870. The medieval canonists were very skilful in mixing the maxims of Roman Law with patristic ideas of a poetical and devotional kind; for instance, it was an old and hallowed notion that the bishop was the father or, sometimes, the spouse of his people, and so the canonists applied to this conception legalistic notions from the Roman law. But not even in the Roman law, and certainly not in the New Testament, was a father's power or authority over his children or a husband's over his wife an absolute authority or power. Notions such as that of Innocent III that the papal *plenitudo potestatis* places the Pope above law itself were as alien to the learned opinion of his day as were the pretensions of Pius IX and his supporters repugnant to learned Roman Catholic opinion in the nineteenth century.

Among the many notions of early piety brought to bear on the democratic development we are now considering was that of the Church as the Mystical Body of Christ. The canonists adapted such devotional ideas, molding them into their own legalistic patterns. But in so doing they evolved the theory that the whole Church is a "corporation," and this view, developed by Cardinal Hostiensis, for instance, in the thirteenth century, provided an excellent groundwork for the ideas of the great fourteenth-century conciliarists, such as John of Paris, whose writings were synthesized in the work of Cardinal Francis Zabarella, perhaps the ablest of all the exponents of conciliarism before the Council of Constance. For it was the emphasis on the notion of the whole Church as a "corporation" that brought into relief the essentially democratic principle in all learned medieval thinking about the structure of the Church and the authority of the Pope, namely, that while the Church is hierarchically organized it is at the same time a corporation, and in the last resort the authority lies in the *congregatio fidelium* in which that corporation consists, although the *congregatio* does not directly exercise its authority in ordinary circumstances.[9]

The Council of Constance, held 1414-18, maintained that a General Council of the Roman Church had authority over even the Pope. Without a single dissentient voice, the Fathers of Constance solemnly decreed that "this Holy Synod . . . has received immediately from Jesus Christ a power to which all persons, no matter of what rank or dignity, the Pope himself not excepted, are bound to submit in those matters that concern the Faith." This was substantially the view of Ockham, to whom Luther owed much, as it was likewise that of the great fifteenth-century divine, John Gerson. The decrees of Constance were never forgotten by learned and pious divines, least of all by the Gallicans in France, despite centuries of effort on the part of the papalists to minimize them.

Less widely known perhaps is the extent to which the full force of the medieval conflict of opinion on the subject came out in the Council of Trent, which, opened on December 11, 1545 under the presidency of Cardinal Del Monte, lasted for nineteen years, and was the longest council in the history of the Roman Church as well as the last to take place for over three hundred years before the Vatican Council. When the Tridentine Fathers eventually assembled after having been kept waiting for months on account of a feud between the papacy and the temporal princes, the principal question they raised at the first session was: who were entitled to vote? It may be surmised that during the months the Pope had kept them idly awaiting the opening of the Council, questions of this kind had been already much before their minds, and possibly disputed with some acrimony. Be that as it may, before any other business was officially transacted, it was such important constitutional points that were raised. The bishops claimed that accord

[9] Conciliar theory was developed from two main sources: (a) the Decretists, who had discussed the limitation of papal power in reference to the early councils, and especially the question of the deposition of a heretical pope; and (b) the Decretalists, who applied corporation theory to the whole Church.

ing to the ancient practice of the Church they had the exclusive right to vote. The abbots asserted that their right was just as good. The significance of this dispute lies, partly at any rate, in the fact that while the office of abbot was recognized to be one of great dignity, since for persons living the monastic life (the way accounted nearer to the counsels of Christ) the abbot often took the place of the bishop and could be independent of the latter's jurisdiction, he was on the whole more likely to be a Pope's man. The price of independence from episcopal jurisdiction is commonly a more special dependence on that of the Pope. The bishops traditionally tended to assert their independence. It was decided that while abbots *as such* were not entitled to vote, this privilege ought to be enjoyed by abbots-general and other heads of religious orders, and such other abbots as were entitled by custom to wear the mitre. This decision, tolerably plausible as it may have seemed, eventually opened the way to abnegating democratic representation altogether. This abnegation became very profitable for the papalists at the Vatican Council.

The Tridentine Fathers next asked point blank what was their relation to the Pope. Did each Father meet as under Christ or, rather, as under Christ through the Pope? Were their acts to be the acts of the Council only, or were they to be the acts of Pope and Council? These were, to the papalists, red-hot questions that they would very much have liked not to have had asked at all. Trent had been designed to crush the doctrines of Luther and bring about in some other way the reforms all men knew were most sorely needed. The one thing Trent required if it was to carry out its work was a show of unity in essential matters, especially those concerning the constitutional bases of the Church itself. How could the Council speak with authority against the Protestant heresies if there were a division of opinion within itself on the nature or locus of its own authority? How could it deal with clerical concubinage and other and worse abuses if its own status was in question? Above all, how could it mold the Roman Church according to the papalist plan if at the very outset it raised so inconvenient a question as that of the relation between Council and Pope?

Del Monte, evidently a watchful president, sent off a courier to Rome to tell the Pope that the bishops were mutinous and that money would be required for the advancement of the papal interests. He had a definite recommendation on the latter point: the tithes of episcopal incomes that were ordinarily paid to the See of Rome should be remitted while the Council continued. The Pope acceded. While some of the bishops expressed their gratitude, most of them looked with some suspicion on the move as suggesting the recognition of the papal right to demand such tithes as well as to forego them. Continuing their discussion of the form the conciliar acts were to take, they made it evident that the general desire was that the decrees to be passed should be in the name of the Council only, with no mention of the Pope at all. The Pope, in turn, suggested that the decrees should be issued as the decrees of the Council presided over by a Legate of the Apostolic See.

This was just what was not wanted. The bishops desired to be accounted representatives. This was the expression of a democratic principle, for it made it clear that though they were not the elected representatives of their respective flocks, as is a modern American congressman the elected representative of the people, they did claim to be the representatives of the faithful, not as merely the assistants of the Pope in the discharge of an autocratic papal function. That many of them probably saw that their claim was more conducive to the exaltation of their own position is beside the point. They were voicing a medieval principle—one that was in grave danger of destruction.

Cardinal Del Monte's manner of dealing with such unwelcome echoes of democracy is illuminating. He appealed to all that was undemocratic in the mind of his hearers. Reminding them that the Church consisted of the laity as well as of the clergy, he drew their attention to what might happen if the view propounded by the bishops should be given out as official. The bishops would be made to appear, he suggested, the representatives of the clergy. Then what if the laity should demand representatives also? It was evidently with reason that he expected the bishops to see in any such prospect nothing but unmitigated disaster. The president's argument was, of course, *ad hominem* and fallacious. For the bishops, if they represented anybody, represented the laity of their dioceses as much as they represented the clergy. But it was not a question of whether the president's exposition of Canon Law was sound or not; it was a practical question, rather, of whether the common people might in fact be incited to some sort of insurrection. One could not but take such a suggestion seriously. The common people included vast masses of illiterates. And in justice to the Tridentine Fathers it must not be forgotten that no society can ever extend a full democratic franchise to an illiterate mob. Sixteenth-century Europe was very far indeed from anything like universal franchise. A properly developed democratic society would, of course, seek to remove the illiteracy as speedily as possible. But that is another question. No one would ever pretend that sixteenth-century Europe was anything in the least like a fully developed democracy. It is contended only that the germs of democracy that had been sown within the medieval Roman Communion had not been, despite the persistent efforts of the papacy, by any means entirely destroyed even by the time of the Council of Trent. The climate of that Council, for all the influence exercised upon it by the papalist faction, was such that it was impossible to exterminate democratic notions entirely. Even after the words "representing the Universal Church," as used at the Councils of Basle and Constance, had been negatived, the principle behind them remained an unsettled question. The democratic tradition survived. There were echoes of it even in the Vatican Council three centuries later, when it eventually received its death-blow, so bringing about the situation that is now familiar to us in contemporary America and throughout the world. This situation will be considered in our concluding chapter.

7

THE FLIGHT FROM DEMOCRACY

MODERN Roman Catholicism is very much a Jesuit creation. The Society of Jesus, founded in the sixteenth century, when the Protestant Reformation seemed to threaten the very survival of the Roman Church, was organized on the most frankly military lines. It was a medieval Salvation Army. Modern Salvationists adopt military terms: prayer becomes "knee-drill," clergy are "officers," and the weekly offering envelopes even become "cartridges." The Jesuits were no less ready to use the picturesque language of medieval chivalry. Loyola, their founder, was determined to use every means in the interest of the cause of the Church. There was a very large element of Spanish romanticism in him, which expresses itself in the Society he founded. St. Paul had told the Corinthians that he and his fellow Apostles were fools for Christ's sake: Loyola would be a Quixote for Christ. It is such a romantic and emotional impulse that lies behind the development of Jesuit ideals. Loyola and his companions laid their swords on the altar of the Virgin and swore to go forth into the world as her knights. The type of piety they nurtured was one the like of which the Roman Church had never quite seen; at any rate not on such a grand scale. And in the war with the Devil, the success of the Jesuit army's tactics seemed so spectacular that the Society could not fail to influence the practice of the whole Church, which has been ever since more and more modeled after the Jesuit pattern.

Romanticism has played an important part in the development of all societies. It brought England rubies from India and led

Americans to the gold that was said to be in their hills. In religion it has played an essential part, for a Church cannot live on its Origens and its Kierkegaards; it needs its Hildebrands and its Booths. Yet all romanticism is dangerous. And when it pretends to enlist the intellect as an aide-de-camp to the emotional ideal of an efficient and fast-moving army of God, it can become a menace even to what is healthy in itself. That all men kill the thing they love may be only a poet's witty exaggeration; but it is true, at any rate, that romantics often kill the thing they love. This is indeed the tragedy of the Jesuit Society.

Nothing could have been more spectacular than the sixteenth-century revival that not only enabled Rome to cut her losses and live, but filled the devout partisans of the old religion with a well-grounded hope of recapturing Europe and inaugurating a new era of splendor and greatness for the Church that had seemed more than half dead from her wounds. The strength of this remarkable revival lay chiefly in the Jesuit Society, though the political might of Spain helped to support it. The Jesuits saw themselves, in accordance with the notions of chivalry they had inherited from the past, as knights of the Blessed Virgin Mary, setting forth to slay the Protestant dragon whose wicked tail had swept off half the House of God. Such a dragon was too much for even the most stalwart knight-errant. It called for an army of them, and such the Jesuit Society was to be. The knights would submit to a rigorous military discipline. They would become an army, and an army must be enlisted under a command. Who else could the commander be but the Pope? All this had become evident to Loyola and his friends after their pilgrimage to Jerusalem. Things had not gone well for them there. No one had seemed to want their services. Well, they would go to the Pope himself. This is a characteristic attitude in romantic adventurers: if everyone spurns you, go to the King—he will be sure to understand, since he must be wiser than all other men. It was in such a spirit that the first Jesuits had offered their services to the Pope. It was in such a spirit that they had fought for him, identifying him with the Church they had set out to save, in fulfilment of Loyola's knightly vow to the Blessed Virgin.

The Jesuit pattern has imposed itself on the Roman Church in ways that would have been unthinkable in earlier times. That the entire Church should be modeled on an army with generals, regimental officers, and sergeant majors, is a notion than which almost nothing could be more repugnant to the ancient doctors of the Church. Yet it was to such a notion that the Vatican Council set its seal. To a modern Jesuit, however, bred in the ecclesiastical militarism that his Society has bequeathed to the modern Roman Church, it seems perfectly natural that the Church of God should be regimented in such a fashion. Father G. H. Joyce, S.J., in an article on the Pope, says:

> It is frequently objected . . . that . . . the Vatican Council destroyed the authority of the diocesan episcopate. . . . To this it is replied that no difficulty is involved in the exercise of immediate jurisdiction over the same subjects by two rulers, provided only that these rulers stand in subordination the one to the other. We constantly see the system at work. In an army the regimental officer and the general both possess immediate authority over the soldiers, yet no one maintains that the inferior authority is thereby annulled. The objection lacks all weight.[1]

To be sure, the objection does lack all weight, once one has suppressed history and has made oneself believe that Jesus Christ not only made Peter Prince of the Apostles but made him General of the Christian army, the other Apostles regimental officers, and the rest of Christendom obedient troopers.[2] Yet such a notion can sound hardly more preposterous to Protestant ears than it would have sounded to an Augustine or a Dante.

The reputation for intellectualism that the Jesuits speedily acquired and still enjoy is, though partly well founded, the occasion

---

[1] *Catholic Encyclopaedia*, art. "Pope."

[2] For a remarkable exposition of the disillusionment of a Jesuit, see Father Tyrrell's letter to the General of the Society, in M. D. Petre, *Autobiography and Life of George Tyrrell*, Vol. II (London, Arnold, 1912), pp. 458-499.

of a fundamental misunderstanding. Certainly Jesuit training has produced skilful and erudite scholars. The influence of their educational system has been felt not only among their own members. For since non-Jesuit priests often have their preliminary training in Jesuit schools, clerical education generally has immensely benefited. But this improvement in quality is due to the indubitable fact that the Jesuit system makes for disciplined minds. This is indeed a useful and noble achievement. But for those of us who deem it to be the supreme aim of all good education to train people to think for themselves, an aim to which mental discipline should but minister, Jesuit education is a conspicuous failure. In contrast to the nineteenth-century tradition of classical education in England and America, based rightly or wrongly on the view that a boy who had to learn Latin and Greek was best fitted to learn to think for himself, the Jesuit emphasis on and success with classical studies entailed, rather, the notion that such a discipline was a good foundation for "right" thinking. The Jesuit conception of "right" thinking consisted largely in the enlistment of the intellect in the service of the Pope. This may be shown from the fact that the intellect is to be disciplined in order that it may be sacrificed: "the sacrifice of the intellect" is the summit of Jesuit piety. Whatever else may be said in favor of Jesuit scholarship, let it not be identified with thought.

In their endeavor to find historical support for the extreme position that was dictated by a romanticism bolstered by a lively but skin-deep scholarly preoccupation, the Jesuit-inspired, post-Reformation papalist party had no difficulty. For they did not have to invent a new philosophy. They found it ready-made in the already strongly developed papalist tradition that had grown up in the Middle Ages. But there was also another tradition in medieval thought which the papalists were bound to suppress. The medieval thinkers, for all the elaborate intellectual edifices they created, were sometimes astonishingly wooly and inconsistent, and even where they were not, they were often sufficiently ambiguous to leave room for opposing interpretations. We find in medieval thought, therefore, radically opposite principles that were never, except in the most superficial fashion, reconciled.

The results of the sixteenth-century Roman Revival were spectacular. While not everything had been on the side of the Reformers, everything was against the old religion. She who had, in Dante's phrase, grafted sword on crook,[3] found the sword gone and the crook much foreshortened. The Roman Revival succeeded in restoring to the old religion a confidence and vitality it had not enjoyed for centuries.

But the Roman Revival had spent its force by the middle of the seventeenth century. Spain had emerged from the Thirty Years' War stripped of the vast power it might have used for Rome. The Jesuits, having lost much of the spiritual fervor as well as the ingenuousness of their early days, had become advisers to a Church that was now perforce content to consolidate her gains. For all that, it was miracle enough that there had been gains to consolidate. The Jesuits, moreover, had not lost *all* the characteristics of their youth. They were still romantic enough to believe they had been the army of Christ's stalwarts whom God had chosen to confound the wisdom of the world. That they had acquired some of this wisdom in the process of confounding it, was believed to be in the good providence of God. The policy was God's policy, and was it surprising that God's policy had been so successful? There was admittedly a lull in the success. No doubt this was why God had allowed them to acquire a greater worldly wisdom than that of the first members of their Society; they needed to bide their time, as men of the world do. Still, God's policy was clear. He evidently wanted an autocratic Church; else he would not have blessed their arms. They would mold the whole Church after the pattern of their own Society. They would exalt the papacy in whose service they had saved the Church.

Meanwhile the papacy hardly rose to the occasion. None of the pontiffs of the seventeenth or eighteenth centuries were great popes.

[3] *Purgatonio* XVI.

Several were men of good intentions and admirable character, such as Innocent XII and Benedict XIV; but they cannot be accounted great leaders. And in face of the growing progress of the civil governments of Roman Catholic lands, not to mention the Protestant countries, they were weak and ineffective. The morale of the papacy was at a low ebb. Under the very strong King Louis XIV of France, a policy was pursued of resisting all papal claims to the utmost. According to a declaration by the French clergy issued in 1682, the usages of the Church in France limited papal interference; civil rulers had full authority in temporal affairs; General Councils were accounted superior to the Pope; and the Pope was in no sense infallible. The King's claim to the possession of certain disputed income accruing from vacant bishoprics was also upheld. The resulting quarrel with the papacy was, however, later patched up. The French clergy practically withdrew their assertions, and as the King kept the disputed income he did not care to press the rest.

The King's policy towards his own subjects, on the other hand, especially after his marriage with Madame de Maintenon in 1684, was largely determined by considerations of national unity. Under Jesuit influence he revoked the Edict of Nantes the following year, making Protestantism illegal and the profession of it liable to the most severe penalties. It was as a result of this disastrously unwise policy that while, on the one hand, thousands of France's most industrious Protestant citizens emigrated to Holland, England, America, and elsewhere, the former alliances of France with Protestant countries were broken, greatly to the detriment of the country's military needs. It was no less at the instigation of the Jesuits that the King pursued his policy of persecuting the Jansenists, who had won to their opinions many of his most deeply religious subjects, including one of the greatest of all France's sons, Blaise Pascal. Certain statements of one of the Jansenist leaders, Pasquier Quesnel, were condemned by Pope Clement XI's bull *Unigenitus*, though some of them were taken literally from St. Augustine. This bull originated in the personal jealousy of the King's Jesuit confessor against Cardinal de Noailles, who had been Quesnel's protector. The Cardinal Archbishop of Paris appealed for a General Council to declare against the Pope. He was unsuccessful; the combination of Jesuit influence and an absolute monarch's pleasure was too strong. By giving France the choice between a Jesuit-jacketed religion or none at all,[4] the Jesuits, turning thousands of France's ablest minds against God, so embittered these that since the Revolution the Church, despite valiant efforts, has never regained her prestige and influence in French life.

Before the French Revolution, feeling against the fanaticism of Jesuit policy and its disastrous effect on the spiritual and temporal welfare of France led to their suppression in 1764. Many of the ablest of the French clergy had opposed them. Three years later they were suppressed in Spain and in Naples, and eventually, in 1773, the Society was abolished by Pope Clement XIV, too impotent to resist the concerted action of the civil governments against the champions of the papalist party. But it was too late. When in 1789 the French Revolution came, people remembered, not the greatness of the Catholic tradition in France, but only the papalist party. In 1798 Pope Pius VI was carried off to France as a prisoner and died there. It was a bitter lesson the papacy had to learn; but the tragedy was, rather, that it did not learn it.

Napoleon, recognizing the use he could make of the old feeling for Catholic piety that was rooted so deeply in the hearts of Frenchmen, entered into a concordat with Pope Pius VII in 1801. Such of the Church's confiscated lands as were in the possession of the State were to be restored to the Church. Appointment of bishops was to be by the Pope, but the State would nominate them. By the Organic Articles, however, added by Napoleon the following year despite the Pope's protest, no papal decrees were

---

[4] Voltaire, contemplating a picture of Christ dressed in the garb of a Jesuit, wrote these lines:

> Admirez l'artifice extrême
> De ces moines industrieux.
> Ils vous ont habillé comme eux,
> Mon Dieu, de peur qu'on ne vous aime.

to be published in France without government permission. Protestants were to have full religious liberty, and their ministers paid by
the government. But Napoleon's policy was to prove a boomerang.
By ignoring Gallican claims, he made it possible for later generations of Frenchmen who kept the old faith, to look "beyond the
mountains" [5] to the Pope, the people's protector. It was to be the
thirteenth century and the friars all over again.

The title of Holy Roman Emperor had for long been but a
reminder of bygone days. When the Emperor Francis II relin-
quished it in 1806, the last echo of the medieval Church-and-State
society vanished. Napoleon's downfall brought in its train a curious
cult of the antique, and a romantic passion for an imaginary age
that had never existed but that the vulgar vaguely called "the
Middle Ages," as one might speak of the age of Homer. The spirit
of the eighteenth century was belittled. It was in this romantic
mood that the Waverley Novels, for example, were read in every
capital in Europe.

Such romanticism was not disadvantageous to the papalist party.
In August 1814 the situation had sufficiently improved to make
it practicable for Pius VII to restore the suppressed Jesuit Society,
which speedily regained an outstanding place in the Church,
though shorn of much of its former political influence. The papacy
itself, having irrevocably lost its political supremacy in the world,
sought more than ever to stress its supremacy over the Church.
By 1830, however, liberal ideas were winning a decisive victory
all over western Europe. On the continent these ideas were,
moreover, often too closely associated with the French Revolution
not to be suspected of leading to worse tyrannies than those from
which they promised salvation. This was not the case in England;
but with England the papacy had very little to do. England was
still *in partibus infidelium!* The liberal movement was a challenge
and a peril, but above all an inevitability. Liberals were often as
extravagant in their claims and programs as were to be the so-

[5] In contrast to the Gallican party, those who looked to Rome, rather than
within France, became known as "ultramontane," because they looked "beyond the mountains" (the Alps).

cialists of a later age. But they all saw in the Roman Church a formidable brake on their rapid progress, and the Church did nothing to allay their suspicions or mitigate their hostility.

At the same time, there can be no doubt that, to many deeply religious persons, inside or outside the Roman Communion, liberalism was fundamentally on the side of the angels. It is not so many years ago since it was the fashion in England to look back with disdain on almost everything pertaining to the age of Queen Victoria. Almost the worst thing you could say of anything, from an armchair to a moral principle, was that it was Victorian. It is true that there was much in English Victorianism to deserve censure. There was also, however, an immense greatness, and now that we have seen some of Europe's experiments in dictatorship in the twentieth century we ought to be more appreciative of some of her nineteenth-century essays in freedom.

Nowhere in Europe was this movement more feared than in papalist circles in the Roman Church. But to the learned minority of Roman Catholic churchmen who were steeped in their own greatest traditions, liberalism was, in spite of its inevitable extravagances, by no means fundamentally alien to Christianity. It was, rather, a righteous reproach to the Church for neglecting her own best traditions and failing to meet the challenge of the age. Could it be that in the liberal movement God had come to Europe and Europe knew it not? In France, men like Montalembert and Lacordaire were ready to believe that God might fulfil himself in many ways, and that the fruits of the French Revolution, for example, though not all good by any means, were far from being altogether the work of the Devil. For such minds, not less devoutly Catholic for being truth-seeking and sensitive to the "inner meaning" of the march of events, acceptance of the changes wrought by liberal attitudes of mind was not something to be merely suffered by the Church till she could muster God's power to stamp them off the face of the earth. They were, rather, to be accepted as God's rebuke to men. Had churchmen followed Christ better, the changes that were taking place would have taken place in a better way.

But since they had not done so, it behoved the Church not to fulminate but to repent. A spirit of humility and repentance is not incompatible with the possession of infallible guidance from the Holy Spirit.[6]

That popes have often been so unlearned as to make it absurd to attribute to them any personal infallibility has been recognized by many Roman theologians and even stressed by some of the most ardent anti-Protestant writers. Alfonso de Castro, for instance, wrote in the sixteenth century: "I do not think there is any man so impudent in his flattery of the Pope as to attribute to him the impossibility of erring or being deceived by his interpretation of Holy Scripture. For since it is well known that many (*plures*) among them have been so illiterate as to be completely ignorant of grammar, how should they be able to interpret Holy Writ?"[7] The infallibility of any pope with such deficiencies could be upheld only on a theory that was not merely "supernatural" but mechanistic. There is no counterpart of such a theory anywhere else in Roman theology. What the priest claims to do in the Mass, for instance, is supernatural indeed; but the priest, in order for it to

[6] The Abbé Bremond has abundantly shown in his encyclopedic work, *Histoire littéraire du sentiment religieux en France,* that there was in the Catholicism of the *ancien régime* in the two or three centuries before the Revolution a very strong spirit of Christian humanism. The whole Salesian tradition would have been as antithetical in spirit to modern Ultramontanism as it was to Jansenism. It is perhaps not inapposite to mention here that the Abbé Bremond himself, born in 1865, worked after the Church had been officially ultramontanized, and though unlike Tyrrell, he left the Jesuit Society peacefully, he incurred ecclesiastical censure on various occasions, not least when, as a result of his conducting a very private funeral ceremony (without ecclesiastical vestments) for his friend Tyrrell, he was punished by being temporarily forbidden to say Mass. And while the French Academy and Oxford both honored him as he deserved, he received no official ecclesiastical recognition.

[7] *Adversus omnes haereses.* Even Cardinal Bellarmine, a Jesuit, a papalist champion, and now a canonized saint, frequently warned Pope Clement VIII not to suppose that he could, being no theologian, understand the Molinist controversy. In 1602 he wrote to that pope saying: "many popes have, without exhausting themselves with study, condemned many errors with the help of councils and universities; others have, through their many studies, brought both themselves and the Church into great difficulties." *Vita,* Bonn 1887.

be valid, must at least know what it is that he is intending to do. A robot could not validly celebrate Mass. But in respect of the exercise of the allegedly infallible *magisterium* of the Pope, a pope such as is portrayed by Alfonso de Castro would be making his infallible judgments almost as would such a robot. His would not be a mind divinely illumined by miraculous, supernatural guidance; he would be, rather, a divinely inspired automaton, a mere microphone for the Holy Ghost. And though the doctrine of papal infallibility is defended by modern Roman theologians as a "supernatural" doctrine, it is not deemed to be "supernatural" in this sense.

Compared with some popes, Pius IX was an unlearned man. Moreover, he was an unlearned Italian aristocrat. Lack of learning is a disadvantage for any ecclesiastic; but it is more dangerous in one of noble birth than it is in a son of the people. For true learning engenders true humility, the lack of which quality is especially disastrous in a man of high rank. Abbot B. C. Butler, in his recent defense of the doctrine of the infallibility of the Pope, does not claim that Pius IX was in any sense a scholarly man. He rightly reminds his readers that it is not for his learning that a pope is accounted infallible; the doctrine springs from a supernatural belief, rather, that divine Providence keeps him from error. Abbot Butler cites Scripture: "Out of the mouths of babes and sucklings thou hast perfected praise. Thou hast concealed these things from the wise and prudent and hast revealed them unto little ones."

This is, in fact, a modern Roman Catholic scholar's best defense of the remarkable doctrine that was defined in 1870. And it is a very poor defense. Little children are, indeed, as the Gospel reminds us, often wiser than their elders. They exhibit flashes of insight that astonish us. It is almost as though some supernatural agency had entered into them and spoken. But what gives little children this strange, occasional superiority in wisdom over their elders is their receptivity and freedom from prejudice. An old man may be very learned; but the cumulative prejudices of a lifetime blind him, making his learning as dust. A pope could very well have that beautiful simplicity of mind and heart that all good men love and admire in children. But if he had, its first manifestation would be an extraordinary willingness to learn from others and a striking pliability of mind. Pius IX's lack of learning was espoused to no such salutary dispositions. He did not have a childlike heart or mind. He was a romantic, and romanticism is, rather, an emotional by-product of adolescence.

8

THE MEANING OF
"EX CATHEDRA"

WE HAVE examined the historical evidence that prevents a reasonable man from admitting the constitutional legality of the Vatican Council. We have further considered some of the practical effects of the illusion created by the papalist party during and after their triumph in 1870. These are perhaps even more shocking to the moral conscience. But after all, it may be argued that, Roman claims to logicality notwithstanding, it is not entirely a matter of reason or even of human conscience. It is a question of faith.

Suppose that you are willing to make "the sacrifice of the intellect" that the Jesuit Fathers recommend. Suppose that you have decided to sacrifice intellect and will, and to affirm your allegiance to the Roman Church, humbly accepting all that may be required of you by the Vatican Decrees. By such an act of faith you are now ready to be in good standing in the Roman Church. Despite the sacrifices you have made in order to achieve this end, you will naturally hope for the consolation of now knowing exactly what to do. You may not feel temperamentally fitted to find authoritarian leadership congenial; but however disinclined for it you may be, you will expect to have the one consolation of knowing precisely what you must do. You will be like a man who has enlisted in the army: while recognizing that you must miss the freedom of civilian life, you will expect at any rate to get clear orders. You will not hope always to get orders when these are needed, and you may have to struggle alone for long stretches as best you can, using

130

THE VATICAN REVOLUTION 131

your own initiative; but when orders do come you should be able to expect to sigh with relief as you say, "It sounds crazy, but anyhow I know what is to be done." Only clear orders can give this sense of moral security, for however soldierly your instincts you cannot exercise these if the orders are ambiguous. So long as the command is clear, it does not matter what it is. To be told to halt is neither easier nor more difficult than to be told to quick-march. No matter how gruff the voice that tells you to present arms, you can obey, for you are determined to be a good soldier. On the other hand, in face of an order such as, "Fire somewhere or other," even the most fanatically loyal soldier would be ready for desertion. How could one do battle if one were constantly in doubt whether the officer who shouted "Fire!" meant you to use your weapon or was only employing the word in a military anecdote? To be left wondering whether a papal judgment were *ex cathedra* or not would be no less intolerable.

Let us now see how clear are the orders in the Church Militant. It is affirmed in the Vatican Decree that the Roman Pontiff is infallible when he speaks *ex cathedra;* that is, when he speaks "in discharge of the office of pastor and doctor of all Christians." [1] It must be remembered that it is claimed that this doctrine of the personal infallibility of the Pope is part of the deposit of faith given by Christ to the Apostles, notably to St. Peter. That is to say, it has always been the implicit faith of the Roman Church that the Pope is infallible. Consequently, it is to be expected that, whatever the troubles that may have beset the Church throughout the ages, and however great the reluctance to make the implicit faith explicit, there should be no difficulty in ascertaining, especially now that the doctrine is defined as eternal truth, whether any papal utterance either before 1870 or afterwards, was made *ex cathedra*. Nothing could be of greater importance, since if anything a pope has said was said *ex cathedra* it must be accepted as if God himself had uttered it, while if it was not said *ex cathedra*

---

[1] See Appendix I: "Concerning the Infallible Teaching of the Roman Pontiff."

it must, though commanding the reverent attention of all the faithful, be nevertheless regarded as having no more an absolute authority than if it were casually offered by a Sicilian peasant as his private opinion. A pope, as much as any other member of the Church, is rightly entitled to express his private opinion without being thereby held responsible for having made an official pronouncement that is to bind all the faithful. It is as a "private doctor" that he makes such unofficial utterances. In the early stages of the Council, for example, Pius himself insisted that it was only as a "private doctor" that he upheld the doctrine of papal infallibility. How, then, could he have known in 1854 that he was making an *ex cathedra* definition of the doctrine of the Immaculate Conception? [2] Can a pope make an infallible definition without knowing what he is doing?

"Before I was Pope," Pius once observed, "I *believed* in papal infallibility; now I *feel* it." Why, then, did not he exercise it in such a way as to leave the faithful in no doubt whether he was exercising it or not? But in fact, according to the Decree, a pope could no more be said to "feel" infallibility in himself than a judge in an American court of law could be said to "feel" justice in himself. A pope does not receive infallibility as a convert receives, say, the gift of faith or charity. It is not a power that can work in him independently of his ordinary mental processes. It is, indeed, just such a "magical" notion of the doctrine that we are warned against by writers such as Monsignor Knox.[3] Nor does a pope get his infallible power as a priest receives, at ordination, the power to consecrate the eucharistic species. He inherits, rather, "the promise to him in blessed Peter" of God's guidance when he requires to make an official utterance to the Church. He might, like any other man, suffer from a neurotic delusion of infallibility in private life. We are not asked to exclude this possibility. What we are asked to admit is, rather, that even a pope so unfortunate

[2] See Appendix II.
[3] *Supra.*

as to suffer from such a personal neurotic disturbance is invested nevertheless with genuine infallibility when he guides the Church officially. Yet he cannot exercise his genuine infallibility in any automatic fashion, any more than a judge in a court of law could dispense justice without knowing that he was so doing. The Pope must therefore always be aware of what he is doing when he is addressing an infallible pronouncement to the Universal Church.

Had the doctrine of the personal infallibility of the Pope been commonly held even by the popes themselves, throughout the ages, they would surely always have made it clear whether they were speaking *ex cathedra* or not. Indeed, before the definition of the doctrine in 1870, the necessity of making this clear would have been particularly obvious to every pope, since plainly, according to the infallibilist view, there was widespread error on the subject throughout the Church before that date, so that popes must have been acutely aware of the need of safeguarding their own and future generations from doubt about which papal utterances were, and which were not, *ex cathedra*.

That it would have been very easy for them to do so is abundantly evident. There is pellucid clarity in the Roman Church concerning certain obligations such as attendance at Mass. A parish priest has no difficulty in making it clear to his parishioners that while he personally may wish that they should attend Benediction on Sundays, they are entirely free to comply with his desires or not, while on the other hand they are required by the law of the Church to attend Mass. So clear is the law of the Church on such matters that if during the Mass there is a sermon, there is no obligation for the faithful to attend this. During the first year of World War II, an English Roman Catholic in New York found the sermons of the Irish rector there so charged with political propaganda against America's possible entry into the war that he informed the priest he would in future leave the church after the singing of the Gospel, take some fresh air, and then return to church as soon as he heard the intoning of the Credo. In this way he would be fulfilling the obligation prescribed by his Mother the

Church without having to endure hebdomadal doses of Irish nationalist politics dispensed under a homiletic guise. His right to do this was incontestable in Canon Law. His right was clear. Why should there have been any greater difficulty for popes in making clear what the faithful ought to believe? It is no answer (yet such an answer has sometimes been offered by ultramontane controversialists) to say that in troubled times men perversely would not have listened to the infallible voice from Peter's throne. Many today do not listen to the Church's command to attend Mass, but this does not prevent modern popes from ordaining that they shall; nor were popes in the past notably reticent in giving orders. Popes could not be expected, of course, to make the whole of the implicit faith (*fides implicita*) into an explicit faith (*fides explicita*) overnight; but when, as now appears, they did either wish or not wish to make the implicit explicit, why did they leave posterity in *any* doubt, let alone such a maze of doubt, about their intention?

Again, a religious superior has no difficulty in making it clear to a monk whether anything he says is an official order in the name of holy obedience, or just a personal request or admonition. If a prior were to say to one of the priests under his jurisdiction, "I want you to go on a mission to China," the priest might conceivably ask, in effect, "Is this an order, or just a personal wish?" The prior need have no difficulty in making his intention clear, should he have failed to do so in the first instance. Indeed, so also does every army officer regularly make it clear whether he is talking officially or just in a casual, friendly fashion. One cannot well imagine being left in any doubt whether an order to make a bayonet charge was official or just the expression of the officer's opinion of what might be done if he happened to be on duty.

This is, however, just the kind of difficulty in which we are left, according to the testimony of modern Roman Catholic theologians, on the subject of whether papal utterances in the past were *ex cathedra* and therefore infallible, or private observations and therefore as fallible as those of anyone else. Hefele, the most learned authority on the subject, took the view[4] that the seventh-century Pope Honorius, who was anathematized by both an ecumenical council and a subsequent pope (Leo II), was giving a doctrinal instruction to the whole Eastern Church and, implicitly, to all Christendom. Leo's language against Honorius is strong: he charges him with making the pure faith into a profane thing (*profana proditione immaculatam fidem subvertere conatus est*). Until the eleventh century, popes were required, according to the *Liber Diurnus*, to take an oath on entering into their office that they acknowledged the Sixth General Council, at which their predecessor Honorius was anathematized for certain pronouncements he made on the Monothelite heresy.

Hefele wrote a special pamphlet on the subject of Honorius[5] and his account of the affair would seem to be fatal to the doctrine of the personal infallibility of popes. Other modern Roman Catholic theologians, therefore, try to escape from the difficulty by contending that Honorius could not have been speaking *ex cathedra* at the time he made the utterance that was subsequently condemned and is now universally held to have been heretical. This is a difficult course for them to have to take; yet not impossible. The point is that it is almost always possible to question whether a pronouncement is *ex cathedra*.

We do not, indeed, have to go as far back as the seventh century to be confronted with doubt whether a papal utterance was given out as *ex cathedra* or not: there is an eminently important example among others that could be cited in our own time. Dom E. C. Butler correctly says[6] that theologians in the 1860's and 1870's very commonly defended the *Syllabus* as an *ex cathedra* and therefore infallible document, though this was questioned by Fessler, the papal secretary at the Vatican Council, but that this view of it is to be dismissed as "being now almost given up." Pius himself maintained, however, that in applying the Vatican Decree there

[4] *History of the Councils,* English edition, Vol. V, p. 61.
[5] See Bibliography.
[6] *History of the Vatican Council,* Vol. II, p. 228.

could be no such difficulty for any man of good will, since the Vatican definition was as clear as daylight.[7] But there were certainly many very sincere persons within the Roman fold who, three-quarters of a century ago, believed the *Syllabus* to be an infallible utterance. There can be no doubt that Pius was aware of this fact, and yet only a generation later very few regarded the notorious *Syllabus* as having this all-important quality.

Modern Roman Catholics commonly imagine that the question is: did or did not the Pope *say* he was making a *definition?* They suppose that one has only to look up a book and see whether the vital words "We define" are, or are not, used. But it is well known to canonists that in ecclesiastical documents the verb *definire* is used in several senses, so that *definimus* is by no means any more exact an expression than *docemus* or *judicamus* or *confirmamus.* There is really nothing more definite about the term "definition" in Canon Law than there is about the term "consideration" in mercantile Law. Such a term may be very important, but it may be quite insignificant: it depends on the context.

On the other hand, the general contention of Abbot B. C. Butler that such is the nature of Christianity that it is only with reluctance that it explicitly affirms doctrines at all [8] is one that merits respectful consideration. But this does not in the least diminish the difficulty that confronts the modern ultramontane. For there is no conceivable reason for having a doctrine of papal infallibility unless it be to ensure perfect clarity and certainty when circumstances force the Church to break her silence and speak. It is a wholly admirable thing to refrain from speech when speech is unnecessary, and it may be an absolute moral duty to speak out clearly when circumstances demand it; but it can never be a good thing to speak obscurely. Let it be admitted (though not all would agree) that Rome does not readily commit the faithful to explicit doctrine, but does so only when so obliged by forces dangerous to the life of

[7] See Appendix I, n. 51.
[8] *The Church and Infallibility,* pp. 67, 83, 167, 200-202.

the Church and all that has been found precious in that life. There is nothing in all this to mitigate the muddle.

"Infallibility," says Dom Chapman, "is, as it were, the apex of a pyramid. The more solemn the utterances of the Apostolic See, the more we can be certain of their truth." [9] Abbot Butler suggests "sure" rather than "certain," "since there can hardly be degrees of strictly intellectual 'certainty.'" Then infallibility does not give certainty after all, but only the least uncertain kind of knowledge; that is, very well-informed opinion. How then can such utterances be "irreformable," as the Decree says they are? It would seem rather, on such a view of infallibility, that the Pope is only, of all members of the teaching Church (the Bishops), the most reliable. Moreover, it must be as a *teacher* that he is so eminently reliable, and the reliability of a teacher must depend on the reliability of his learning. The notion that a pope whose theological learning is, compared with that of many other bishops and priests and laymen, quite mediocre, can be the most reliable teacher, is even more difficult than the notion that he can be, by virtue of his office, oracular. No theological professor in the world ever claims infallibility, so that when a pope claims it he must claim it, not in virtue of his erudition, but in virtue of a special divine power which, hiding the truth from the wise, can reveal it unto babes.[10] It is intolerably difficult to suppose that a special divine power could so ill equip its recipient that he could not even express clearly to the faithful for whose enlightenment it was intended, whether he was speaking as one who had such guidance or was speaking only as a private teacher.

In spite of the early recognition of the importance of the See of Rome and the consequent prestige of its bishop, there is not even a hint of the *ex cathedra* notion before the eleventh century. Even in the fourteenth, in the lively debates on the nature of papal pronouncements, no such common notion was ever being either com-

[9] Quoted by Abbot B. C. Butler, *op. cit.*, p. 201.
[10] Matt. xi. 25.

batted or upheld. In the fifteenth century, the distinction between the *persona publica* and the *persona privata* of the Pope is made, and when, two centuries later, the Jesuit Cardinal Bellarmine affirms that the Pope speaks *ex cathedra* when he speaks to the whole Church, he is plainly thinking of the future rather than the past. It is a novel doctrine. Yet it is not for the invention of a novelty that Bellarmine is to be blamed. The poems of Ossian may be quite interesting in themselves; this does not, however, make the hoax, by means of which they were originally palmed off as translations of ancient poems, any less a hoax.

The average modern Roman Catholic is innocent of such difficulties about the meaning of the words *ex cathedra*. The distinction between certainty and well-grounded opinion can hardly be expected to trouble his mind.[11] The very notion of such a distinction, so familiar to readers of the history of modern philosophy, is not likely to occur to him even as an academic question, since most of the classics of modern philosophy, the French rationalists as well as the British empiricists, are on the Papal Index of Prohibited Books. The reading of the *Meditations* of Descartes is forbidden, "till it be corrected" (*donec corrigatur*), by a Decree of the Holy Office, October 10, 1663; Locke's *Essay concerning Human Understanding* is forbidden by a Papal Brief of Clement XII, June 19, 1734; Berkeley's *Alciphron* is forbidden by a Decree, November 17, 1742 and the entire works of Hume are forbidden by a Decree, January 19, 1761, and by a further Decree, September 10, 1827. All these prohibitions against almost all the post-medieval classics commonly prescribed to first-year philosophy students in reputable universities throughout the world, have continued in force for Roman Catholics in the present twentieth century. Except to the extent that he has been dispensed by the Church from the ban on intellectual influences of which it officially disapproves, even the intelligent modern Roman Catholic is not very likely to draw any distinction between infallibility and anything else that looks

---

[11] The old scholastic distinction between certainty and probability would not help, even if he knew it.

at all like it. For practical purposes, therefore, such a layman commonly believes everything the Pope puts in writing, on subjects in any way related to faith or morals, to be as infallible as if he had heard it uttered by Jesus Christ.

One looks in vain in the Codex of Canon Law for any commentary on the meaning of the words *ex cathedra*. Instead, one reads that it is the function both of Ecumenical Councils and of the Roman Pontiff speaking *ex cathedra* to pronounce judgment on matters of faith[12]—a proposition which can hardly be accounted very informative in view of even those difficulties we have already noticed. It is no more than Dryden said.[13] Here is what Canon 1323 says:

> s.1: The divine and Catholic faith to be believed by all consists of those things which are contained in the Word of God, written or handed down, and set forth by the Church, either in solemn judgment or in her ordinary and universal teaching, as divinely revealed.
> s.2: It belongs to both the ecumenical council and (*tum . . . tum*) to the Roman Pontiff speaking *ex cathedra* to pronounce solemn judgment after this manner.
> s.3: Nothing is to be understood as declared or defined unless it has been clearly established.

The interpretations of the Vatican Decree offered to the intellectual world at large are, moreover, remarkably different from the simple explanations offered in Catholic Truth Society pamphlets and the like. It is almost as commonly imagined by non-Romanists as it is by modern Roman Catholics who are ill informed about their religion (a very much larger class than is commonly supposed) that, whatever is to be said against the Vatican Decree, there is this to be said in its favor: it gives the ordinary man or woman a sense of security, since he may lay his intellectual difficulties on an infinitely roomy tiara. But in fact it seems that the nearer one gets to the tiara the less roomy it appears. Dom E. C. Butler considers the question whether there had indeed been any

---

[12] *Codex Jur. Can.*, Lib. III, Pars iv, De Magisterio Ecclesiastico, Canon 1323.
[13] *Supra.*

infallible pronouncements from the time of the Vatican Decree till the date of his writing, some sixty years later.[14] According to two of the experts he cites on this question, Père Choupin and Père Dublanchy, there probably were none. Nevertheless, some have supposed that the declaration, by Leo XIII, of the nullity of Anglican Orders, was an infallible pronouncement. Dom Cuthbert Butler doubts, however, whether that pronouncement was really invested with this character. Neither the word "define" nor the expression *ex cathedra* was used, so that there is ample room for doubt. Ought Leo to have left such room? Much less conspicuous officials of both Church and State are accustomed to feel it their duty to take considerable precaution in making clear whether they are speaking *ex officiis* or "off the record."

We now turn for enlightenment, not unnaturally, to the bishop who was papal secretary at the Vatican Council itself. But Fessler only tells us blandly that we are not to expect easily to discern an *ex cathedra* utterance. No mere circumstances suffice in themselves, he says, to enable us to recognize whether that which a pope proclaims is or is not an *ex cathedra* definition. It is only, he affirms, when it is *acknowledged* that the circumstances and the words and the pronouncement itself *all* support the view that it has been the papal intention to make an *ex cathedra* definition that the pronouncement may be presumed to be *ex cathedra*.

By whom is this acknowledgment to be made? It might be imagined that the most obvious person to make it would be the Pope, since he is presumably the most likely person to know his own intention. But evidently this is not to be expected of him. Indeed, Fessler seems almost to imply that it is unreasonable to expect anything of the sort. We are to look instead to the theologians and canonists. Who, precisely, are these doctors, whose function it is to determine, if possible, whether a papal definition is, or is not, *ex cathedra*? Plainly, they must be in the first place persons who accept the Vatican Decree. It is a little difficult to see how they could be laymen, since, whenever a priest is in

[14] *History of the Vatican Council*, Vol. I, pp. 220 ff.

serious trouble with the ecclesiastical hierarchy, the regular remedy
for what might become a scandal to the faithful is that he should
obtain "reduction to the lay state" in order that he may be able
more freely to express his private opinions without giving the impression that he is speaking with the authority of the Church behind him. So we should hardly expect to find any layman, even
a learned Roman Catholic thinker such as, say, Monsieur Gilson,
determining for the episcopate whether they should believe a certain papal definition to be infallible or not. For it is not by any
means simply a question of learning. The simplest priest from a
country parish in Sardinia speaks with more authority than all the
laymen in the world, and it is by no means easy to see how all of
these banded together could legitimately set themselves up against
him. They might appeal to a bishop. A bishop speaks not only
with greater authority than any priest, but presumably with greater
authority than all the priests in the world. But then, does not the
Bishop of Rome speak with greater authority than all the other
members of the episcopate? Who is to speak with greater authority concerning the interpretation of the intention of the Pope but
the Pope himself, who evidently is not to be expected to do so?
The interpretation, therefore, must always be left to others whose
authority to make it is limited, and so, while having an infallible
Pope, we can never know infallibly whether his definition is infallible or not. It is true, however, that one man's guess is not quite
as good as another's: a priest's is better than a layman's guess; a
bishop's is a comparatively good guess; the guess of a whole
assembly of bishops is a really first-class guess.

So, at the end of this not very simple process, we are still
uncertain whether the papal definition is *ex cathedra* or not. Suppose, for example, that the Pope were to make what seemed like
an *ex cathedra* definition of a doctrine of the Assumption of St.
John the Evangelist. (Such a definition is by no means impossible,
however unlikely it may appear to be at the present time.)[15] He
uses neither the word "define" nor the phrase *ex cathedra:* the

[15] See Appendix II.

pronouncement itself is slightly vague; and finally the circumstances might be interpreted either in favor of or against the view that an *ex cathedra* definition has been made. Bishops, priests, and people are to be indefinitely engaged in a guessing-game, in the full knowledge that without the Pope, who is silent on the subject, their guess can never be more than a guess, and a guess is indisputably less than a certainty. One cannot make infallible guesses. But this would not be merely to say that in such a case the members of the Roman Church would be no better off than heretics on the subject of whether or not St. John the Evangelist had been assumed corporeally into heaven. They would be worse off. For, having no more certainty than a non-Romanist, they would be plainly compelled to consider the question very seriously, since it *might* be an infallible definition that had been made. It is true that it is sufficient for salvation, according to modern Roman Catholic theologians, to believe in general in "all the Church doth teach," which is a very beautiful notion, but one that does nothing to diminish the fact that it is very annoying to belong to a Church that teaches so obscurely. It is especially unsatisfactory when (a) one is assured by the Vatican Decree that the teaching of the Pope, however obscure, may be infallible and yet may not be, and (b) one is at the same time aware that the Pope is reigning in Rome and will not say whether he is being infallible or not. It is even more baffling and much less comfortable than the view, which has actually been put forward, that hell exists but there is no certainty that there is anybody in it. For the notion that hell exists, coupled with agnosticism about whether it is inhabited, might have some attraction for a person who did not claim to enjoy infallible guidance from God through the Pope as the mouthpiece of the Church; but a person who does claim to enjoy such guidance cannot but find it remarkably unsatisfactory to have guidance which might, and yet might not, be the kind of guidance he needs. There is something to be said for having guidance that purports to be infallible, and there is something to be said for having no such guidance; but it is difficult to see what can be said for having guidance which may be infallible and may not be, while one at the same time believes that the guide who has given the guidance is able to say which it is, and does not say. Surely no state in which the Roman Church was before 1870 could be so bad that this is an improvement.

9

THE ISSUE IN MODERN AMERICA

NOT long after I came to live permanently in this country, I happened to attend a ceremony in a Roman Catholic university. The large audience was addressed by a well-known prelate; a stylized sort of address, for it was a formal occasion. On one side of the platform was the American flag; on the other side the yellow-and-white flag of the Holy See.

Throughout the speech I kept wondering what sort of impression it would have made on me if I had been, say, a simple-minded farm lad from Ireland or Spain who had recently arrived here for a fresh start in life. I think I should have supposed the United States of America to be both traditionally and actually an almost entirely Roman Catholic country. Not as devoutly Catholic, to be sure, as the hierarchy was praying it might become; afflicted, like France, by the presence of a certain number of godless men and women; but, despite such shortcomings, a fine, fresh, great Catholic land. A grand-scale, rejuvenated Ireland; or, perhaps, an English-speaking New Spain. Mary's Own Country. Discovered by a Catholic explorer some five hundred years ago, it was more fully penetrated by other Catholics: John and Sebastian Cabot, John Ponce de Leon, and the like; Pineda, who first set eyes on the Mississippi and called it the River of the Holy Ghost; Hennepin, Joliet, Marquette, De Soto, Tristan de Luna, and other fine Catholic explorers, who opened up the mid-west and the south. Gradually the country was developed by successive generations of splendid Catholic heroes. Not without difficulties, of course; there was a certain amount of godlessness in those days, too. One must be careful, so to speak, to avoid supposing that the Mayflower was packed with Franciscans or that the War of Independence was entirely a Catholic enterprise designed to free America from a Protestant king so that she might be more truly dedicated to the service of the Pope. Nevertheless, one might have concluded from the speech, had one been learning one's American history for the first time, that all the good America had ever accomplished, not least its scientific achievements, was due to the untiring efforts of Roman Catholic heroes throughout the centuries. Still, there was no room for complacency. For despite America's glorious Catholic heritage and the special favors the Blessed Virgin had been pleased to shower upon these United States, you had only to look around you to find on every hand evidence of the havoc wrought by godlessness, indifference, and other "non-Catholic" forces. The monuments of pride and lust and greed—all that is evil in America—rise high in our cities and should challenge rather than surprise us: are they not due indeed to lack of Catholic vigilance in overcoming the "non-Catholic" forces that are an ever-present danger even in a land that is Mary's Own?

It was a simple message the prelate had to give. The audience evidently accepted it as somewhat conventional. Not all Roman Catholic propaganda is as ingenuously crude; on the contrary, much of it is exceedingly well disguised. But the impression it is calculated to make is generally the same: the Roman Faith is the *norm* for all civilized people, for the Pope's judicial powers in faith and morals extend over the length and breadth of the universe. Not all who deviate from this norm are the agents of the Devil; they are often, rather, the dupes. Nevertheless, but for the inspiration of the Devil there would no more be a Baptist or an Episcopal Church at the top of the street than there would be a dope-den or a brothel. True, there are many Roman Catholics in America whose spirit is more tolerant and whose minds are less easily controlled by what the hierarchy says; but this is due in considerable measure to their inevitable intake of ideas from the "non-Catholic" atmosphere that the bishops so fanatically deplore. Yet what else could these do but deplore and condemn it? They are the leaders of what purports to be a fundamentalist Church. For Roman Catholicism, since 1870, is avowedly fundamentalist in the sense that it has deliberately turned against all "modernism," not least all Biblical criticism that is conducted in a spirit of free inquiry, and has set its face rigidly against symbolical interpretations of and investigations into religious ideas such as those that are increasingly occupying the attention of earnest and thoughtful Christians throughout the world, outside the Roman Obedience. Since the papalist triumph at the Vatican Council that ensured obscurantist policies on many of the most deeply Christian problems of today, Rome has been content to lose thousands of her most thoughtful people, including some of her most distinguished scholars, and to repel thousands more of equal mental caliber who might otherwise have been eager to enter her fold. She has preferred to pursue instead a policy of outbreeding the "non-Catholic" world, by means of which policy she may expect to control the democracies by creating and using a weapon to kill these, namely, a political majority determined to do so.

Already, in America, the numerical strength of the Roman Church is amply sufficient to produce some remarkable results. One of the most striking is the censorship of literature and art. That children should be subjected to a reasonable amount of book and movie censorship by their parents is widely recognized by responsible Americans. Nor would many deny, I think, that if an adult wishes to place himself, for one reason or another, under some form of censorship in his reading or playgoing, such a person has the right to do so. One might not admire such a person; but his right to act in this way would hardly be questioned. There are timid and undecided persons in every society who like to be guided more than do other people, and surely the strong-minded and independent are not the only people, or even the first, in the Kingdom of Heaven. There should be no objection in principle, therefore, and there is probably little in fact among intelligent Americans, to the notion that members of a group, even a group as large as the Roman Church in America, are entitled to include among their religious duties the obligation of reading only those books that their spiritual advisers allow them to read, and seeing only those movies that are likewise accounted not injurious to their spiritual digestion. However we may disapprove such censorship, we may concede this much. But in practice what inevitably happens is far more than this.

For the Roman Catholic faithful, docile as they may be, are not as obedient as some non-Romanists imagine. Nor is the power of the hierarchy over them as absolute as is sometimes supposed. It is a stock reply of Roman Catholic controversialists, when asked why the Pope did not take action in this or that matter, that the Pope, for all the reverence accorded him, is not omnipotent; far from it. So in practice the Roman hierarchy cannot effectively prevent a great many of the faithful seeing certain plays and reading certain books, except by using its influence to prevent *everybody* from doing so, or at any rate making this extremely inconvenient for ordinary people. Comparatively few books, nowadays, are put on the notorious Papal Index: local censorship and boycott are, in the modern world, much more effective. This means that the local Church censors' powers may often be wielded in an arbitrary fashion. What is accounted dangerous in Ireland may be deemed harmless in Belgium. A book of my own that was gently commended by a Jesuit in a learned Spanish journal was attacked by the *Catholic Times* in England as "dangerous to Faith and morals." It should not be forgotten that while such unofficial pronouncements are not taken seriously by Roman Catholic scholars, they have a great effect on ordinary priests and laymen.

This arbitrariness of the local censor's use of his powers together with the fact that the very limitations of his powers as well as the Church's claim to universal jurisdiction compel him to impose a sectarian censorship over the whole community—all this serves to indicate the predicament of a modern democracy that is trying to uphold a principle of religious toleration. But there are other, more flagrant exhibitions of modern Roman Catholic arrogance towards "non-Catholics" in such a society. The systematic though less successful attempts of the hierarchy to discourage the practice of scientific methods of birth control among married couples of all faiths is widely known. Here also the Church cannot legislate for her own people without legislating for the nation, as, needless to say, she would most eagerly do much more thoroughly if she could, since she claims to be "by right the Mother of all men." Nor can she confine her laws on annulment and divorce to her own faithful: these laws cannot but affect, as they do, a considerable number of other persons.[1]

The modern papacy has emphatically and persistently denounced all secular education, that is, education organized and controlled by a public authority such as national or municipal government, and not specifically based on any religious principles. It makes little or no difference, from the papalist viewpoint, whether the educational authority encourages the parents to supplement such education with religious instruction of their own choosing, or publicly jeers at all religious indoctrination. For in principle the education of the young is as much an exclusive monopoly of the priesthood as is the use of the pulpit or the confessional. In general, a Roman Catholic convent will employ a secular, lay teacher only as a physician might have to use non-qualified assistance in an emergency. At any rate, whoever does the teaching, it must be under the direction of the Church. Otherwise it is to be vilified as godless education. In such circumstances, a country such as America cannot expect to come to any reasonable terms with the Roman Catholic hierarchy on the subject of education. The Church is avowedly opposed not only to public schools but also to independent schools and universities that are not under the control of the Roman Catholic Church, to which alone, it is affirmed, belongs the right to teach anything.[2]

----

[1] I am, of course, not concerned here with the ethics of divorce, birth control, and the like, but only with the effect that a "regimented" society can have within a democratic State.

[2] It is not only in the United States that Roman Catholic control of public education is distrusted. There is no less antipathy to it among, say, French university professors, even those who are practicing Roman Catholics.

In practice, however, in a country such as the United States, the Church is unable, for obvious reasons, to enforce this principle. So the hierarchy has to content itself with the more practical aim of securing Roman Catholic parochial schools at the public expense. With a view to this, it has hindered measures for educational reform in this country so long as these measures seemed to hold out no hope of financial support, or other advantage, to sectarian education, and it has welcomed the same measures whenever they seemed to hold out any such hope. The need for federal aid for the American public schools, for instance, was long recognized, to diminish the great disparity in educational facilities between rich states such as California and New York and poor ones such as Mississippi. Though Mississippi was spending more on education, proportionately to its income, than was New York, the latter was actually able to spend four or five times more per pupil than was the former. So great a disparity in so important a service was obviously against the national interest. The hierarchy, however, was for long against the obvious remedy. But as soon as there was a prospect of the parochial schools getting the indirect but very considerable benefit of grants for auxiliary services such as transport and textbooks, the policy of the hierarchy changed.

The parochial school system that is an integral part of Roman Catholic expansion endeavor in America, is too expensive for the Church to keep up by herself. If the Church ever did manage to make its own educational system a charge on the American public, there would therefore be two consequences. Not only would the American people as a whole be compulsorily paying for the religious indoctrination of the offspring of parents who are being diligently encouraged to outbreed "non-Catholics"; the actual financial assets of the Roman Church in this country would be enormously improved, since they would be relieved of one of their principal burdens. Financially, it would hardly be better news to the hierarchy, if Congress were to pass a bill appropriating public money from the Treasury for the payment of mass stipends to all Roman Catholic clergy throughout the country. Public funds for sectarian schools would bring about a repetition on a vast scale of what has happened in small countries such as Scotland [3] and the Netherlands where the State's educational system includes provision for schools which, though subject to government inspection, are controlled by the Roman Catholic Church.

All these familiar phenomena in modern America are as one should expect. They are the outcome of a pragmatistic attitude; the attitude of men who say, "It is not a question of what is 'true' or 'constitutional' within the Roman Church's history and tradition, since there is no such truth: what is opportune will become true if we work hard to make it so." Already, the Roman Catholic Church that has inherited this attitude of the papalist party at the Vatican Council has shown that an autocratically-governed Church at work in a democratically-governed country can be extremely successful; so successful that its leaders have been able to predict, as some of them have done, that within the lifetime of today's children the United States will have become a Roman Catholic country. In doing so they refer not merely to the expected results of the outbreeding process. As a matter of fact, these results, remarkable as they are, are said to have been, in the cities at any rate, a disappointment to the hierarchy. In any case an outbreeding policy is never in itself sufficient, however useful it may be as a basis for other policies. Numerical strength is not everything, and even if there were a Roman Catholic majority in America, America might be far from being a Roman Catholic land; perhaps even further than it now is from this. Minorities are notoriously vigorous; large minorities can often be exceedingly effective, as the large Roman Catholic minority has already proved. It is, rather, by means of censorship and boycott, and, above all, educational indoctrination at the public expense, that it is hoped to transform America into a country that is predominantly Roman Catholic in spirit; that is to say, one in which it would be very imprudent to

[3] The situation in Scotland is set forth, with its historical background, in a British government memorandum presented in Parliament in February 1943. Published by H. M. Stationery Office (Cmd. 6426), 1943; reprinted 1949.

speak openly against anything uttered by a Roman Catholic bishop, and exceedingly dangerous to speak even privately in favor of anything uttered by anyone who was explicitly under the ban of the Church.

That which, far more than anything else, makes for the cleavage between the Roman Church and the rest of Christendom and stands in the way of even attempts at that full Christian reconciliation that is the prayer of all sincere Christians, is this: Rome is, according to the decrees of the Vatican Council, essentially non-democratic in her conception of Church government, while much of the rest of Christendom is susceptible to a genuinely democratic Church order. This is why virtually all groups in non-Roman Christendom are able, despite their not inconsiderable differences, to parley freely in ecumenical conferences, while Roman Catholics cannot participate in these. The *kind* of democracy that is proper to Christ's Church may be a matter of very considerable controversy in ecumenical discussions. After all, much the same is to be said in the secular realm: Americans and British and French, for instance, have different conceptions of democracy. But the fact that they all accept certain fundamental democratic principles not only makes them able to discuss their differences freely and constructively, but enables them to be, not least when faced with a totalitarian foe, very close friends indeed. Between a nation that has such democratic foundations and one that has not there can never be any such friendship, and the costly consequences of the slightest flirtation with dictator-ruled nations are now too well known to need to be elaborated. The only hope for eventual cooperation and friendship lies in the development or recovery of democratic principles in the dictatorship. This is no less true of an autocratic Church than it is of an autocratic State.

The hope of such an eventual reconciliation with the Roman Church, distant as it is on any human reckoning, would be out of the question if the decrees of the Vatican Council represented the only tradition within the Roman Church. But all is not entirely dark if there is a democratic ideal that might be recovered by Roman Catholics themselves, however long and arduous the process of recovery.

One has only to read the pages of *Commonweal,* the organ of a group of thoughtful Roman Catholic laymen in this country, to appreciate some of the possibilities. A series of articles that appeared in that weekly review during 1953[4] show on almost every page evidences of a very different spirit from that which prevails in Spain or Ireland. In a criticism of the results of Roman Catholic censorship of movies, for example, Walter Kerr complains that it is the "well-meaning second-rate" that gets the acclamation of the Church. *Quo Vadis,* for instance, which he calls an "essay in calculated vulgarity," got the most publicized accolade of the Church in 1952, and Father Keller, in presenting the award, praised the film frankly because of what evidently seemed to him to be its proselytizing effect. "The sort of judgment which at best reveals an alarming innocence of the very texture of art," writes Kerr, "and which at worst smacks suspiciously of cant, has pretty much become a rule-of-thumb for the American Catholic moviegoer. A film featuring a saint is a film of majestic technical excellence. A film showing a nun driving a jeep is a superbly made comedy. . . . When there is no recent film of obviously Catholic sympathies—no priest in the pulpit, no nun in the backfield, no early-Christian Deborah Kerr in the jaws of a Technicolor lion—the next-best bet, in the current practice of Catholic criticism, is to play it safe. . . . The identification of good will with good work is commonplace in the Catholic press. Unfortunately, the sort of art which Catholics are urged to admire is commonplace too and the power which Catholic spokesmen have come to wield over the motion picture even more commonplace than it need have been."

This is certainly not the sort of language one would find in the clerical press in America. One would look long indeed for it in *any* press in Ireland or Spain. But despite the vigor of the criticism

---

[4] Published in book form under the title, *Catholicism in America* (New York, Harcourt, Brace & Co., 1954).

there is a curious lack of concern about the roots of the disease. Throughout the whole series of articles there are healthy lamentations about the astonishing inferiority of Roman Catholic achievement in art, literature, and science in modern America. Figures are reported showing that Roman Catholic scientific writers are on the whole quite astonishingly inferior in originality. It is admitted with sadness that "the most pure-minded reading of literature is done, generally speaking, at the non-Catholic universities," and that talk of a Roman Catholic literary revival in America is wishful thinking. Similar uneasiness, almost resentment, is to be found in Joseph Cunneen's criticism of the hierarchy's policy on the school question in America.

But it must not be supposed that such voices of criticism in themselves betoken a widespread knowledge of what is at the heart of the matter. For they betray no real concern about what, we shall see, must most trouble every historian: the loss of the democratic element in the Roman Catholic tradition itself. The death-knell of this element was sounded at the Vatican Council in 1870, and the present generation of thoughtful young members of the Roman Church in this country have evidently little if any notion of the extraordinary circumstances and repercussions of that upheaval. Having come to take it for granted that their Church is essentially autocratic in its form of government and its organization, they seem to feel no special distaste for the notion of the Pope arbitrarily condemning everything of which he disapproves, and they have an ingenuous confidence that all would be well if only he were to be better informed. Luther himself once shared this confidence. He lost it. And yet intelligent modern Roman Catholics are naturally puzzled at the echoes of a very different spirit that they occasionally hear, however dimly, within their own Church itself. "Let the bishop know, and in the last resort let it be reported to the Pope," might be all very well in a Church led by a constitutional papacy in which the Pope spoke as the mouthpiece of the Church by the authority he derived from it. But it can be of no avail in an organization in which such a view is explicitly condemned in favor of a thoroughly undemocratic interpretation of Roman Catholic Church government. With the authors of such an undemocratic policy neither Americans as such nor Christians as such can have any useful parleys.

It is primarily among the intelligent laymen of the Roman Catholic Church that the knowledge of what happened in 1870 must be spread. For theirs is, we shall also see, a most privileged position. A layman may speak his mind more freely than a priest, let alone a bishop, by reason of the very fact that he is not, and cannot be, an officer of the Church. Deprived of the possibility of having any commission in the Church Militant, he is in many ways more powerful, especially in a country such as this, than is any prelate. He might use his power if, less ignorant of her history, not least her recent history, he were to discover the immense constitutional rights of his Church against the papacy. Then, it is not inconceivable, the whole texture of the Roman Church might be altered, and her relations to the rest of Christendom immensely modified both to the advantage of Roman Catholics themselves and to other Christians in America and elsewhere who are outside the Roman fold. There is much one can do in a democracy, however unwieldy, that is impossible under an autocracy, however benevolent. Nor need one be discouraged by the indisputable fact that such education of modern Roman Catholics, so long cut off from all genuine understanding of liberal institutions, and from even the remoter effects of liberal scholarship, would be likely to take a long time. Were it to take many generations the prospect would still be rosier than it is now. The fact that a good tree is slow-growing ought not to prevent one from planting it.

The doctrine of Papal Infallibility has become congenial to the Church in the measure that it has fostered what Tyrrell called "Authority-fever." [5] Only the Pope's judgments can ever be infal-

---

[5] See M. D. Petre, *Autobiography and Life of George Tyrrell* (E. Arnold, 1912) Vol. II, p. 146, where Tyrrell in a letter written in 1900 mischievously suggests that it might be useful to have every Monsignor in Rome declared infallible. So the evil might spend itself. The whole chapter (Chap. VII, "The Joint-Pastoral") is relevant.

lible, according to the theory, but the authority of the subordinate officers of the Church is, in practice, thereby enhanced rather than diminished. The simplest priest speaks with infallible authority behind him, so that he quickly acquires a sense of being infallible to the extent that he is obedient to his canonical superiors. As for the layman, his role, as Lord Halifax complained,[6] is to "pay his fare and take his seat as so much ballast in the bark of Peter, while the clergy pull him across the ferry."

This feverishly authoritarian attitude of the modern Roman Church today betokens a peculiar state of mind. The hyperanxiety in the official policies of the Church in contemporary America and elsewhere reveals a fear that is at variance with the faith and confidence so characteristic of the Christian life in every age. It is not surprising, however, to find this curious nervousness in the hierarchy's attitude. We have already seen how the temper of the Vatican Fathers and the motives behind their remarkable decisions revealed a pragmatistic outlook. Underlying all pragmatism there is skepticism of one sort or another. The modern Roman Catholic spokesman is afflicted with tremendous doubts about the whole structure of his Church's system; doubts which he is not permitted by that system openly to declare. Often they are pushed below the level of his consciousness; always they are there. The more intelligent he is, the more troublesome the doubts. We can have no constructive, effective policy on the problem till we have taken this fully into account.

It should not have escaped our notice that the intense preoccupation of the Majority at the Vatican Council with the question of infallibility, and their curious craving for anything, however confused, that would have the appearance of locating the seat of infallibility and giving an easy sense of security to the faithful, was a sign of their own misgivings. Men of greater confidence in the abiding power of God with his people are less preoccupied with trying to find such reassurances on the subject. The pragmatism of these papalists in 1870, radically at variance with the Church's

[6] *Op. cit.*, p. 155.

professed theory of truth, has been abundantly confirmed in subsequent history. It is this attitude that makes Roman Catholicism capable of having a policy so different in Spain, for instance, from what it has in the United States; one policy in England and another in France.[7] In an article in the Jesuit magazine *America,* in 1946, Father John Courtney Murray, S.J., argues that it is not merely for the sake of expediency that Roman Catholics ought to acquiesce in the American principle of religious freedom and lack of legal establishment of religion: they ought to uphold this as good in itself. It is well known that in Spain anyone, even a layman, who talked like this would be accounted disloyal, perhaps even heretical. Cardinal Pla y Deniel, Archbishop of Toledo and Primate of Spain, referring to the Concordat between Spain and the Holy See,[8] wrote in an article in *Ecclesia,* the official organ of Spanish Catholic Action, that there must be no expansion of the toleration of Protestants allowed under this Concordat. On the contrary, such expansion of toleration is forbidden by the terms of the Concordat. Permission had been given to Protestants[9] to worship privately in their own fashion; but any public meeting or street gathering or external sign of a Protestant place of worship or even a poster advertising its whereabouts would "contravene public order and the common good of our Catholic Spain."

It is not that the ultramontanized Church teaches one doctrine as true in America and another doctrine as true in Spain. It is, rather, that whatever works for the "liberty and exaltation of our holy Mother the Church" must be true. If the condition of Spain be such that the notions of religious toleration expounded by the Cardinal Archbishop of Toledo seem most conducive to the exaltation

[7] On this subject, see a well-informed article in the *Quarterly Review,* Vol. CCXCII, No. 601, July 1954, "The Roman Church in Differing Cultures," by J. W. Poynter.

[8] Signed at the Vatican, August 27, 1953. It was designed to give toleration to the *private* practice of religions other than Roman Catholicism.

[9] Protestants in Spain may be estimated to number about 20,000 (of whom 10,000 are foreigners) out of a population of 28,000,000. This makes the percentage of Spanish Protestants 0.036.

of the Church, the notions are "true" wherever this condition exists. But where, as in America, the historical background and other circumstances make it evident that other notions of religious toleration are more efficacious for the exaltation of the Church, these are the "true" notions. It is not that a different truth is taught in America from that which is taught in Spain. In either case the notions are "true" because they *are in process of being made true*. Like so much else in the utterances of Rome, they are expressions of policy rather than of belief. The apparent "literalism" of Roman doctrine is a veil between the people and the thought of the ultramontanized hierarchy. This "thought" is in many ways essentially pragmatic.

It would be absurd, nevertheless, to suppose that "the exaltation of our holy Mother the Church" could be Rome's sole norm of truth. A certain type of secular politician might perhaps be said to recognize no standard or measure other than his party's success at the polls. His own profit-and-loss account is the sole norm of a business man, *as such*. But it can never be, even in extreme cases, the total life of any man to be a man of business or a professional politician. And the life of a servant of the Church is such a total life. No one, however miserly or power-hungry, is ever devoted to his business or his party as thousands of priests and nuns and others are consecrated to the service of God in the Church. It is the nature of Mammon to enlist careerists among its votaries. The Church's demands are too comprehensive and too exacting to be psychologically or otherwise adapted to the aims of any but the most narrow or perverted careerist.

The pragmatistic outlook of the Roman hierarchy must be understood, then, in its context. It is not the pragmatism of the materialistic business man or the self-seeking politician. It is a pragmatism combined with an intense desire to conserve certain values, and this desire springs from a set of metaphysical beliefs. There may be doubts in the minds of Roman theologians concerning the official doctrines of the Church; but, except in the comparatively rare case of incorrigible hypocrites, there is also a metaphysical belief that implies that the Roman Church is the earthly institution that is preeminently worth conserving. Her spread, her "exaltation" is, therefore, on such a view, a good-in-itself.

Modern Roman Catholic pragmatism is largely an unconscious attitude. Roman Catholics are more sensitive than most other Christians to success and failure as measured by external manifestations. They are not commonly aware of their own craving for such external ratifications of their beliefs. But their belief in the infallibility of the Church (much weaker, we have seen, than is their external profession of it) is in fact constantly being tested by them, albeit unconsciously, in "results." If these results are such as to corroborate their belief (weakening of Protestant influence, for example, attended by a corresponding increase of Roman Catholic agencies and strengthening of Roman Catholic power), that belief in the infallibility of the Roman Church is fortified. If they are not so corroborated, it is diminished.

The results of the victory of the papalist party in 1870 have since in many ways exceeded their reasonable expectation. The Revolution of 1789 had dealt a blow to the Church in France from which she never recovered. France remained *catholique de mœurs et d'habitudes,* but by 1870 the influence of the Church seemed irreparably weakened.[10] The indignities suffered by France in the Franco-Prussian War, however, encouraged the development of a patriotic right wing which, looking in disgust at the work of the Revolution, turned towards Rome with an intense devotion, hoping to find there the means of recovering in some measure the spirit of the *ancien régime* for which it nostalgically craved. Truly, the Pope had turned out to be the fount of the Church's life, which life, though it had waned in France, could be restored by Rome. The result might be in some ways novel; but it was, to those who thought along such lines, acceptable *faute de mieux,* and certainly much more congenial than anything inherited from the Revolution of 1789. The ultramontanists had been right: the infallibility did

---

[10] Cf. A. Débidour, *Histoire des rapports de l'Eglise et de l'Etat en France de 1789 à 1870,* pp. 643-649.

reside in the papacy, without which France, it seemed, would have lost the faith altogether. The price of the reaction was the creation of a tension between "right" and "left." This tension developed into what is now characteristic of most traditionally Roman Catholic lands—a choice between Rome and Moscow. Nevertheless, at the time, the price did not seem exorbitant.

The effect of the now acutely centralized spiritual authority of Rome was felt wherever Roman Catholic piety had survived. The Vatican Revolution of 1870 injected vigor into the Church. The new spirit, with its strongly Jesuitical preoccupations, transformed piety in all lands. Zealous Roman Catholics increasingly seemed almost to enjoy the idea of the Pope "clamping down" on recalcitrant members, as if this reassured them of the vitality of the Church. History has been, more than ever before, perverted under the influence of the modern, Jesuit-inspired Roman Catholic teaching, so that there is more than a grain of truth in the story of the child who, being asked "Why did our Lord come to earth?" replied glibly, "To bring us the Blessed Sacrament." It would have been hardly less venial an error had the child replied, "So that our Blessed Lady might be conceived without sin." This is, indeed, a distortion of Roman Catholic doctrine; yet it is a distortion that would offend ultramontane piety less than would, say, the notion that the Pope derives his authority from the Church rather than by virtue of "the promise to blessed Peter." It is the *emphases* of this piety that are so peculiarly offensive to historically-minded Christians. But they are the emphases that "work" in the modern Roman Church, confirming to the average person in that Communion that the doctrine of Papal Infallibility defined in 1870 must be true.

There is no doubt that despite the defections and lapses that are a constant grief to the hierarchy, Roman Catholicism has flourished since 1870 in comparison with almost all other types of Christianity, especially among the masses. The spate of conversions that was so remarkable a century ago, in Newman's England, has much abated, but the position of Roman Catholicism in England today is immeasurably more secure than it was in his, and its prospects brighter. Because of the existence, moreover, of old English families who remained loyal to Rome despite the Reformation, conversion to Rome has generally been socially a little less difficult in England than it has been in the United States. The Battle of the Cradle, as it has been called in Canada, has been profitable for the Roman Church, which has gained more power throughout the United States as a whole, since 1870, than it acquired in any comparable period of time since the landing of Columbus.[11]

Since there are virtually no countries in the world where it could be shown that the fortunes of the Roman Church might have in any way suffered from the decrees of the Vatican Council, and since the contrary is in many cases so abundantly evident, it is only to be expected that Roman Catholics should see, as they do, the hand of God in the Vatican Decrees. The gloomy prognostications of the so-called Inopportunist party have seemed very ill founded, with the natural result that it has been possible for the hierarchy to ignore them and allow them to be gently forgotten.

The slightest misgiving on this score, however, tends to raise questionings among educated Roman Catholics. Any widespread check in the success of the ultramontane policy could very well cause the bishops to reinvestigate the constitutional legality of the Vatican Council and to reconsider the foundations of the Church's faith. This need not be a check in numerical increase: a check in the political influence or, better still, in the apparent spiritual vitality of the Church, would be even more efficient. A Roman Catholic laity determined to be intelligently critical while at the same time insisting on its own essential loyalty could produce spectacular results. Not even bishops are impervious to determined bombardment from an educated laity.

There would be nothing entirely new in the notion of educating the papalist party in the Roman Church. The existence of Roman

[11] The estimated Roman Catholic population in 1800 was about 100,000; by 1870, in spite of the enormous Irish immigrations, it was only 4,500,000. (So great were the defections among immigrants that in the fifties Bishop Reynolds of Charleston discouraged the immigration of Irish Roman Catholics, "lest they should lose their immortal souls.") Today there are about 25,-000,000.

Catholics of the Eastern Uniate Rites[12] is a testimony to the fact that even popes can sometimes "talk turkey" when people "talk turkey" to them. For these Rites (or Churches within a Church) commonly owe their peculiarities and privileges to concessions by Rome on the return of schismatic groups, conditional on these receiving special treatment. The modern Roman Catholic contention that such concessions and compromises have been made in disciplinary and liturgical matters, not doctrinal ones, is less impressive than appears. Doctrinal compromises have been made throughout the Church's history. They were made even at the Vatican Council, at which over a hundred extremists wanted the *Ave Maria* changed to include a special mention of the Immaculate Conception.[13] Their wish was frustrated by the moderation imposed by the climate of opinion in the Council. Nor, of course, is there really anything sacrosanct about the notion that the Vatican Decrees, having been defined both by the Pope *ex cathedra* and by a General Council, are immutable. That the Pope can define doctrine on his own authority was questionable enough to make Pius IX insist on the Council taking the initiative in deciding that he could. The constitutional legality of the Council is, of course, what has been in question in the present study.

It is by no means fundamentally impossible for the Roman Church to be liberated from its papalist party and reformed accordingly. But there is no use talking to the papalist party in language they cannot understand. At the Council of Trent itself, in the sixteenth century, there was a strong party that wished for the reform of the Roman Church on very different lines from those ultimately determined by the Council. This party was led by the

[12] That is, those who worship after the manner of the Eastern Schismatic Churches, using the same liturgical languages, e.g., Greek, Ruthenian, etc., and whose secular clergy may marry before ordination, but who are nevertheless in full communion with the Pope.

[13] This prayer is repeated one hundred and fifty times in the course of the full recitation of the Rosary. The revised version of the relevant part of the prayer would have been:

"Holy Mary, *Immaculate Virgin*, Mother of God, pray for us sinners, now and at the hour of our death."

aristocratic Venetian Cardinal Gasparo Contarini, and received also
the support of Reginald Pole. There were other parties (they included some important Spanish prelates), which, resenting every
effort by the Pope to control the Council, insisted that while the
Pope was *primus inter pares,* each bishop drew his authority independently from Christ through the apostolic succession, as Cyprian
had said over a thousand years earlier, and not through Rome. Others
wanted to keep off doctrinal questions, so as not further to alienate
the Protestants, and would have had the Council accomplish reforms such as the marriage of the clergy, the reduction of the papal
power, and the singing of vernacular hymns in church. Contarini
was sympathetic, on theological (chiefly Augustinian) grounds, to
the Lutheran doctrine of justification by faith. Though it was the
counsels of the Jesuits and of Caraffa (later Pope Paul IV) that
prevailed over those of Contarini, it might have been otherwise.
The papalists could not have resisted the efforts of such parties,
even had the interests of the curia been equally at stake, if only
the efforts had been sufficiently determined and impressive. But
in dealing with the members of a thoroughly power-minded party
it is useless to appeal to history or theology. One must confront
them with the only language they can understand. They are no
less vulnerable to influence and pressure than are historians to
historical argument.

On the other hand, nothing could be more unimpressive to hierarchy and faithful alike than the negative, dog-in-the-manger attitude of some Protestants. The Protestant who, not content with
rushing past his own church doors on the way to the golf course,
complains of or even jeers at the fact that Roman Catholics are
required to go to Mass, is not likely to have much influence in
purifying the Roman Church. More zealous Protestants, however
narrow they might be, could make a better impression. Yet no
amount of zeal is of much avail unless it is joined to a deep and
genuine understanding of the doctrine, ethos, and piety of the
modern Roman Church.

Perhaps not many Protestants are sufficiently inclined to appreciate the immense complexity of the Roman Catholic heritage or the richness of the Church's life. Seeing only what seems to be a vitality greater than their own, associated with an autocratic form of Church government, they too readily attribute the vitality to the autocratic rule, without stopping to consider whether the real vitality in Roman Catholicism might not be in spite of rather than because of the autocracy. It is a deep awareness of the vitality of their Church, rather than any certainty or lack of anxiety about its own doctrinal position that keeps intelligent modern Roman Catholics loyal to Rome. They are unable to see such vitality elsewhere, partly because their religious training ill fits them to appreciate the type of vitality, richer in some ways and in many ways much stronger, that the Christian life can display outside the Roman Communion.

The anxieties that torment the hierarchy disturb the whole Church, manifesting themselves, for example, in the preoccupation of the ordinary worshiper with all sorts of devotional trivialities, a restlessness that expresses the same *malaise* that we have seen expressed in the papalist power-mania. But it must not be forgotten that with all these pathological features is mixed a genuine vision. If one is to make any headway in reforming Rome by undermining the papalistic forces that help to make her what she is, one must distinguish the evil in her from the good. The Roman Catholic faithful are in some measure aware of the distinction; sometimes, indeed, more acutely conscious than are those outside that all is not well with their Church. And yet so long as the papalist policies are successful they will certainly prevail and the Roman Church will be held in her present captivity.

It must be the business of others who are sufficiently able to enjoy the privilege of free inquiry to halt the success of the papalist policy. This should be done in no spirit of vengeance, but in a spirit of love. Christians in the United States of America are in a position of unique opportunity, for if the papalist program is defeated here it is unlikely to be triumphant elsewhere, and the Roman Church throughout the world will be obliged to re-examine her own constitution, and this, let us remember, not for the first time in human history. The outcome of such a set-back to the papalist party aims would be of incalculable benefit to Christendom and mankind, and the role America can play in it is one that every American might well be proud to have recorded in the annals of the human race and the pages of Christian history. Christian Faith, which is ever born of controversy, has nothing to lose by doubt. *Plus profuit nobis dubitatio Thomae quam citissima fides Mariae.* (The doubt of Thomas has been more helpful to us than the most ready faith of Mary.") [14]

[14] St. Augustine, Sermo LXI.

APPENDIX I

The Text of the Vatican Decrees,
with an English Translation and Notes

The text is from the *Acta et decreta sacrosancti œcumenici Concilii Vaticani*, Rome, 1872. The translation is by Cardinal Manning. The notes revise and augment the notes to the text in the *Acta*.

The proceedings of the earlier sessions, being of a formal character only, are omitted here.

DECRETA DOGMATICA CONCILII VATICANI DE FIDE CATHOLICA ET DE EC-
CLESIA CHRISTI.

CONSTITUTIO DOGMATICA DE FIDE CATHOLICA.

Sessio III.

PIUS EPISCOPUS, SERVUS SERVORUM DEI, SACRO APPROBANTE CONCILIO, AD
PERPETUAM REI MEMORIAM.

Dei Filius et generis humani Redemptor, Dominus Noster Jesus
Christus, ad Patrem cœlestem rediturus, cum Ecclesia sua in terris mi-
litante omnibus diebus usque ad consummationem sæculi futurum se
esse promisit. Quare dilectæ sponsæ præsto esse, adsistere docenti,
operanti benedicere, periclitanti opem ferre nullo unquam tempore
destitit. Hæc vero salutaris ejus providentia, cum ex aliis beneficiis
innumeris continenter apparuit, tum iis manifestissime comperta est
fructibus, qui orbi Christiano e Conciliis œcumenicis, ac nominatim
e Tridentino, iniquis licet temporibus celebrato, amplissimi provene-
runt. Hinc enim sanctissima religionis dogmata pressius definita uberius-
que exposita, errores damnati atque cohibiti; hinc ecclesiastica disciplina
restituta firmiusque sancita, promotum in clero scientiæ et pietatis
studium, parata adolescentibus ad sacram militiam educandis collegia,
Christiani denique populi mores et accuratiore fidelium eruditione et
frequentiore sacramentorum usu instaurati. Hinc præterea arctior mem-
brorum cum visibili Capite communio, universoque corpori Christi
mystico additus vigor; hinc religiosæ multiplicatæ familiæ aliaque
Christianæ pietatis instituta; hinc ille etiam assiduus et usque ad
sanguinis effusionem constans ardor in Christi regno late per orbem
propagando.

Verumtamen hæc aliaque insignia emolumenta, quæ per ultimam
maxime œcumenicam Synodum divina clementia Ecclesiæ largita est,
dum grato, quo par est, animo recolimus, acerbum compescere haud
possumus dolorem ob mala gravissima, inde potissimum orta, quod
ejusdem sacrosanctæ Synodi apud permultos vel auctoritas contempta,
vel sapientissima neglecta fuere decreta.

Nemo enim ignorat, hæreses, quas Tridentini Patres proscripserunt,
dum, rejecto divino Ecclesiæ magisterio, res ad religionem spectantes
privati cujusvis judicio permitterentur, in sectas paullatim dissolutas
esse multiplices, quibus inter se dissentientibus et concertantibus, omnis
tandem in Christum fides apud non paucos labefactata est. Itaque ipsa
Sacra Biblia, quæ antea Christianæ doctrinæ unicus fons et judex
asserebantur, jam non pro divinis haberi, imo mythicis commentis
accenseri coeperunt.

THE DOGMATIC DECREES OF THE VATICAN COUNCIL CONCERNING THE CATH-
OLIC FAITH AND THE CHURCH OF CHRIST.

DOGMATIC CONSTITUTION ON THE CATHOLIC FAITH.

Published in the Third Session, held April 24, 1870.

PIUS, BISHOP, SERVANT OF THE SERVANTS OF GOD, WITH THE APPROVAL
OF THE SACRED COUNCIL, FOR PERPETUAL REMEMBRANCE.

Our Lord Jesus Christ, the Son of God, and Redeemer of Mankind,
before returning to his heavenly Father, promised that he would be
with the Church Militant on earth all days, even to the consummation
of the world. Therefore, he has never ceased to be present with his be-
loved Spouse, to assist her when teaching, to bless her when at work,
and to aid her when in danger. And this his salutary providence, which
has been constantly displayed by other innumerable benefits, has been
most manifestly proved by the abundant good results which Christendom
has derived from ecumenical Councils, and particularly from that of
Trent, although it was held in evil times. For, as a consequence, the
sacred doctrines of the faith have been defined more closely, and set
forth more fully, errors have been condemned and restrained, ecclesiastical discipline has been restored and more firmly secured, the love
of learning and of piety has been promoted among the clergy, colleges
have been established to educate youth for the sacred warfare, and the
morals of the Christian world have been renewed by the more accurate
training of the faithful, and by the more frequent use of the sacraments.
Moreover, there has resulted a closer communion of the members with
the visible head, an increase of vigour in the whole mystical body of
Christ, the multiplication of religious congregations, and of other institutions of Christian piety, and such ardour in extending the kingdom of
Christ throughout the world as constantly endures, even to the sacrifice
of life itself.

But while we recall with due thankfulness these and other signal benefits which the divine mercy has bestowed on the Church, especially by
the last ecumenical Council, we can not restrain our bitter sorrow for
the grave evils, which are principally due to the fact that the authority
of that sacred Synod has been contemned, or its wise decrees neglected,
by many.

No one is ignorant that the heresies proscribed by the Fathers of
Trent, by which the divine magisterium of the Church was rejected, and
all matters regarding religion were surrendered to the judgment of each
individual, gradually became dissolved into many sects, which disagreed
and contended with one another, until at length not a few lost all faith
in Christ. Even the Holy Scriptures, which had previously been declared the sole source and judge of Christian doctrine, began to be held
no longer as divine, but to be ranked among the fictions of mythology.

Tum nata est et late nimis per orbem vagata illa rationalismi seu naturalismi doctrina, quæ religioni Christianæ utpote supernaturali instituto per omnia adversans, summo studio molitur, ut Christo, qui solus Dominus et Salvator noster est, a mentibus humanis, a vita et moribus populorum excluso, meræ quod vocant rationis vel naturæ regnum stabiliatur. Relicta autem projectaque Christiana religione, negato vero Deo et Christo ejus, prolapsa tandem est multorum mens in Pantheismi, Materialismi, Atheismi barathrum, ut jam ipsam rationalem naturam, omnemque justi rectique normam negantes, ima humanæ societatis fundamenta diruere connitantur.

Hac porro impietate circumquaque grassante, infeliciter contigit, ut plures etiam e Catholicæ Ecclesiæ filiis a via veræ pietatis aberrarent, in iisque, diminutis paullatim veritatibus, sensus Catholicus attenuaretur. Variis enim ac peregrinis doctrinis abducti, naturam et gratiam, scientiam humanam et fidem divinam perperam commiscentes, genuinum sensum dogmatum, quem tenet ac docet sancta mater Ecclesia, depravare, integritatemque et sinceritatem fidei in periculum adducere comperiuntur.

Quibus omnibus perspectis, fieri qui potest, ut non commoveantur intima Ecclesiæ viscera? Quemadmodum enim Deus vult omnes homines salvos fieri, et ad agnitionem veritatis venire; quemadmodum Christus venit, ut salvum faceret, quod perierat, et filios Dei, qui erant dispersi, congregaret in unum: ita Ecclesia, a Deo populorum mater et magistra constituta, omnibus debitricem se novit, ac lapsos erigere, labantes sustinere, revertentes amplecti, confirmare bonos et ad meliora provehere parata semper et intenta est. Quapropter nullo tempore a Dei veritate, quæ sanat omnia, testanda et prædicanda quiescere potest, sibi dictum esse non ignorans: Spiritus meus, qui est in te, et verba mea, quæ posui in ore tuo, non recedent de ore tuo amodo et usque in sempiternum.[1]

Nos itaque, inhærentes prædecessorum nostrorum vestigiis, pro supremo nostro Apostolico munere veritatem Catholicam docere ac tueri perversasque doctrinas reprobare nunquam intermissimus. Nunc autem, sedentibus nobiscum et judicantibus universi orbis Episcopis, in hanc œcumenicam Synodum auctoritate nostra in Spiritu Sancto congregatis, innixi Dei verbo scripto et tradito, prout ab Ecclesia Catholica sancte custoditum et genuine expositum accepimus, ex hac Petri Cathedra, in conspectu omnium, salutarem Christi doctrinam profiteri et declarare constituimus, adversis erroribus potestate nobis a Deo tradita proscriptis atque damnatis.

Then there arose, and too widely overspread the world, that doctrine of rationalism, or naturalism, which opposes itself in every way to the Christian religion as a supernatural institution, and works with the utmost zeal in order that, after Christ, our sole Lord and Saviour, has been excluded from the minds of men, and from the life and moral acts of nations, the reign of what they call pure reason or nature may be established. And after forsaking and rejecting the Christian religion, and denying the true God and his Christ, the minds of many have sunk into the abyss of Pantheism, Materialism, and Atheism, until, denying rational nature itself, and every sound rule of right, they labour to destroy the deepest foundations of human society.

Unhappily, it has yet further come to pass that, while this impiety prevailed on every side, many even of the children of the Catholic Church have strayed from the path of true piety, and by the gradual diminution of the truths they held, the Catholic sense became weakened in them. For, led away by various and strange doctrines, utterly confusing nature and grace, human science and divine faith, they are found to deprave the true sense of the doctrines which our holy Mother Church holds and teaches, and endanger the integrity and the soundness of the faith.

Considering these things, how can the Church fail to be deeply stirred? For, even as God wills all men to be saved, and to arrive at the knowledge of the truth, even as Christ came to save what had perished, and to gather together the children of God who had been dispersed, so the Church, constituted by God the mother and teacher of nations, knows its own office as debtor to all, and is ever ready and watchful to raise the fallen, to support those who are falling, to embrace those who return, to confirm the good and to carry them on to better things. Hence, it can never forbear from witnessing to and proclaiming the truth of God, which heals all things, knowing the words addressed to it: "My Spirit that is in thee, and my words that I have put in thy mouth, shall not depart out of thy mouth, from henceforth and forever." [1]

We, therefore, following the footsteps of our predecessors, have never ceased, as becomes our supreme Apostolic office, from teaching and defending Catholic truth, and condemning doctrines of error. And now, with the Bishops of the whole world assembled round us, and judging with us, congregated by our authority, and in the Holy Spirit, in this ecumenical Council, we, supported by the Word of God written and handed down as we received it from the Catholic Church, preserved with sacredness and set forth according to truth, have determined to profess and declare the salutary teaching of Christ from this Chair of Peter, and in sight of all, proscribing and condemning, by the power given to us of God, all errors contrary thereto.

CAPUT I.

De Deo rerum omnium Creatore.

Sancta Catholica Apostolica Romana Ecclesia credit et confitetur, unum esse Deum verum et vivum, Creatorem ac Dominum cœli et ter-ræ, omnipotentem, æternum, immensum, incomprehensibilem, intel-lectu ac voluntate omnique perfectione infinitum; qui cum sit una sin-gularis, simplex omnino et incommutabilis substantia spiritualis, prædi-candus est re et essentia a mundo distinctus, in se et ex se beatissimus, et super omnia, quæ præter ipsum sunt et concipi possunt, ineffabiliter excelsus.

Hic solus verus Deus bonitate sua et omnipotenti virtute non ad augen-dam suam beatitudinem, nec ad acquirendam, sed ad manifestandam perfectionem suam per bona, quæ creaturis impertitur, liberrimo con-silio simul ab initio temporis utramque de nihilo condidit creaturam, spiritualem et corporalem, angelicam videlicet et mundanam, ac deinde humanam quasi communem ex spiritu et corpore constitutam.[2]

Universa vero, quæ condidit, Deus providentia sua tuetur atque gubernat, attingens a fine usque ad finem fortiter, et disponens omnia suaviter.[3] Omnia enim nuda et aperta sunt oculis ejus,[4] ea etiam, quæ libera creaturarum actione futura sunt.

CAPUT II.

De Revelatione.

Eadem sancta mater Ecclesia tenet et docet, Deum, rerum omnium principium et finem, naturali humanæ rationis lumine e rebus creatis certo cognosci posse; invisibilia enim ipsius, a creatura mundi, per ea quæ facta sunt, intellecta, conspiciuntur:[5] attamen placuisse ejus sapientiæ et bonitati, alia, eaque supernaturali via se ipsum ac æterna voluntatis suæ decreta humano generi revelare, dicente Apostolo: Multi-fariam, multisque modis olim Deus loquens patribus in Prophetis: no-vissime, diebus istis locutus est nobis in Filio.[6]

Huic divinæ revelationi tribuendum quidem est, ut ea, quæ in rebus divinis humanæ rationi per se impervia non sunt, in præsenti quoque generis humani conditione ab omnibus expedite, firma certitudine et nullo admixto errore cognosci possint. Non hac tamen de causa revelatio absolute necessaria dicenda est, sed quia Deus ex infinita bonitate sua ordinavit hominem ad finem supernaturalem, ad partici-panda scilicet bona divina, quæ humanæ mentis intelligentiam omnino superant; siquidem oculus non vidit, nec auris audivit, nec in cor hominis ascendit, quæ præparavit Deus iis, qui diligunt illum.[7]

CHAPTER I.

Of God, the Creator of all Things.

The holy Catholic Apostolic Roman Church believes and confesses that there is one true and living God, Creator and Lord of heaven and earth, almighty, eternal, immense, incomprehensible, infinite in intelligence, in will, and in all perfection, who, as being one, sole, absolutely simple and immutable spiritual substance, is to be declared as really and essentially distinct from the world, of supreme beatitude in and from himself, and ineffably exalted above all things which exist, or are conceivable, except himself.

This one only true God, of his own goodness and almighty power, not for the increase or acquirement of his own happiness, but to manifest his perfection by the blessings which he bestows on creatures, and with absolute freedom of counsel, created out of nothing, from the very first beginning of time, both the spiritual and the corporeal creature, to wit, the angelical and the mundane, and afterwards the human creature, as partaking, in a sense, of both, consisting of spirit and of body.[2]

God protects and governs by his providence all things which he hath made, "reaching from end to end mightily, and ordering all things sweetly." [3] For "all things are bare and open to his eyes," [4] even those which are yet to be by the free action of creatures.

CHAPTER II.

Of Revelation.

The same holy Mother Church holds and teaches that God, the beginning and end of all things, may be certainly known by the natural light of human reason, by means of created things; "for the invisible things of him from the creation of the world are clearly seen, being understood by the things that are made," [5] but that it pleased his wisdom and bounty to reveal himself, and the eternal decrees of his will, to mankind by another and a supernatural way: as the Apostle says, "God, having spoken on divers occasions, and many ways, in times past, to the Fathers by the Prophets; last of all, in these days, hath spoken to us by his Son." [6]

It is to be ascribed to this divine revelation, that such truths among things divine as of themselves are not beyond human reason, can, even in the present condition of mankind, be known by every one with facility, with firm assurance, and with no admixture of error. This, however, is not the reason why revelation is to be called absolutely necessary; but because God of his infinite goodness has ordained man to a supernatural end, viz., to be a sharer of divine blessings, which utterly exceed the intelligence of the human mind; for "eye hath not seen, nor ear heard, neither hath it entered into the heart of man, what things God hath prepared for them that love him." [7]

Hæc porro supernaturalis revelatio, secundum universalis Ecclesiæ fidem, a sancta Tridentina Synodo declaratam, continetur in libris scriptis et sine scripto traditionibus quæ ipsius Christi ore ab Apostolis acceptæ, aut ab ipsis Apostolis Spiritu Sancto dictante quasi per manus traditæ, ad nos usque pervenerunt.[8] Qui quidem veteris et Novi Testamenti libri integri cum omnibus suis partibus, prout in ejusdem Concilii decreto recensentur, et in veteri vulgata latina editione habentur, pro sacris et canonicis suscipiendi sunt.[9] Eos vero Ecclesia pro sacris et canonicis habet, non ideo, quod sola humana industria concinnati, sua deinde auctoritate sint approbati; nec ideo dumtaxat, quod revelationem sine errore contineant, sed propterea, quod Spiritu Sancto inspirante conscripti Deum habent auctorem, atque ut tales ipsi Ecclesiæ traditi sunt.

Quoniam vero, quæ sancta Tridentina Synodus[10] de interpretatione divinæ Scripturæ ad coërcenda petulantia ingenia salubriter decrevit, a quibusdam hominibus prave exponuntur, nos, idem decretum renovantes, hanc illius mentem esse declaramus, ut in rebus fidei et morum, ad ædificationem doctrinæ Christianæ pertinentium, is pro vero sensu Scripturæ habendus sit, quem tenuit ac tenet sancta mater Ecclesia, cujus est judicare de vero sensu et interpretatione Scripturarum sanctarum; atque ideo nemini licere contra hunc sensum aut etiam contra unanimem consensum Patrum ipsam Scripturam sacram interpretari.

CAPUT III.

De Fide.

Quum homo a Deo tamquam Creatore et Domino suo totus dependeat, et ratio creata increatæ veritati penitus subjecta sit, plenum revelanti Deo intellectus et voluntatis obsequium fide præstare tenemur. Hanc vero fidem, quæ humanæ salutis initium est, Ecclesia Catholica profitetur, virtutem esse supernaturalem, qua, Dei aspirante et adjuvante gratia, ab eo revelata vera esse credimus, non propter intrinsecam rerum veritatem naturali rationis lumine perspectam, sed propter auctoritatem ipsius Dei revelantis, qui nec falli nec fallere potest. Est enim fides, testante Apostolo, sperandarum substantia rerum, argumentum non apparentium.[11]

Ut nihilominus fidei nostræ obsequium rationi consentaneum esset, voluit Deus cum internis Spiritus Sancti auxiliis externa jungi revelationis suæ argumenta, facta scilicet divina, atque imprimis miracula et prophetias, quæ cum Dei omnipotentiam et infinitam scientiam luculenter

Further, this supernatural revelation, according to the universal belief of the Church, declared by the sacred Synod of Trent, is contained in the written books and unwritten traditions which have come down to us, having been received by the Apostles from the mouth of Christ himself; or from the Apostles themselves, by the dictation of the Holy Spirit, have been transmitted, as it were, from hand to hand.[8] And these books of the Old and New Testament are to be received as sacred and canonical, in their integrity, with all their parts, as they are enumerated in the decree of the said Council, and are contained in the ancient Latin edition of the Vulgate.[9] These the Church holds to be sacred and canonical, not because, having been carefully composed by mere human industry, they were afterwards approved by her authority, nor merely because they contain revelation, with no admixture of error; but because, having been written by the inspiration of the Holy Ghost, they have God for their author, and have been delivered as such to the Church herself.

And as the things which the holy Synod of Trent[10] decreed for the good of souls concerning the interpretation of Divine Scripture, in order to curb rebellious spirits, have been wrongly explained by some, we, renewing the said decree, declare this to be their sense, that, in matters of faith and morals, appertaining to the building up of Christian doctrine, that is to be held as the true sense of Holy Scripture which our holy Mother Church hath held and holds, to whom it belongs to judge of the true sense and interpretation of the Holy Scripture; and therefore that it is permitted to no one to interpret the Sacred Scripture contrary to this sense, nor, likewise, contrary to the unanimous consent of the Fathers.

CHAPTER III.

On Faith.

Man being wholly dependent upon God, as upon his Creator and Lord, and created reason being absolutely subject to uncreated truth, we are bound to yield to God, by faith in his revelation, the full obedience of our intelligence and will. And the Catholic Church teaches that this faith, which is the beginning of man's salvation, is a supernatural virtue, whereby, inspired and assisted by the grace of God, we believe that the things which he has revealed are true; not because of the intrinsic truth of the things, viewed by the natural light of reason, but because of the authority of God himself, who reveals them, and who can neither be deceived nor deceive. For faith, as the Apostle testifies, is "the substance of things hoped for, the conviction of things that appear not." [11]

Nevertheless, in order that the obedience of our faith might be in harmony with reason, God willed that to the interior help of the Holy Spirit there should be joined exterior proofs of his revelation; to wit, divine facts, and especially miracles and prophecies, which, as they manifestly display the omnipotence and infinite knowledge of God, are

commonstrent, divinæ revelationis signa sunt certissima et omnium intelligentiæ accommodata. Quare tum Moyses et Prophetæ, tum ipse maxime Christus Dominus multa et manifestissima miracula et prophetias ediderunt; et de Apostolis legimus: Illi autem profecti prædicaverunt ubique, Domino cooperante et sermonem confirmante sequentibus signis.[12] Et rursum scriptum est: Habemus firmiorem propheticum sermonem, cui bene facitis attendentes quasi lucernæ lucenti in caliginoso loco.[13]

Licet autem fidei assensus nequaquam sit motus animi cæcus: nemo tamen evangelicæ prædicationi consentire potest, sicut oportet ad salutem consequendam, absque illuminatione et inspiratione Spiritus Sancti, qui dat omnibus suavitatem in consentiendo et credendo veritati.[14] Quare fides ipsa in se, etiamsi per caritatem non operetur, donum Dei est, et actus ejus est opus ad salutem pertinens, quo homo liberam præstat ipsi Deo obedientiam, gratiæ ejus, cui resistere posset, consentiendo et cooperando.

Porro fide divina et Catholica ea omnia credenda sunt, quæ in verbo Dei scripto vel tradito continentur, et ab Ecclesia sive solemni judicio sive ordinario et universali magisterio tamquam divinitus revelata credenda proponuntur.

Quoniam vero sine fide impossibile est placere Deo,[15] et ad filiorum ejus consortium pervenire; ideo nemini unquam sine illa contigit justificatio, nec ullus, nisi in ea perseveraverit usque in finem, vitam æternam assequetur. Ut autem officio veram fidem ampletendi, in eaque constanter perseverandi satisfacere possemus, Deus per Filium suum unigenitum Ecclesiam instituit, suæque institutionis manifestis notis instruxit, ut ea tamquam custos et magistra verbi revelati ab omnibus posset agnosci. Ad solam enim Catholicam Ecclesiam ea pertinent omnia, quæ ad evidentem fidei Christianæ credibilitatem tam multa et tam mira divinitus sunt disposita. Quin etiam Ecclesia per se ipsa, ob suam nempe admirabilem propagationem, eximiam sanctitatem et inexhaustam in omnibus bonis fœcunditatem, ob Catholicam unitatem, invictamque stabilitatem, magnum quoddam et perpetuum est motivum credibilitatis et divinæ suæ legationis testimonium irrefragabile.

Quo fit, ut ipsa veluti signum levatum in nationes,[16] et ad se invitet, qui nondum crediderunt, et filios suos certiores faciat, firmissimo niti fundamento fidem, quam profitentur. Cui quidem testimonio efficax subsidium accedit ex superna virtute. Etenim benignissimus Dominus et errantes gratia sua excitat atque adjuvat, ut ad agnitionem veritatis venire possint, et eos, quos de tenebris transtulit in admirabile lumen suum, in hoc eodem lumine ut perseverent, gratia sua confirmat, non deserens, nisi deseratur. Quocirca minime par est conditio eorum, qui per cœleste

most certain proofs of his divine revelation, adapted to the intelligence of all men. Wherefore, both Moses and the Prophets, and most especially, Christ our Lord himself, showed forth many and most evident miracles and prophecies; and of the Apostles we read: "But they going forth preached everywhere, the Lord working withal, and confirming the word with signs that followed." [12] And again, it is written: "We have the more firm prophetical word, whereunto you do well to attend, as to a light shining in a dark place." [13]

But though the assent of faith is by no means a blind action of the mind, still no man can assent to the Gospel teaching, as is necessary to obtain salvation, without the illumination and inspiration of the Holy Spirit, who gives to all men sweetness in assenting to and believing in the truth.[14] Wherefore, faith itself, even when it does not work by charity, is in itself a gift of God, and the act of faith is a work appertaining to salvation, by which man yields voluntary obedience to God himself, by assenting to and co-operating with his grace, which he is able to resist.

Further, all those things are to be believed with divine and Catholic faith which are contained in the Word of God, written or handed down, and which the Church, either by a solemn judgment, or by her ordinary and universal magisterium, proposes for belief as having been divinely revealed.

And since, without faith, it is impossible to please God,[15] and to attain to the fellowship of his children, therefore without faith no one has ever attained justification, nor will any one obtain eternal life unless he shall have persevered in faith unto the end. And, that we may be able to satisfy the obligation of embracing the true faith, and of constantly persevering in it, God has instituted the Church through his only-begotten Son, and has bestowed on it manifest notes of that institution, that it may be recognized by all men as the guardian and teacher of the revealed Word; for to the Catholic Church alone belong all those many and admirable tokens which have been divinely established for the evident credibility of the Christian faith. Nay, more, the Church by itself, with its marvelous extension, its eminent holiness, and its inexhaustible fruitfulness in every good thing, with its Catholic unity and its invincible stability, is a great and perpetual motive of credibility, and an irrefutable witness of its own divine mission.

And thus, like a standard set up unto the nations,[16] it both invites to itself those who do not yet believe, and assures its children that the faith which they profess rests on the most firm foundation. And its testimony is efficaciously supported by a power from on high. For our most merciful Lord gives his grace to stir up and to aid those who are astray, that they may come to a knowledge of the truth; and to those whom he has brought out of darkness into his own admirable light he gives his grace to strengthen them to persevere in that light, deserting none who desert not him. Therefore there is no parity between the condition of those

fidei donum Catholicæ veritati adhæserunt, atque eorum, qui ducti opinionibus humanis, falsam religionem sectantur; illi enim, qui fidem sub Ecclesiæ magisterio susceperunt, nullam unquam habere possunt justam causam mutandi, aut in dubium fidem eamdem revocandi. Quæ cum ita sint, gratias agentes Deo Patri, qui dignos nos fecit in partem sortis sanctorum in lumine,[17] tantam ne negligamus salutem,[8] sed aspicientes in auctorem fidei et consummatorem Jesum,[19] teneamus spei nostræ confessionem indeclinabilem.[20]

CAPUT IV.

De Fide et Ratione.

Hoc quoque perpetuus Ecclesiæ Catholicæ consensus tenuit et tenet, duplicem esse ordinem cognitionis, non solum principio, sed objecto etiam distinctum: principio quidem, quia in altero naturali ratione, in altero fide divina cognoscimus; objecto autem, quia præter ea, ad quæ naturalis ratio pertingere potest, credenda nobis proponuntur mysteria in Deo abscondita, quæ, nisi revelata divinitus, innotescere non possunt. Quocirca Apostolus, qui a gentibus Deum per ea, quæ facta sunt, cognitum esse testatur, disserens tamen de gratia et veritate, quæ per Jesum Christum facta est,[21] pronunciat: Loquimur Dei sapientiam in mysterio, quæ abscondita est, quam prædestinavit Deus ante sæcula in gloriam nostram, quam nemo principum hujus sæculi cognovit: nobis autem revelavit Deus per Spiritum suum: Spiritus enim omnia scrutatur, etiam profunda Dei.[22] Et ipse Unigenitus confitetur Patri, quia abscondit hæc a sapientibus et prudentibus, et revelavit ea parvulis.[23]

Ac ratio quidem, fide illustrata, cum sedulo, pie et sobrie quærit, aliquam, Deo dante, mysteriorum intelligentiam eamque fructuosissimam assequitur, tum ex eorum, quæ naturaliter cognoscit, analogia, tum e mysteriorum ipsorum nexu inter se et cum fine hominis ultimo; nunquam tamen idonea redditur ad ea perspicienda instar veritatum, quæ proprium ipsius objectum constituunt. Divina enim mysteria suapte natura intellectum creatum sic excedunt, ut etiam revelatione tradita et fide suscepta, ipsius tamen fidei velamine contecta et quadam quasi caligine obvoluta maneant, quamdiu in hac mortali vita peregrinamur a Domino: per fidem enim ambulamus, et non per speciem.[24]

Verum etsi fides sit supra rationem, nulla tamen unquam inter fidem et rationem vera dissensio esse potest: cum idem Deus, qui mysteria revelat et fidem infundit, animo humano rationis lumen indiderit; Deus autem negare seipsum non possit, nec verum vero unquam contradicere. Inanis autem hujus contradictionis species inde potissimum oritur, quod

who have adhered to the Catholic truth by the heavenly gift of faith, and of those who, led by human opinions, follow a false religion; for those who have received the faith under the magisterium of the Church can never have any just cause for changing or doubting that faith. Therefore, giving thanks to God the Father who has made us worthy to be partakers of the lot of the Saints in light,[17] let us not neglect so great salvation,[18] but with our eyes fixed on Jesus,[19] the author and finisher of our faith, let us hold fast the confession of our hope without wavering.[20]

CHAPTER IV.

On Faith and Reason.

The Catholic Church, with one consent, has also ever held and does hold that there is a twofold order of knowledge distinct both in principle and also in object; in principle, because our knowledge in the one is by natural reason, and in the other by divine faith; in object, because, besides those things to which natural reason can attain, there are proposed to our belief mysteries hidden in God, which unless divinely revealed, can not be known. Wherefore, the Apostle, who testifies that God is known by the Gentiles through created things, still, when discoursing of the grace and truth which come by Jesus Christ,[21] says: "We speak the wisdom of God in a mystery, a wisdom which is hidden, which God ordained before the world unto our glory; which none of the princes of this world knew . . . but to us God hath revealed them by his Spirit. For the Spirit searcheth all things, yea, the deep things of God." [22] And the only-begotten Son himself gives thanks to the Father, because he has hid these things from the wise and prudent, and has revealed them to little ones.[23]

Reason, indeed, enlightened by faith, when it seeks earnestly, piously, and calmly, attains by a gift from God some, and that a very fruitful, understanding of mysteries; partly from the analogy of those things which it naturally knows, partly from the relations which the mysteries bear to one another and to the last end of man; but reason never becomes capable of apprehending mysteries as it does those truths which constitute its proper object. For the divine mysteries by their own nature so far transcend the created intelligence that, even when delivered by revelation and received by faith, they remain covered with the veil of faith itself, and shrouded in a certain degree of darkness, so long as we are pilgrims in this mortal life, not yet with God; "for we walk by faith and not by sight." [24]

But although faith is above reason, there can never be any real discrepancy between faith and reason, since the same God who reveals mysteries and infuses faith has bestowed the light of reason on the human mind; and God can not deny himself, nor can truth ever contradict truth. The false appearance of such a contradiction is mainly due, either to the

vel fidei dogmata ad mentem Ecclesiæ intellecta et exposita non fuerint, vel opinionum commenta pro rationis effatis habeantur. Omnem igitur assertionem veritati illuminatæ fidei contrariam omnino falsam esse definimus.[25] Porro Ecclesia, quæ una cum apostolico munere docendi, mandatum accepit fidei depositum custodiendi, jus etiam et officium divinitus habet falsi nominis scientiam proscribendi, ne quis decipiatur per philosophiam et inanem fallaciam.[26] Quapropter omnes Christiani fideles hujusmodi opiniones, quæ fidei doctrinæ contrariæ esse cognoscuntur, maxime si ab Ecclesia reprobatæ fuerint, non solum prohibentur tanquam legitimas scientiæ conclusiones defendere, sed pro erroribus potius, qui fallacem veritatis speciem præ se ferant, habere tenentur omnino.

Neque solum fides et ratio inter se dissidere nunquam possunt, sed opem quoque sibi mutuam ferunt, cum recta ratio fidei fundamenta demonstret, ejusque lumine illustrata rerum divinarum scientiam excolat; fides vero rationem ab erroribus liberet ac tueatur, eamque multiplici cognitione instruat. Quapropter tantum abest, ut Ecclesia humanarum artium et disciplinarum culturæ obsistat, ut hanc multis modis juvet atque promoveat. Non enim commoda ab iis ad hominum vitam dimanantia aut ignorat aut despicit; fatetur imo, eas, quemadmodum a Deo, scientiarum Domino, profectæ sunt, ita si rite pertractentur, ad Deum, juvante ejus gratia, perducere. Nec sane ipsa vetat, ne hujusmodi disciplinæ in suo quæque ambitu propriis utantur principiis et propria methodo; sed justam hanc libertatem agnoscens, id sedulo cavet, ne divinæ doctrinæ repugnando errores in se suscipiant, aut fines proprios transgressæ, ea, quæ sunt fidei, occupent et perturbent.

Neque enim fidei doctrina, quam Deus revelavit, velut philosophicum inventum proposita est humanis ingeniis perficienda, sed tanquam divinum depositum Christi Sponsæ tradita, fideliter custodienda et infallibiliter declaranda. Hinc sacrorum quoque dogmatum is sensus perpetuo est retinendus, quem semel declaravit sancta mater Ecclesia, nec unquam ab eo sensu, altioris intelligentiæ specie et nomine, recedendum. Crescat igitur et multum vehementerque proficiat, tam singulorum, quam omnium, tam unius hominis, quam totius Ecclesiæ, ætatem ac sæculorum gradibus, intelligentia, scientia, sapientia; sed in suo dumtaxat genere, in eodem scilicet dogmate, eodem sensu, eademque sententia.[27]

dogmas of faith not having been understood and expounded according to the mind of the Church, or to the inventions of opinion having been taken for the verdicts of reason. We define, therefore, that every assertion contrary to a truth of enlightened faith is utterly false.[25] Further, the Church, which, together with the Apostolic office of teaching, has received a charge to guard the deposit of faith, derives from God the right and the duty of proscribing false science, lest any should be deceived by philosophy and vain fallacy.[26] Therefore all faithful Christians are not only forbidden to defend, as legitimate conclusions of science, such opinions as are known to be contrary to the doctrines of faith, especially if they have been condemned by the Church, but are altogether bound to account them as errors which put on the fallacious appearance of truth.

And not only can faith and reason never be opposed to one another, but they are of mutual aid one to the other; for right reason demonstrates the foundations of faith, and, enlightened by its light, cultivates the science of things divine; while faith frees and guards reason from errors, and furnishes it with manifold knowledge. So far, therefore, is the Church from opposing the cultivation of human arts and sciences, that it in many ways helps and promotes it. For the Church neither ignores nor despises the benefits of human life which result from the arts and sciences, but confesses that, as they came from God, the Lord of all science, so, if they be rightly used, they lead to God by the help of his grace. Nor does the Church forbid that each of these sciences in its sphere should make use of its own principles and its own method; but, while recognizing this just liberty, it stands watchfully on guard, lest sciences, setting themselves against the divine teaching, or transgressing their own limits, should invade and disturb the domain of faith.

For the doctrine of faith which God hath revealed has not been proposed, like a philosophical invention, to be perfected by human ingenuity, but has been delivered as a divine deposit to the Spouse of Christ, to be faithfully kept and infallibly declared. Hence, also, that meaning of the sacred dogmas is perpetually to be retained which our holy mother the Church has once declared; nor is that meaning ever to be departed from, under the pretense or pretext of a deeper comprehension of them. Let, then, the intelligence, science, and wisdom of each and all, of individuals and of the whole Church, in all ages and all times, increase and flourish in abundance and vigour; but simply in its own proper kind, that is to say, in one and the same doctrine, one and the same sense, one and the same judgment.[27]

CANONES

I.

De Deo rerum omnium Creatore.

1. Si quis unum verum Deum visibilium et invisibilium Creatorem et Dominum negaverit: anathema sit.

2. Si quis præter materiam nihil esse affirmare non erubuerit: anathema sit.

3. Si quis dixerit, unam eandemque esse Dei et rerum omnium substantiam vel essentiam: anathema sit.

4. Si quis dixerit, res finitas, tum corporeas tum spirituales aut saltem spirituales, e divina substantia emanasse; aut divinam essentiam sui manifestatione vel evolutione fieri omnia; aut denique Deum esse ens universale seu indefinitum, quod sese determinando constituat rerum universitatem in genera, species et individua distinctam: anathema sit.

5. Si quis non confiteatur, mundum, resque omnes, quæ in eo continentur, et sprituales et materiales, secundum totam suam substantiam a Deo ex nihilo esse productas; aut Deum dixerit non voluntate ab omni necessitate libera, sed tam necessario creasse, quam necessario amat seipsum; aut mundum ad Dei gloriam conditum esse negaverit: anathema sit.

II.

De Revelatione.

1. Si quis dixerit, Deum unum et verum, Creatorem et Dominum nostrum, per ea, quæ facta sunt, naturali rationis humanæ lumine certo cognosci non posse: anathema sit.

2. Si quis dixerit, fieri non posse, aut non expedire ut per revelationem divinam homo de Deo cultuque ei exhibendo edoceatur: anathema sit.

3. Si quis dixerit, hominem ad cognitionem et perfectionem, quæ naturalem superet, divinitus evehi non posse, sed ex seipso ad omnis tandem veri et boni possessionem jugi profectu pertingere posse et debere: anathema sit.

4. Si quis sacræ Scripturæ libros integros cum omnibus suis partibus, prout illos sancta Tridentina Synodus recensuit, pro sacris et canonicis non susceperit, aut eos divinitus inspiratos esse negaverit: anathema sit.

CANONS.

I.

Of God, the Creator of all things.

1. If any one shall deny one true God, Creator and Lord of things visible and invisible: let him be anathema.

2. If any one shall not be ashamed to affirm that, except matter, nothing exists: let him be anathema.

3. If any one shall say that the substance and essence of God and of all things is one and the same: let him be anathema.

4. If any one shall say that finite things, both corporeal and spiritual, or at least spritual, have emanated from the divine substance; or that the divine essence by the manifestation and evolution of itself becomes all things; or, lastly, that God is universal or indefinite being, which by determining itself constitutes the universality of things, distinct according to genera, species, and individuals: let him be anathema.

5. If any one confess not that the world, and all things which are contained in it, both spiritual and material, have been, in their whole substance, produced by God out of nothing; or shall say that God created, not by his will, free from all necessity, but by a necessity equal to the necessity whereby he loves himself; or shall deny that the world was made for the glory of God: let him be anathema.

II.

Of Revelation.

1. If any one shall say that the one true God, our Creator and Lord, can not be certainly known by the natural light of human reason through created things: let him be anathema.

2. If any one shall say that it is impossible or inexpedient that man should be taught by divine revelation concerning God and the worship to be paid to him: let him be anathema.

3. If any one shall say that man can not be raised by divine power to a higher than natural knowledge and perfection, but can and ought, by a continuous progress, to arrive at length, of himself, to the possession of all that is true and good: let him be anathema.

4. If any one shall not receive as sacred and canonical the books of Holy Scripture, entire with all their parts, as the holy Synod of Trent has enumerated them, or shall deny that they have been divinely inspired: let him be anathema.

III.

De Fide.

1. Si quis dixerit, rationem humanam ita independentem esse, ut fides ei a Deo imperari non possit: anathema sit.

2. Si quis dixerit, fidem divinam a naturali de Deo et rebus moralibus scientia non distingui, ac propterea ad fidem divinam non requiri, ut revelata veritas propter auctoritatem Dei revelantis credatur: anathema sit.

3. Si quis dixerit, revelationem divinam externis signis credibilem fieri non posse, ideoque sola interna cujusque experientia aut inspiratione privata homines ad fidem moveri debere: anathema sit.

4. Si quis dixerit, miracula nulla fieri posse, proindeque omnes de iis narrationes, etiam in sacra Scriptura contentas, inter fabulas vel mythos ablegandas esse; aut miracula certo cognosci nunquam posse, nec iis divinam religionis Christianæ originem rite probari: anathema sit.

5. Si quis dixerit, assensum fidei Christianæ non esse liberum, sed argumentis humanæ rationis necessario produci; aut ad solam fidem vivam, quæ per caritatem operatur, gratiam Dei necessariam esse: anathema sit.

6. Si quis dixerit, parem esse conditionem fidelium atque eorum, qui ad fidem unice veram nondum pervenerunt, ita ut Catholici justam causam habere possint, fidem, quam sub Ecclesiæ magisterio jam susceperunt, assensu suspenso in dubium vocandi, donec demonstrationem scientificam credibilitatis et veritatis fidei suæ absolverint: anathema sit.

IV.

De Fide et Ratione.

1. Si quis dixerit, in revelatione divina nulla vera et proprie dicta mysteria contineri, sed universa fidei dogmata posse per rationem rite excultam e naturalibus principiis intelligi et demonstrari: anathema sit.

2. Si quis dixerit, disciplinas humanas ea cum libertate tractandas esse, ut earum assertiones, etsi doctrinæ revelatæ adversentur, tanquam veræ retineri, neque ab Ecclesia proscribi possint: anathema sit.

3. Si quis dixerit, fieri posse, ut dogmatibus ab Ecclesia propositis, aliquando secundum progressum scientiæ sensus tribuendus sit alius ab eo, quem intellexit et intelligit Ecclesia: anathema sit.

III.

On Faith.

1. If any one shall say that human reason is so independent that faith can not be enjoined upon it by God: let him be anathema.

2. If any one shall say that divine faith is not distinguished from natural knowledge of God and of moral truths, and therefore that it is not requisite for divine faith that revealed truth be believed because of the authority of God, who reveals it: let him be anathema.

3. If any one shall say that divine revelation can not be made credible by outward signs, and therefore that men ought to be moved to faith solely by the internal experience of each, or by private inspiration: let him be anathema.

4. If any one shall say that miracles are impossible, and therefore that all the accounts regarding them, even those contained in Holy Scripture, are to be dismissed as fabulous or mythical; or that miracles can never be known with certainty, and that the divine origin of Christianity can not be proved by them: let him be anathema.

5. If any one shall say that the assent of Christian faith is not a free act, but inevitably produced by the arguments of human reason; or that the grace of God is necessary for that living faith only which worketh by charity: let him be anathema.

6. If any one shall say that the condition of the faithful, and of those who have not yet attained to the only true faith, is on a par, so that Catholics may have just cause for doubting, with suspended assent, the faith which they have already received under the magisterium of the Church, until they shall have obtained a scientific demonstration of the credibility and truth of their faith: let him be anathema.

IV.

On Faith and Reason.

1. If any one shall say that in divine revelation there are no mysteries, truly and properly so called, but that all the doctrines of faith can be understood and demonstrated from natural principles, by properly cultivated reason: let him be anathema.

2. If any one shall say that human sciences are to be so freely treated that their assertions, although opposed to revealed doctrine, are to be held as true, and can not be condemned by the Church: let him be anathema.

3. If any one shall assert it to be possible that sometimes, according to the progress of science, a sense is to be given to doctrines propounded by the Church different from that which the Church has understood and understands: let him be anathema.

Itaque supremi pastoralis Nostri officii debitum exequentes, omnes Christi fideles, maxime vero eos, qui præsunt vel docendi munere funguntur, per viscera Jesu Christi obtestamur, necnon ejusdem Dei et Salvatoris nostri auctoritate jubemus, ut ad hos errores a Sancta Ecclesia arcendos et eliminandos, atque purissimæ fidei lucem pandendam studium et operam conferant.

Quoniam vero satis non est, hæreticam pravitatem devitare, nisi ii quoque errores diligenter fugiantur, qui ad illam plus minusve accedunt; omnes officii monemus, servandi etiam Constitutiones et Decreta, quibus pravæ ejusmodi opiniones, quæ isthic diserte non enumerantur, ab hac Sancta Sede proscriptæ et prohibitæ sunt.

Datum Romæ in publica Sessione in Vaticana Basilica solemniter celebrata, anno Incarnationis Dominicæ millesimo octingentesimo septuagesimo, die vigesima quarta Aprilis. Pontificatus Nostri anno vigesimo quarto.

CONSTITUTIO DOGMATICA PRIMA DE ECCLESIA CHRISTI.

Sessio IV.

PIUS EPISCOPUS, SERVUS SERVORUM DEI SACRO APPROBANTE CONCILIO AD PERPETUAM REI MEMORIAM.

Pastor æternus et Episcopus animarum nostrarum, ut salutiferum Redemptionis opus perenne redderet, sanctam ædificare Ecclesiam decrevit, in qua veluti in domo Dei viventis fideles omnes unius fidei et caritatis vinculo continerentur. Quapropter, priusquam clarificaretur, rogavit Patrem non pro Apostolis tantum, sed et pro eis, qui credituri erant per verbum eorum in ipsum, ut omnes unum essent, sicut ipse Filius et Pater unum sunt.[28] Quemadmodum igitur Apostolos, quos sibi de mundo elegerat, misit, sicut ipse missus erat a Patre: ita in Ecclesia sua pastores et doctores usque ad consummationem sæculi esse voluit. Ut vero episcopatus ipse unus et indivisus esset, et per cohærentes sibi invicem sacerdotes credentium multitudo universa in fidei et communionis unitate conservaretur, beatum Petrum cæteris Apostolis præponens in ipso instituit perpetuum utriusque unitatis principium ac visibile fundamentum, super cujus fortitudinem æternum exstrueretur templum, et Ecclesiæ cœlo inferenda sublimitas in hujus fidei firmitate consurgeret.[29] Et quoniam portæ inferi ad evertendam, si fieri posset, Ecclesiam, contra ejus fundamentum divinitus positum majori in dies odio undique insurgunt, Nos ad Catholici gregis custodiam, incolumitatem, augmentum, necessarium esse judicamus, sacro approbante Concilio, doctrinam de

Therefore, we, fulfilling the duty of our supreme pastoral office, entreat, by the mercies of Jesus Christ, and, by the authority of the same, our God and Saviour, we command, all the faithful of Christ, and especially those who are set over others, or are charged with the office of instruction, that they earnestly and diligently apply themselves to ward off and eliminate these errors from holy Church, and to spread the light of pure faith.

And since it is not sufficient to shun heretical pravity, unless those errors also be diligently avoided which more or less nearly approach it, admonish all men of the further duty of observing those constitutions and decrees by which such erroneous opinions as are not here specifically enumerated, have been proscribed and condemned by this Holy See.

Given at Rome in public Session solemnly held in the Vatican Basilica in the year of our Lord one thousand eight hundred and seventy, on the twenty-fourth day of April, in the twenty-fourth year of our Pontificate.

FIRST DOGMATIC CONSTITUTION ON THE CHURCH OF CHRIST.

Published in the Fourth Session of the holy Ecumenical Council of the Vatican.

PIUS BISHOP, SERVANT OF THE SERVANTS OF GOD, WITH THE APPROVAL OF THE SACRED COUNCIL, FOR AN EVERLASTING REMEMBRANCE.

The eternal Pastor and Bishop of our souls, in order to continue for all time the life-giving work of his Redemption, determined to build up the holy Church, wherein, as in the house of the living God, all who believe might be united in the bond of one faith and one charity. Wherefore, before he entered into his glory, he prayed unto the Father, not for the Apostles only, but for those also who through their preaching should come to believe in him, that all might be one even as he the Son and the Father are one.[28] As then he sent the Apostles whom he had chosen to himself from the world, as he himself had been sent by the Father: so he willed that there should ever be pastors and teachers in his Church to the end of the World. And in order that the Episcopate also might be one and undivided, and that by means of a closely united priesthood the multitude of the faithful might be kept secure in the oneness of faith and communion, he set blessed Peter over the rest of the Apostles, and fixed in him the abiding principle of this twofold unity, and its visible foundation, in the strength of which the everlasting temple should arise, and the Church in the firmness of that faith should lift her majestic front to heaven.[29] And seeing that the gates of hell, with daily increase of hatred, are gathering their strength on every side to upheave the foundation laid by God's own hand, and so, if that might be, to overthrow the Church: we, therefore, for the preservation, safe-keeping, and increase of

institutione, perpetuitate, ac natura sacri Apostolici primatus, in quo totius Ecclesiæ vis ac soliditas consistit, cunctis fidelibus credendam et tenendam, secundum antiquam atque constantem universalis Ecclesiæ fidem, proponere, atque contrarios, dominico gregi adeo perniciosos, errores proscribere et condemnare.

CAPUT I.

De Apostolici Primatus in beato Petro institutione.

Docemus itaque et declaramus, juxta Evangelii testimonia primatum jurisdictionis in universam Dei Ecclesiam immediate et directe beato Petro Apostolo promissum atque collatum a Christo Domino fuisse. Unum enim Simonem, cui jam pridem dixerat: Tu vocaberis Cephas,[30] postquam ille suam edidit confessionem inquiens: Tu es Christus, Filius Dei vivi, solemnibus his verbis allocutus est Dominus: Beatus es, Simon Bar-Jona, quia caro et sanguis non revelavit tibi, sed Pater meus, qui in cœlis est: et ego dico tibi, quia tu es Petrus, et super hanc Petram ædificabo Ecclesiam meam, et portæ inferi non prævalebunt adversus eam: et tibi dabo claves regni cœlorum: et quodcumque ligaveris super terram, erit ligatum et in cœlis: et quodcumque solveris super terram, erit solutum et in cœlis.[31] Atque uni Simoni Petro contulit Jesus post suam resurrectionem summi pastoris et rectoris jurisdictionem in totum suum ovile dicens: Pasce agnos meos: Pasce oves meas.[32] Huic tam manifestæ sacrarum Scripturarum doctrinæ, ut ab Ecclesia Catholica semper intellecta est, aperte opponuntur pravæ eorum sententiæ, qui, constitutam a Christo Domino in sua pervertentes, negant, solum Petrum præ cæteris Apostolis, sive seorsum singulis sive omnibus simul, vero proprioque jurisdictionis primatu fuisse a Christo instructum; aut qui affirmant, eundem primatum non immediate directeque ipsi beato Petro, sed Ecclesiæ, et per hanc illi ut ipsius Ecclesiæ ministro delatum fuisse.

Si quis igitur dixerit, beatum Petrum Apostolum non esse a Christo Domino constitutum Apostolorum omnium principem et totius Ecclesiæ militantis visibile caput; vel eundem honoris tantum, non autem veræ propri que jurisdictionis primatum ab eodem Domino nostro Jesu Christo directe et immediate accepisse: anathema sit.

CAPUT II.

De perpetuitate Primatus beati Petri in Romanis Pontificibus.

Quod autem in beato Apostolo Petro princeps pastorum et pastor magnus ovium Dominus Christus Jesus in perpetuam salutem ac perenne bonum

the Catholic flock, with the approval of the sacred Council, do judge it to be necessary to propose to the belief and acceptance of all the faithful, in accordance with the ancient and constant faith of the universal Church, the doctrine touching the institution, perpetuity, and nature of the sacred Apostolic Primacy, in which is found the strength and solidity of the entire Church, and at the same time to proscribe and condemn the contrary errors, so hurtful to the flock of Christ.

CHAPTER I.

Of the Institution of the Apostolic Primacy in blessed Peter.

We therefore teach and declare that, according to the testimony of the Gospel, the primacy of jurisdiction over the universal Church of God was immediately and directly promised and given to blessed Peter the Apostle by Christ the Lord. For it was to Simon alone, to whom he had already said: "Thou shalt be called Cephas," [30] that the Lord after the confession made by him, saying: "Thou art the Christ, the Son of the living God," addressed these solemn words: "Blessed art thou, Simon Bar-Jona, because flesh and blood have not revealed it to thee, but my Father who is in heaven. And I say to thee that thou art Peter; and upon this rock I will build my Church, and the gates of hell shall not prevail against it. And I will give to thee the keys of the kingdom of heaven. And whatsoever thou shalt bind on earth, it shall be bound also in heaven; and whatsoever thou shalt loose on earth, it shall be loosed also in heaven." [31] And it was upon Simon alone that Jesus after his resurrection bestowed the jurisdiction of chief pastor and ruler over all his fold in the words: "Feed my lambs; feed my sheep." [32] At open variance with this clear doctrine of Holy Scripture as it has been ever understood by the Catholic Church are the perverse opinions of those who, while they distort the form of government established by Christ the Lord in his Church, deny that Peter in his single person, preferably to all the other Apostles, whether taken separately or together, was endowed by Christ with a true and proper primacy of jurisdiction; or of those who assert that the same primacy was not bestowed immediately and directly upon blessed Peter himself, but upon the Church, and through the Church on Peter as her minister.

If any one, therefore, shall say that blessed Peter the Apostle was not appointed the Prince of all the Apostles and the visible Head of the whole Church Militant; or that the same directly and immediately received from the same our Lord Jesus Christ a primacy of honour only, and not of true and proper jurisdiction: let him be anathema.

CHAPTER II.

On the Perpetuity of the Primacy of blessed Peter in the Roman Pontiff.

That which the Prince of Shepherds and great Shepherd of the sheep, Jesus Christ our Lord, established in the person of the blessed Apostle

Ecclesiæ instituit, id eodem auctore in Ecclesia, quæ fundata super petram ad finem sæculorum usque firma stabit, jugiter durare necesse est. Nulli sane dubium, imo sæculis omnibus notum est, quod sanctus beatissimusque Petrus, Apostolorum princeps et caput fideique columna, et Ecclesiæ Catholicæ fundamentum, a Domino nostro Jesu Christo, Salvatore humani generis ac Redemptore, claves regni accepit: qui ad hoc usque tempus et semper in suis successoribus, episcopis sanctæ Romanæ Sedis, ab ipso fundatæ, ejusque consecratæ sanguine, vivit et præsidet et judicium exercet.[33] Unde quicumque in hac Cathedra Petro succedit, is secundum Christi ipsius institutionem primatum Petri in universam Ecclesiam obtinet. Manet ergo dispositio veritatis, et beatus Petrus, in accepta fortitudine petræ perseverans, suscepta Ecclesiæ gubernacula non reliquit.[34] Hac de causa ad Romanam Ecclesiam propter potentiorem principalitatem necesse semper fuit omnem convenire Ecclesiam, hoc est, eos, qui sunt undique fideles, ut in ea Sede, e qua venerandæ communionis jura in omnes dimanant, tamquam membra in capite consociata, in unam corporis compagem coalescerent.[35]

Si quis ergo dixerit, non esse ex ipsius Christi Domini institutione, seu jure divino, ut beatus Petrus in primatu super universam Ecclesiam habeat perpetuos successores; aut Romanum Pontificem non esse beati Petri in eodem primatu successorem: anathema sit.

De vi et ratione Primatus Romani Pontificis.

Quapropter apertis innixi sacrarum litterarum testimoniis, et inhærentes tum Prædecessorum Nostrorum, Romanorum Pontificum, tum Conciliorum generalium disertis perspicuisque decretis, innovamus œcumenici Concilii Florentini[36] definitionem, qua credendum ab omnibus Christi fidelibus est, sanctam Apostolicam Sedem, et Romanum Pontificem in universum orbem tenere primatum, et ipsum Pontificem Romanum successorem esse beati Petri, principis Apostolorum, et verum Christi Vicarium, totiusque Ecclesiæ caput, et omnium Christianorum patrem ac doctorem existere; et ipsi in beato Petro pascendi, regendi ac gubernandi universalem Ecclesiam a Domino nostro Jesu Christo plenam potestatem traditam esse; quemadmodum etiam in gestis œcumenicorum Conciliorum et sacris canonibus continetur.

Docemus proinde et declaramus, Ecclesiam Romanam, disponente Domino, super omnes alias ordinariæ potestatis obtinere principatum, et hanc Romani Pontificis jurisdictionis potestatem, quæ vere episcopalis

Peter to secure the perpetual welfare and lasting good of the Church, must, by the same institution, necessarily remain unceasingly in the Church; which, being founded upon the Rock, will stand firm to the end of the world. For none can doubt, and it is known to all ages, that the holy and blessed Peter, the Prince and Chief of the Apostles, the pillar of the faith and foundation of the Catholic Church, received the keys of the kingdom from our Lord Jesus Christ, the Saviour and Redeemer of mankind, and lives, presides, and judges, to this day and always, in his successors the Bishops of the Holy See of Rome, which was founded by him, and consecrated by his blood.[33] Whence, whosoever succeeds to Peter in this See, does by the institution of Christ himself obtain the Primacy of Peter over the whole Church. The disposition made by Incarnate Truth therefore remains, and blessed Peter, abiding through the strength of the Rock in the power that he received, has not abandoned the direction of the Church.[34] Wherefore it has at all times been necessary that every particular Church—that is to say, the faithful throughout the world—should agree with the Roman Church, on account of the greater authority of the princedom which this has received; that all being associated in the unity of that See whence the rights of communion spread to all, might grow together as members of one Head in the compact unity of the body.[35]

If, then, any should deny that it is by the institution of Christ the Lord, or by divine right, that blessed Peter should have a perpetual line of successors in the Primacy over the universal Church, or that the Roman Pontiff is the successor of blessed Peter in this primacy: let him be anathema.

CHAPTER III.

On the Power and Nature of the Primacy of the Roman Pontiff.

Wherefore, resting on plain testimonies of the Sacred Writings, and adhering to the plain and express decrees both of our predecessors, the Roman Pontiffs, and of the General Councils, we renew the definition of the ecumenical Council of Florence,[36] in virtue of which all the faithful of Christ must believe that the holy Apostolic See and the Roman Pontiff possesses the primacy over the whole world, and that the Roman Pontiff is the successor of blessed Peter, Prince of the Apostles, and is true vicar of Christ, and head of the whole Church, and father and teacher of all Christians; and that full power was given to him in blessed Peter to rule, feed, and govern the universal Church by Jesus Christ our Lord; as is also contained in the acts of the General Councils and in the sacred Canons.

Hence we teach and declare that by the appointment of our Lord the Roman Church possesses a superiority of ordinary power over all other churches, and that this power of jurisdiction of the Roman Pontiff, which

est, immediatam esse: erga quam cujuscumque ritus et dignitatis pastores atque fideles, tam seorsum singuli quam simul omnes, officio hierarchiæ subordinationis veræque obedientiæ obstringuntur, non solum in rebus, quæ ad fidem et mores, sed etiam in iis, quæ ad disciplinam et regimen Ecclesiæ per totum orbem diffusæ pertinent; ita ut, custodita cum Romano Pontifice tam communionis, quam ejusdem fidei professionis unitate, Ecclesiæ Christi sit unus grex sub uno summo pastore. Hæc est Catholicæ veritatis doctrina, a qua deviare salva fide atque salute nemo potest.

Tantum autem abest, ut hæc Summi Pontificis potestas officiat ordinariæ ac immediatæ illi episcopalis jurisdictionis potestati, qua Episcopi, qui positi a Spiritu Sancto in Apostolorum locum successerunt,[37] tamquam veri pastores assignatos sibi greges, singuli singulos, pascunt et regunt, ut eadem a supremo et universali Pastore asseratur, roboretur ac vindicetur, secundum illud sancti Gregorii Magni: Meus honor est honor universalis Ecclesiæ. Meus honor est fratrum meorum solidus vigor. Tum ego vere honoratus sum, cum singulis quibusque honor debitus non negatur.[38]

Porro ex suprema illa Romani Pontificis potestate gubernandi universam Ecclesiam jus eidem esse consequitur, in hujus sui muneris exercitio libere communicandi cum pastoribus et gregibus totius Ecclesiæ, ut iidem ab ipso in via salutis doceri ac regi possint. Quare damnamus ac reprobamus illorum sententias, qui hanc supremi capitis cum pastoribus et gregibus communicationem licite impediri posse dicunt, aut eandem reddunt sæculari potestati obnoxiam, ita ut contendant, quæ ab Apostolica Sede vel ejus auctoritate ad regimen Ecclesiæ constituuntur, vim ac valorem non habere, nisi potestatis sæcularis placito confirmentur.

Et quoniam divino Apostolici primatus jure Romanus Pontifex universæ Ecclesiæ præest, docemus etiam et declaramus, eum esse judicem supremum fidelium,[39] et in omnibus causis ad examen ecclesiasticum spectantibus ad ipsius posse judicium recurri;[40] Sedis vero Apostolicæ, cujus auctoritate major non est, judicium a nemine fore retractandum, neque cuiquam de ejus licere judicare judicio.[41] Quare a recto veritatis tramite aberrant, qui affirmant, licere ab judiciis Romanorum Pontificum ad œcumenicum Concilium tamquam ad auctoritatem Romano Pontifice superiorem appellare.

Si quis itaque dixerit, Romanum Pontificem habere tantummodo officium inspectionis vel directionis, non autem plenam et supremam potestatem jurisdictionis in universam Ecclesiam, non solum in rebus, quæ ad fidem et mores, sed etiam in iis, quæ ad disciplinam et regimen Ecclesiæ per totum orbem diffusæ pertinent; aut eum habere tantum

is truly episcopal, is immediate; to which all, of whatever rite and dignity, · both pastors and faithful, both individually and collectively, are bound, by their duty of hierarchical subordination and true obedience, to submit not only in matters which belong to faith and morals, but also in those that appertain to the discipline and government of the Church throughout the world, so that the Church of Christ may be one flock under one supreme pastor through the preservation of unity both of communion and of profession of the same faith with the Roman Pontiff. This is the teaching of Catholic truth, from which no one can deviate without loss of faith and of salvation.

But so far is this power of the Supreme Pontiff from being any prejudice to the ordinary and immediate power of episcopal jurisdiction, by which Bishops, who have been set by the Holy Ghost to succeed and hold the place of the Apostles,[37] feed and govern, each his own flock, as true pastors, that this their episcopal authority is really asserted, strengthened, and protected by the supreme and universal Pastor; in accordance with the words of St. Gregory the Great: "My honour is the honour of the whole Church. My honour is the firm strength of my brethren. I am truly honoured when the honour due to each and all is not withheld." [38]

Further, from this supreme power possessed by the Roman Pontiff of governing the universal Church, it follows that he has the right of free communication with the pastors of the whole Church, and with their flocks, that these may be taught and ruled by him in the way of salvation. Wherefore we condemn and reject the opinions of those who hold that the communication between this supreme head and the pastors and their flocks can lawfully be impeded; or who make this communication subject to the will of the secular power, so as to maintain that whatever is done by the Apostolic See, or by its authority, for the government of the Church, can not have force or value unless it be confirmed by the assent of the secular power.

And since by the divine right of apostolic primacy the Roman Pontiff is placed over the universal Church, we further teach and declare that he is the supreme judge of the faithful,[39] and that in all causes, the decision of which belongs to the Church, recourse may be had to his tribunal,[40] and that none may re-open the judgment of the Apostolic See, than whose authority there is no greater, nor can any lawfully review its judgment.[41] Wherefore they err from the right course who assert that it is lawful to appeal from the judgments of the Roman Pontiffs to an ecumenical Council, as to an authority higher than that of the Roman Pontiff.

If, then, any shall say that the Roman Pontiff has the office merely of inspection or direction, and not full and supreme power of jurisdiction over the universal Church, not only in things which belong to faith and morals, but also in those which relate to the discipline and government of the Church spread throughout the world; or assert that he possesses

potiores partes, non vero totam plenitudinem hujus supremæ potestatis;
aut hanc ejus potestatem non esse ordinariam et immediatam sive in omnes
ac singulas ecclesias, sive in omnes et singulos pastores et fideles: anathema sit.

CAPUT IV.

De Romani Pontificis infallibili magisterio.

Ipso autem Apostolico primatu, quem Romanus Pontifex, tamquam
Petri principis Apostolorum successor, in universam Ecclesiam obtinet,
supremam quoque magisterii potestatem comprehendi, hæc Sancta Sedes
semper tenuit, perpetuus Ecclesiæ usus comprobat, ipsaque œcumenica
Concilia, ea imprimis, in quibus Oriens cum Occidente in fidei caritatisque
unionem conveniebat, declaraverunt. Patres enim Concilii Constantino-
politani quarti, majorum vestigiis inhærentes, hanc solemnem ediderunt
professionem: Prima salus est, rectæ fidei regulam custodire. Et quia
non potest Domini nostri Jesu Christi prætermitti sententia dicentis:
Tu es Petrus, et super hanc petram ædificabo Ecclesiam meam,[42] hæc,
quæ dicta sunt, rerum probantur effectibus, quia in Sede Apostolica
immaculata est semper Catholica reservata religio, et sancta celebrata doctrina. Ab hujus ergo fide et doctrina separari minime cupientes, speramus,
ut in una communione, quam Sedes Apostolica prædicat, esse mereamur, in
qua est integra et vera Christianæ religionis soliditas.[43] Approbante vero
Lugdunensi Concilio secundo, Græci professi sunt: Sanctam Romanam
Ecclesiam summum et plenum primatum et principatum super universam
Ecclesiam Catholicam obtinere, quem se ab ipso Domino in beato Petro,
Apostolorum principe sive vertice, cujus Romanus Pontifex est successor,
cum potestatis plenitudine recepisse veraciter et humiliter recognoscit;
et sicut præ cæteris tenetur fidei veritatem defendere, sic et, si quæ de
fide subortæ fuerint quæstiones, suo debent judicio definiri.[44] Florentinum
denique Concilium definivit:[45] Pontificem Romanum, verum Christi
Vicarium, totiusque Ecclesiæ caput et omnium Christianorum patrem ac
doctorem existere; et ipsi in beato Petro pascendi, regendi ac gubernandi
universalem Ecclesiam a Domino nostro Jesu Christo plenam potestatem
traditam esse.[46]

Huic pastorali muneri ut satisfacerent, Prædecessores Nostri indefessam
semper operam dederunt, ut salutaris Christi doctrina apud omnes terræ
populos propagaretur, parique cura vigilarunt, ut, ubi recepta esset,
sincera et pura conservaretur. Quocirca totius orbis Antistites, nunc singuli,
nunc in Synodis congregati, longam ecclesiarum consuetudinem[47] et
antiquæ regulæ formam[48] sequentes, ea præsertim pericula, quæ in

merely the principal part, and not all the fulness of the supreme power;
or that this power which he enjoys is not ordinary and immediate, both
over each and all the churches, and over each and all the pastors and the
faithful: let him be anathema.

CHAPTER IV.

Concerning the Infallible Teaching of the Roman Pontiff.

Moreover, that the supreme power of teaching is also included in the
apostolic primacy, which the Roman Pontiff, as the successor of Peter,
Prince of the Apostles, possesses over the whole Church, this Holy See
has always held, the perpetual practice of the Church confirms, and
ecumenical Councils also have declared, especially those in which the
East with the West met in the union of faith and charity. For the Fathers
of the Fourth Council of Constantinople, following in the footsteps of
their predecessors, gave forth this solemn profession: The first condition
of salvation is to keep the rule of the true faith. And because the sentence
of our Lord Jesus Christ can not be passed by, who said: "Thou art
Peter, and upon this rock I will build my Church," [42] these things which
have been said are approved by events, because in the Apostolic See the
Catholic religion and her holy and well-known doctrine has always been
kept undefiled. Desiring, therefore, not to be in the least degree separated
from the faith and doctrine of that See, we hope that we may deserve to
be in the one communion, which the Apostolic See preaches, in which
is the entire and true solidity of the Christian religion.[43] And, with the
approval of the Second Council of Lyons, the Greeks professed that the
holy Roman Church enjoys supreme and full primacy and pre-eminence
over the whole Catholic Church, which it truly and humbly acknowledges
that it has received with the plenitude of power from our Lord himself
in the person of blessed Peter, Prince or Head of the Apostles, whose
successor the Roman Pontiff is; and as the Apostolic See is bound before
all others to defend the truth of faith, so also, if any questions regarding
faith shall arise, they must be defined by its judgment.[44] Finally, the
Council of Florence defined:[45] That the Roman Pontiff is the true vicar of
Christ, and the head of the whole Church, and the father and teacher of all
Christians; and that to him in blessed Peter was delivered by our Lord
Jesus Christ the full power of feeding, ruling, and governing the whole
Church.[46]

To satisfy this pastoral duty, our predecessors ever made unwearied
efforts that the salutary doctrine of Christ might be propagated among all
the nations of the earth, and with equal care watched that it might be
preserved genuine and pure where it had been received. Therefore the
Bishops of the whole world, now singly, now assembled in Synod, following the long-established custom of churches,[47] and the form of the ancient
rule,[48] sent word to this Apostolic See of those dangers especially which

negotiis fidei emergebant, ad hanc Sedem Apostolicam retulerunt, ut ibi potissimum resarcirentur damna fidei, ubi fides non potest sentire defectum.[49] Romani autem Pontificis, prout temporum et rerum conditio suadebat, nunc convocatis œcumenicis Conciliis aut explorata Ecclesiæ per orbem dispersæ sententia, nunc per Synodos particulares, nunc aliis, quæ divina suppeditabat providentia, adhibitis auxiliis, ea tenenda definiverunt, quæ sacris Scripturis et apostolicis traditionibus consentanea, Deo adjutore, cognoverant. Neque enim Petri successoribus Spiritus Sanctus promissus est, ut eo revelante novam doctrinam patefacerent, sed ut, eo assistente, traditam per Apostolos revelationem seu fidei depositum sancte custodirent et fideliter exponerent. Quorum quidem apostolicam doctrinam omnes venerabiles Patres amplexi et sancti doctores orthodoxi venerati atque secuti sunt; plenissime scientes, hanc sancti Petri Sedem ab omni semper errore illibatam permanere, secundum Domini Salvatoris nostri divinam pollicitationem discipulorum suorum principi factam: Ergo rogavi pro te, ut non deficiat fides tua, et tu aliquando conversus confirma fratres tuos.[50]

Hoc igitur veritatis et fidei numquam deficientis charisma Petro ejusque in hac Cathedra successoribus divinitus collatum est, ut excelso suo munere in omnium salutem fungerentur, ut universus Christi grex per eos ab erroris venenosa esca aversus, cœlestis doctrinæ pabulo nutriretur, ut, sublata schismatis occasione, Ecclesia tota una conservaretur, atque suo fundamento innixa, firma adversus inferi portas consisteret.

At vero cum hac ipsa ætate, qua salutifera Apostolici muneris efficacia vel maxime requiritur, non pauci inveniantur, qui illius auctoritati obtrectant; necessarium omnino esse censemus, prærogativam, quam unigenitus Dei Filius cum summo pastorali officio conjungere dignatus est, solemniter asserere.

Itaque Nos traditioni a fidei Christianæ exordio perceptæ fideliter inhærendo, ad Dei Salvatoris nostri gloriam, religionis Catholicæ exaltationem et Christianorum populorum salutem, sacro approbante Concilio, docemus et divinitus revelatum dogma esse definimus: Romanum Pontificem, cum ex Cathedra loquitur, id est, cum omnium Christianorum pastoris et doctoris munere fungens pro suprema sua Apostolica auctoritate doctrinam de fide vel moribus ab universa Ecclesia tenendam definit, per assistentiam divinam, ipsi in beato Petro promissam, ea infallibilitate[51] pollere, qua divinus Redemptor Ecclesiam suam in definienda doctrina de fide vel moribus instructam esse voluit; ideoque ejusmodi Romani Pontificis definitiones ex sese, non autem ex consensu Ecclesiæ, irreformabiles[52] esse.

Si quis autem huic Nostræ definitioni contradicere, quod Deus avertat, præsumpserit: anathema sit.

sprang up in matters of faith, that there the losses of faith might be most effectually repaired where the faith can not fail.[49] And the Roman Pontiffs, according to the exigencies of times and circumstances, sometimes assembling ecumenical Councils, or asking for the mind of the Church scattered throughout the world, sometimes by particular Synods, sometimes using other helps which Divine Providence supplied, defined as to be held those things which with the help of God they had recognized as conformable with the sacred Scriptures and apostolic traditions. For the Holy Spirit was not promised to the successors of Peter, that by his revelation they might make known new doctrine; but that by his assistance they might inviolably keep and faithfully expound the revelation or deposit of faith delivered through the Apostles. And, indeed, all the venerable Fathers have embraced, and the holy orthodox doctors have venerated and followed, their apostolic doctrine; knowing most fully that this See of holy Peter remains ever free from all blemish of error according to the divine promise of the Lord our Saviour made to the Prince of his disciples: "I have prayed for thee that thy faith fail not, and when thou art converted, confirm thy brethren." [50]

This gift, then, of truth and never-failing faith was conferred by heaven upon Peter and his successors in this chair, that they might perform their high office for the salvation of all; that the whole flock of Christ, kept away by them from the poisonous food of error, might be nourished with the pasture of heavenly doctrine; that the occasion of schism being removed, the whole Church might be kept one, and resting on its foundation, might stand firm against the gates of hell.

But since in this very age, in which the salutary efficacy of the apostolic office is most of all required, not a few are found who take away from its authority, we judge it altogether necessary solemnly to assert the prerogative which the only-begotten Son of God vouchsafed to join with the supreme pastoral office.

Therefore faithfully adhering to the tradition received from the beginning of the Christian faith, for the glory of God our Saviour, the exaltation of the Catholic religion, and the salvation of Christian people, the sacred Council approving, we teach and define that it is a dogma divinely revealed: that the Roman Pontiff, when he speaks *ex cathedra,* that is, when in discharge of the office of pastor and doctor of all Christians, by virtue of his supreme apostolic authority, he defines a doctrine regarding faith or morals to be held by the universal Church, by the divine assistance promised to him in blessed Peter, is possessed of that infallibility[51] with which the divine Redeemer willed that his Church should be endowed for defining doctrine regarding faith or morals; and that therefore such definitions of the Roman Pontiff are irreformable[52] of themselves, and not from the consent of the Church.

But if any one—which may God avert—presume to contradict this our definition: let him be anathema.

Datum Romæ, in publica Sessione in Vaticana Basilica solemniter celebrata, anno Incarnationis Dominicæ millesimo octingentesimo septuagesimo, die decima octava Julii. Pontificatus Nostri anno vigesimo quinto.

NOTES ON THE TEXT OF THE VATICAN DECREES

1. Isaiah lix. 21.
2. Lateran Council, IV, 1215, c. 1 (Mansi XXII, 981).
3. Wisd. viii. 1.
4. Heb. iv. 13.
5. Rom. i. 20.
6. Heb. i. 1-2.
7. 1 Cor. ii. 9.
8. Council of Trent, Sess. IV, 1546, *Decretum de Canonicis Scripturis.*
9. See Leo XIII, Encyclical *Providentissimus Deus,* Nov. 18, 1893,
on the study of Holy Scripture.
10. Council of Trent, Sess. IV, *Decretum de editione et usu sacrorum
librorum.*
11. Heb. xi. 1.
12. Mark xvi. 20.
13. 2 Peter i. 19.
14. Synod of Orange (confirmed by Pope Boniface II), 529, c. 7,
against the Semipelagians (*Hefele* II, 728).
15. Heb. xi. 6.
16. Isaiah xi. 12.
17. Coloss. i. 12.
18. Heb. ii. 3.
19. Heb. xii. 2.
20. Heb. xii. 2, and x. 23.
21. John i. 17.
22. 1 Cor. ii. 7-10.
23. Matt. xi. 25.
24. 2 Cor. v. 7.
25. Leo X, Bull *Apostolici regiminis;* Lateran Council V, Sess. VIII.
26. Coloss. ii. 8.
27. Vincent of Lérins, *Commonitorium,* 434, c. 23.
28. John xvii. 21.
29. Leo the Great, Sermon IV, c. 2 (*Migne* LIV, 150).
30. John i. 42.
31. Matt. xvi. 16-19.
32. John xxi. 15-17.
33. Council of Ephesus, III, 431 (*Mansi* IV, 1295).
34. Leo the Great, Sermon III, 3 (*Migne* LIV, 146).
35. Irenæus, *Adv. hæreses* III, 3.
36. *Hefele* VII, 659 ff.

Given at Rome in public Session solemnly held in the Vatican Basilica in the year of our Lord one thousand eight hundred and seventy, on the eighteenth day of July, in the twenty-fifth year of our Pontificate.

37. Council of Trent, XXIII, c. 4.

38. Gregory the Great, Reg. VIII, 29 (July 598).

39. Pius VI, Brief *Super soliditate*, Nov. 28, 1786.

40. Council of Lyons, 1274 (*Mansi* XXIV, 71).

41. Nicholas I., *Epist.* 86, to the Emperor Michael (*Migne* CXIX, 954).

42. Matt. xvi. 18.

43. From the Formula of St. Hormisdas, subscribed by the Fathers of the Eighth General Council (Fourth of Constantinople), 869 (*Mansi* XVI, 28).

44. Council of Lyons, 1274 (*Labbe* XIV, 512).

45. Council of Florence, 1438 (*Labbe* XVIII, 526).

46. John xxi. 15-17.

47. Cyril of Alexandria, letter to Celestine I., 422.

48. Rescript of Innocent I. to the Council of Milevis, 402 (*Labbe* III, 47).

49. St. Bernard of Clairvaux, *Epist.* 190, to Innocent II, 1130 (*Migne* CLXXXII, 1053).

50. Luke xxii. 32; see also Sixth General Council, 680 (*Labbe* VII, 659).

51. In a speech of Pius IX, July 20, 1871, he said that some people wanted him to make the conciliar definition broader and more exact, but he would not do so. It was clear enough, he said, and needed no further commentaries or explanations. Whoever read the Decree with a sincere intention would find it as clear as the light of day.

52. In the words used by Pope Nicholas I. and in the Synod of Quedinburg, 1085, "It is allowed to none to revise its judgment, or to sit in judgment upon what it has judged" (*Labbe* XII, 679). The words, *ex sese, non autem ex consensu Ecclesiæ*, were added two days before the promulgation of the Decree. They were peculiarly odious to the Opposition and had been proposed at the instigation of some of the extremists on the infallibilist side.

APPENDIX II

Note on the Doctrines of the Immaculate Conception and of the Assumption of Mary

THE IMMACULATE CONCEPTION

The New Testament affirms that all men have sinned (e.g., Rom. iii, 23; v, 12 and 18; 2 Cor. v, 14), and St. Augustine, in common with the Fathers generally, held that this included every human being except Jesus Christ, who, though fully human, was unique in that his human nature was united, in the hypostatic union, to his divine nature. (Cf. St. Augustine, *De Peccatorum Meritis*, ii, cc. 20, 29, 35; *Contra Julian.*, vi, 7; *De Natura et Gratia*, c. 4; *de Perfectione Institiæ*, c. 21.) It is expressly affirmed by St. Augustine that Mary's flesh was "flesh of sin." (*De Peccatorum Meritis*, ii, c. 24.) Fulgentius says her flesh was "conceived in sin according to the usual law of human nature." (*De Incarnatione et Gratia*, Epist. xvii, c. 6.) St. Paschasius Radbertus says that she was born and procreated of flesh of sin, and was herself flesh of sin. (*In opusc. de Parta Virginali*, i — Migne cxx, 1371.)

Jesuit theologians have argued, however, that even these propositions are not incompatible with the doctrine of the Immaculate Conception, and that this might have been held even by their authors.[1] For, the Jesuits suggest, the Fathers commonly assumed, alongside of a "latent" doctrine of the Immaculate Conception, two now discarded "psychological" notions and one now discredited theological opinion, viz. (1) that in the human embryo there are three successive souls, (a) the vegetative soul, which comes first and is then supplanted by (b) the sentient or animal soul, succeeded by (c) the rational soul (cf. St. Thomas Aquinas, *Contra Gentiles*, II, c. 89, n. 6); (2) the "traducianist" theory, expounded by Tertullian, that in the act of generation the spiritual as well as the physical nature of man is handed on by the parents (which theory is rejected by both Aquinas and Calvin in favor of "creationism," the view that every time a conception takes place God creates a new soul); and (3) that the concupiscence excited in the conjugal act is itself the vehicle

[1] See article *Immaculée Conception*, by X. Le Bachelet, S.J., in *Dictionnaire de Théologie Catholique*, Vol. 7, cols. 1167-1168.

of original sin (cf. St. Augustine, *De nuptiis et concupiscentia*, i, cc. 23-24, nn. 25-27).

In an endeavor to make the doctrine of the Immaculate Conception not contradictory to the plain utterances of the Fathers on the subject of Mary's inheritance of original sin, the Jesuits distinguish between the debt of contracting original sin and the actual contracting of it: Mary ought to have incurred original sin, but was by a special favor exempted from it. The admission of this distinction, together with the recognition of the aforementioned assumptions underlying the patristic utterances that seem so plainly against the doctrine of the Immaculate Conception, makes it possible, the Jesuits hold, to say that the Fathers could have believed in the Immaculate Conception even while saying that Mary was "born and procreated of flesh of sin and was herself flesh of sin." The necessity of making such a distinction was kept well in mind by Pius IX when, in his bull, he explicitly distinguished Mary's freedom from original sin from that of Jesus: Mary was preserved from its stain by God's pure grace, Jesus in his own right. ("Mary, the most holy Mother of God, was, by virtue of the merits of the Redeemer Christ our Lord, which were foreknown, never subject to original sin, but altogether preserved from the stain of her origin, and therefore redeemed *in a more sublime manner*"). Christ redeemed Mary with the rest of humanity, but redeemed her *sublimiori modo*. It was necessary to say this in view of the Pauline statement that Christ died for all (2 Cor. v, 15).

Even such arguments, however, cannot cloud the fact that most of the great medieval schoolmen, including St. Thomas and St. Bonaventure, categorically opposed the opinion that Mary was immaculately conceived. St. Thomas mentions that "some keep the Feast of the Conception of the Blessed Virgin" (*Summa Theol.*, III, 27, 2, obj. 3); but "although the Church of Rome does not celebrate the Conception of the Blessed Virgin, yet it tolerates the custom of certain churches that do keep that feast; wherefore this is not to be entirely reprobated. Nevertheless the celebration of this feast does not give us to understand that she was holy in her conception. But since it is not known when she was sanctified [i.e., at what precise moment between her conception and her birth], the feast of her sanctification, rather than the feast of her conception, is kept on the day of her conception [i.e., the day popularly so called in certain churches]" (*Ibid.* ad 3). St. Thomas explicitly affirms that while Christ did not contract original sin in any way whatsoever, nevertheless "the Blessed Virgin did contract orginal sin, but was cleansed therefrom before her birth from the womb" (*Ibid.* ad 2). "Non potuit Virgo sanctificari nisi post conceptionem" (3 *Sent.* 3, 1, 1). What then would have been Mary's state should she have died before the Passion of Christ? Would she, unlike the Patriarchs and Prophets, have been admitted to heaven at once by virtue of her special position? St. Thomas replies negatively: "If the Blessed Virgin had died before the Passion of Christ, she would not have been admitted to the vision of God (i.e., heaven) (3 *Sent.* 3, 1, 2, solutio 1 ad 1). "It is to be held therefore, that she was conceived in original sin, but was cleansed from it in a special manner" (*Compendium Theol.*, 224).

Moreover, even the Council of Trent, assembled to reform the Church and to combat Protestantism, expressly declined to declare in favor of the Immaculate Conception, in spite of the explicit devotion to it encouraged by Pope Sixtus IV. Cardinal del Monte had wanted to add to the decree concerning original sin a declaration about Mary's conception. This was read and discussed on June 14, 1546, and Cardinal Pacheco desired that an exception should be made, in favor of Mary, to the affirmation that all creatures are conceived in original sin. But this motion failed to get the support of the majority. Even though it might have been admitted that the faithful commonly believed in this doctrine of Mary's immaculate conception, the theological difficulties were evidently too great. The Council, preferring the *status quo* to the definition they could have so easily made, especially since so many Protestant opinions were being officially condemned by them, declared as follows expressly against affirming the Immaculate Conception: "This Sacred Synod declares that in this decree on original sin it is not intended to include the Blessed and Immaculate Virgin Mary, Mother of God, but it is to be understood that the constitutions of Pope Sixtus IV (of happy memory) on this subject are to be observed" (Hefele, *Histoire des Conciles,* Vol. X, Paris, 1938, p. 58 f.).

Cardinal Pacheco had desired a phrase that would have hinted at the Immaculate Conception without affirming it. Seventeen bishops supported him, while eleven desired a clear affirmation of this opinion. Among these was Balthazar of Heredia, Bishop of Bosa, one of the rare Dominicans who favored the opinion. He asked that it be not treated with a pinch of salt (*ne tam sicce et cum grano salis*). But the Council, while recognizing the popularity of the opinion among the faithful, preferred the conservative view they finally adopted. In doing so they not only favored the preponderance of learned opinion but also respected the two authorities pre-eminently before them, *sc.*, the Bible, which lent no support to the notion of the Immaculate Conception, and St. Thomas, who explicitly opposed it.

By the nineteenth century there was, however, much popular clamor for the recognition of the Immaculate Conception. In 1830, Catherine Labouré, a novice in the Rue Bac, Paris, saw Mary in a vision, she claimed, and this did much to foster the popular movement.

Pius IX, in promulgating as defined doctrine, on his own authority, without a council, a theological opinion that the Council of Trent had after such careful deliberation so clearly declined to confirm, chose an excellent field, from the papalist viewpoint, for his experiment in infallibility. For if he could establish a precedent here, the destruction of all conciliar claim to control the definition of doctrine was not far off. Within sixteen years it was to be accomplished by assembling a body which, purporting to be an ecumenical council, would, in effect, declare itself and all future ecumenical councils unnecessary, since there was nothing they could do that the Pope could not do alone in his own private apartments.

THE ASSUMPTION

The term *assumptio* was used by the Fathers in an untechnical sense, to indicate, in a very general fashion, the entry of anyone to heaven. St. Augustine speaks, for instance, of the assumption of the Apostles (*Contra Faustum*, xxxiii, 3), by which he certainly did not mean that they escaped death. Gregory of Tours similarly writes of the assumption of St. Martin (*De miraculis Sancti Martini*, i, 32). Nothing, therefore, may be concluded from the mere use of the term in reference to Mary. But in fact there is a remarkable silence about Mary's departure from this earth, even by the fourth century, by which time popular piety was already exalting her far above all other creatures, and the Fathers wrote of her, after the manner of Irenæus, as the "second Eve." St. Ambrose, praising the Virgin, in such a passage in his commentary on St. Luke, contents himself with the routine observation that St. Luke's reference to a sword piercing Mary's soul (Luke ii. 35) is not to be interpreted as signifying that she was to suffer martyrdom. Epiphanius explicitly points out (*Adv. Haer.*, lxxviii, 11) that there is no indication in the Scriptures concerning the question of whether Mary died or did not die, and discusses, much in the manner of Ambrose, the passage that seems to have suggested to some that she was martyred. His conclusion is that there is definitely no evidence about the question of her death, and it is clear from what he says that there was by about the year 400 A.D. nothing in the least like even a persistent pious rumor that she had been "translated" bodily into heaven. In view of the immense reverence for Mary by that time and the readiness of popular piety to accept miraculous stories it would not be in the least surprising to find such a legend; yet there is none.

By the fifth century, however, there appears such a legend, in many versions and languages. It is very probable that this legend arose in Egypt, where there were several versions of it. The Sahidic version purports to have been written by Cyril, archbishop of Jerusalem, and narrates that when the Apostles were in the act of carrying Mary's body for burial, the Jews pursued them, intending to burn it so that no one should ever be able to point to the tomb of Mary. The Apostles fled, but the Jews, when they had overtaken the bier, could not find the body and supposed that the Apostles must have escaped with it. A sweet fragrance, however, issued from the bier, and a heavenly voice announced to the Jews that it was useless to look for the Virgin's body till the Day of Judgment.

The Bohairic version, on the other hand, gives a much more colorful story. Christ himself appeared to the Apostles when Mary was present, weeping at the prospect of her own death. Then Death appeared, and when Mary beheld him, her soul leapt from her body into the arms of Christ. In accordance with Christ's command, the Apostles Peter and John lifted up the body while the other Apostles sang, keeping watch for three and a half days. Then Christ came in a chariot of light, drawn by cherubim, and put the soul of Mary into the body again before setting her, "wearing the flesh," beside him on the chariot. Finally, Christ and Mary went up into heaven in glory, preceded by singing angels.

The Greek version, claiming the authorship of St. John the Evangelist himself, recounts a similar tale, and some other versions even have the twelve Apostles also carried to heaven on twelve beams of light.

The first writer in Western Christendom to assert the corporeal assumption of Mary into heaven is Gregory of Tours (already mentioned) who, in the *De Gloria martyrum*, written towards the end of the sixth century, recounts that Christ appeared to the Apostles and commanded that Mary's body be lifted up to heaven where it was reunited with her soul. It is evident that Gregory has simply accepted one of the accounts that by his time were available. He gives no argument for it. By the end of the seventh century there is a reference in the Gallican liturgy to the corporeal assumption of Mary, while in the Roman liturgies there seems to be very much greater reserve. In the ninth century, when Charlemagne cites some sixteen other feasts of first-rate importance, he remarks that in regard to the assumption of Mary, the matter is to be left open for further consideration (*Capitula de presbyteris*, xix, Migne xcvii, 326). Even Usuard's Martyrology, used at that time, declines to give any recognition to the notion, on the ground that it is better to be silent than to teach anything "frivolum et apocryphum." The feast appears, however, in the list approved in 813 by the Council of Mainz. In the East, reputable opinion on the subject was even more vague and uncertain.

There is no record of Mary's tomb in the accounts of early pilgrimages to the Holy Land, though among the various traditions on the subject there is one, whose precise meaning is doubtful, that she was taken by John to Ephesus. In the sixth century there is a reference to a church in the valley of Josaphat, dedicated to Mary, and this, later on, attracted many pilgrims. Among these was the Venerable Bede, who writes somewhat casually about an empty tomb there, where "the Mother of God is said to have reposed for a time." He adds that no one knows by whom or at what time the body was taken away. This is remarkable reticence on Bede's part, in view of the fact that by his time the festival was being observed in that part of Christendom whence he had come. For many centuries afterwards there was a similar caution among many of the most reputable writers on the subject. It was, of course, well known to these that what credence the doctrine had among the faithful had grown, *in spite* of the silence of Scripture and the Fathers, along with many other picturesque but discredited miraculous legends. There were Jewish legends of a similar sort recounted in Hebrew apocryphal literature such as the *Apocalypse of Abraham* and the *Ascension of Isaiah,* and the Muslims were not without legends of the translation of Muhammad. Even in canonical Hebrew Scripture there is the story of the translation of Elijah. Such corporeal assumption into heaven came to be widely deemed a mark of special favor. Moreover, on the basis of Christ's words (John xxi. 22) there was a not inconsiderable tradition that St. John the Evangelist was favored in such a manner. St. Ambrose refers to this. Later there are similar legends about other New Testament figures, so that the very paucity of them in regard to Mary is all the more astonishing.

With the intense, universal devotion to Mary in the Middle Ages it is almost inconceivable that, if any of these numerous legends were to be believed, the one relating to Mary should remain widely disbelieved. By the thirteenth century it was in fact so generally accepted without any particular evidence seeming to be required, that St. Thomas's own master, Albert the Great, simply affirms it without much ado. Unlike the question of the Immaculate Conception, it was not a lively subject of controversy in the Middle Ages, but rather a pious opinion about which theological or other argument seemed to be, in general, somewhat beside the point. Furthermore, it was an ideal subject for painters. Nevertheless, the notion did occasionally provide grounds for controversy, especially after the Council of Trent, which had left it an open question. There was a remarkable dispute about it in the seventeenth century, in ecclesiastical circles in Paris. But with the militant devotion to Mary fostered by the Jesuits in the post-Tridentine world, the slightest tendency to derogate in any way from her glory savored of heresy, since such refusal to give adequate honor to Mary was, of course, associated with Protestantism.

By the time of the Vatican Council, when the doctrine of the Immaculate Conception had already been defined by Pius sixteen years earlier, it seemed natural to ultramontane extremists to use the occasion to define the Corporeal Assumption of the Virgin, and there was in fact a proposal made to this effect. The Council, however, did not make any such definition. Presumably the time was not accounted ripe, though it is difficult to see what doubts could have been entertained on the subject in 1870 that could have been removed by the Feast of All Saints, 1950, on which date the doctrine was solemnly defined by Pope Pius XII, in the Apostolic Constitution *Munificentissimus Deus,* as part of the Catholic Faith which none may doubt without loss of salvation. But the Council's neglect in this is understandable. There was no need for them to define the Assumption, since this could safely be left, together with everything else, to the care of the Supreme Pontiff. Acknowledging that they could not even commit to him the power to define it, since every pope from the time of Peter had possessed that power, they retired from the scene, patiently waiting the papal definition that came some eighty years later.

BIBLIOGRAPHY

The bibliography on the Vatican Council itself is enormous. In the Vatican Palace, whole rooms were set aside for the shorthand and long-hand notes of the speeches. About twelve copies of the printed proceedings were also deposited in the archives. In theological circles there was a tremendous spate of writing about it, both for and against the infallibilist side. Those against this wrote from two different viewpoints, viz., that of the "outside" observer, and that of the Roman theologians who, loyal to the papacy, were much perturbed by the immense historical and theological difficulties of the infallibilist position, as well as by the methods used at the Council in the name of the Roman Church they deeply loved.

But since the question at issue involves much of the history of Christian doctrine and practice, the relevant bibliography is indefinitely large. All the literature on the Gallican Church, for instance, is immediately relevant to the question of Papal Infallibility, and so also are numerous documents in primitive and medieval Christian literature. Not only is a complete bibliography, therefore, out of the question; even a tolerably comprehensive one would be impracticable to compile. What is provided here is, mainly, a list of source books, together with such commentaries, histories, and essays, learned and popular, on the subject, as may adequately represent the various standpoints and be useful for further study. From these sources the specialist may verify the evidence for the interpretation offered in the foregoing essay, while the more general reader may be guided to points of view other than the one taken here.

A. ACTS OF THE VATICAN COUNCIL

Acta et Decreta sacrorum Conciliorum Recentiorum (Collectio Lacensis, Vol. VII). Friburg, 1890. Contains unofficial documents, including speeches and letters of Pius, and various commentaries outside the proceedings of the Council.

Acta sacrosancti œcumenici Concilii Vaticani. Arnhem, 1923. (Vols. XLIX-LIII of the *Amplissima Collectio* of Mansi.) Contains the speeches in the General Congregations and all official documents.

B. ACTS OF PIUS IX

Acta Sanctæ Sedis. For the papal pronouncements after the year 1865.
Atti del Sommo Pontefice Pio IX. Rome, 1857, etc. Papal State documents; contains the *motu-proprii* and *chirografi.*
Pii Pontificis Maxima Acta. Contains the Encyclicals, Allocutions, etc.

C. OTHER WORKS

Acton (Lord). *The History of Freedom and Other Essays.* Macmillan,
   1909. There is an important chapter on the Vatican Council from
   an anti-papalist standpoint.
————. *Selections from the Correspondence of the First Lord Acton.*
   London, Longmans, 1917. Vol. I contains letters to Gladstone, *q.v.*
   Acton, one of the most hostile and influential critics of the Vatican
   Decree, held communion with Rome to be "dearer than life."
Adam, Karl. *The Spirit of Catholicism.* New York, Macmillan, 1936.
   The methods used in presenting the story of the Vatican Council in
   this persuasive defense of modern Roman Catholicism should be
   studied in the light of the known facts.
Addone. *Concili ecumenici e vicende del Concilio Vaticano.* Milan, 1934.
[Anonymous]. *Ce qui se passe au Concile.* Paris, 1870. A pamphlet
   showing inside information about the secret proceedings; condemned
   formally by the Council, July 1870.
[Anonymous]. *Le Pape et le Congrès.* Paris, 1860 (60 pp.). Contains
   also Dupanloup's reply, followed by a reply to him. Attributed to
   Louis Etienne Arthur Dubreuil-Hélion, vicomte de La Guéronnière.
Arthur, William. *The Pope, the Kings, and the People.* London, 1903.
Aubert, R. *Le Pontificat de Pie IX.* Paris, Bloudet Gay, 1952. Vol. XXI
   of the *Histoire de l'Eglise* (ed. Fliche et Martin). There is an ex-
   cellent bibliography.
Augustine, St. *De Civitate Dei.* English trans. in Fathers of the Church
   Edit., Vols. VI-VIII. New York, 1952.
Ballerini. *Il Concilio ecumenico Vaticano.* Milan, 1880.
Bellarmine, Robert (Cardinal; S.J.). De Romano Pontifice (III *Contro-*
   versia in the *Disputationes de controversiis Christianæ Fidei ad-*
   versus hujus temporis hæreticos, 3 vols; 1581-1593). Bellarmine was
   beatified by Pius XI on May 13, 1923, and later canonized.
Bianchi, R. *De constitutione monarchica Ecclesiæ et de infallibilitate*
   Romani Pontificis. Rome, 1870.
Bickel, G. *Gründe für die Unfehlbarkeit des Kirchenoberhauptes nebst*
   Widerlegung der Einwürfe. Munster, 1870. From the papalist side.
Bliemetzrieder, Franz. *Das General Konzil im grossen abendländischen*
   Schisma. Paderborn, 1904. Shows the academic ancestry of the
   Conciliar movement.

Bossuet. *Defensio declarationis conventus cleri gallicani* (in *Œuvres,* edit. Guillaume, Vol. X). Paris, 1885.

Bottalla, P. *L'autorità infallibile del papa nella Chiesa.* Palermo. 1880.

Bungener, F. *Rome and the Council in the 19th Century.* Edinburgh, 1870.

Butler, Basil Christopher (Abbot). *The Church and Infallibility.* London, Sheed and Ward, 1954 (230 pp.). A reply to the abridged edition of Salmon's *The Infallibility of the Church.*

Butler, Edward Cuthbert (Abbot). *The Vatican Council.* London, Longmans, 1930. Based on the diary of Bishop Ullathorne. The best account in English from the papalist side. It ignores, however, much evidence given by writers from the other side.

Campana, E. *Il Concilio Vaticano.* Lugano-Bellinzona, 1926.

Carbonero y Sol, León. *Crónica del Concilio ecuménico del Vaticano.* Madrid, 1869-70 (4 vols.). Vol. III contains (pp. 5-321) a critical bibliography.

Cardoni, Joseph. *Elucubratio de dogmatica Romani Pontificis Infallibilitate ejusque Definibilitate.* Rome, typis Civilitatis Catholica, May 1870 (174 pp.). A semi-official work on the papalist side. The author was Archbishop of Edessa (*in partibus*).

Cebada, Emilio Moreno. *El santo Concilio ecuménico del Vaticano: Historia de esta augusta Asamblea.* Barcelona (2 vols.).

Cecconi, E. *Storia del concilio ecumenico Vaticano scritta sui documenti originali.* Rome, 1872-79 (2 vols.). Contains 260 documents relative to the antecedents of the Council.

Cesare, R. de. *The Last Days of Papal Rome, 1850-1870.* London, 1909. Translated by H. Zimmern.

Ciasca. *Examen critico-apologeticum super Constitutionem dogmaticam de Fide catholica editam in sessione tertia SS. Œcumenici Concilii Vaticani.* Rome, 1872.

Congar, Ives M.-J. *Vraie et Fausse Réforme dans l'Eglise.* Paris, Editions du Cerf, 1950 (648 pp.). A most important recent work by a learned Dominican. Bearing the *imprimi potest* of the Dominican authorities and the *imprimatur* of the Vicar General of the archdiocese of Paris, it was subsequently withdrawn from circulation.

Coulton, George Gordon. *Papal Infallibility.* London, 1932. Coulton was an indefatigable controversialist on the Protestant side. His personal story is told in his autobiography, *Fourscore Years* (Cambridge, 1944).

Dante. *De Monarchia.* English translation by Aurelia Henry. Cambridge, Mass., 1904.

Darboy, Georges (Archbishop). *La Liberté du Concile et l'infaillibilité.* Fifty copies of this pamphlet were printed. It was attributed to Darboy, and was, if not his work, due, at any rate, to his inspiration. It is reprinted in Friedrich (*q.v.*), *Documenta,* pp. 129-186.

Deschamps, V. *L'Infaillibilité et le concile général.* Paris, 1869. From the papalist side.

Diez, A. Machuca. *Los sacrosanctos œcuménicos Concilios de Trento y Vaticano.* Madrid, 1903.

Döllinger, Johann Joseph Ignaz von. *Das Papsttum.* Munich, 1892.

————. *Einige Wörte über die Unfehlbarkeits adresse.* Munich, 1870.

————. *Erwägunger für die Bischöfe des Consiliums über die Frage der päpstlichen Unfehlbarkeit.* Munich, 1869. Döllinger, a leading opponent of the infallibilist position, was excommunicated. See Janus; Quirinus.

Dupanloup, Félix-Antoine-Philibert (Bishop). *La Convention du 15 septembre et l'Encyclique du 8 décembre.* Paris, 1865. A pamphlet in defense of the *Syllabus.* Dupanloup, in spite of his loyalty to the papacy, was the leader of the Minority.

————. *Observations sur la controverse soulevée relativement à la définition de l'infaillibilité au futur concile.* Paris 1869. A pamphlet. See Lagrange; Maynard.

Durand de Maillane, Pierre-Toussaint. *Les Libertés de l'église gallicane, prouvées et commentées.* Lyons, 1771.

Fessler, Joseph. *Das Vaticanische Concilium, dessen aüssere Bedentung und innerer Verlauf.* Vienna, 1871.

————. *Die wahre und die falsche Unfehlbarkeit der Päpste.* Vienna, 1871. From the papalist side, against Schulte. Fessler was papal secretary at the Council.

Franciscis, Pasquale de (Don). *Discorsi del Sommo Pontefice Pio IX.* Rome, 1872, etc. The speeches to pilgrims after 1870.

Frayssinous, D. *Vraies Principes de l'Eglise Gallicane.* Paris, 1818; 2nd edit. 1843. The author was Bishop of Hermopolis. An attempt to reconcile the Ultramontane and the Gallican elements in the Church in France.

Friedberg, E. *Sammlung der Aktenstücke zum ersten vaticanischen Concil, mit einem grundrisse der Geschichte desselben.* Tübingen, 1872.

Friedhoff, Franz. *Gegen-Erwägungen über die päpstliche Unfehlbarkeit.* Munster, 1869 (21 pp.). From the papalist side.

Friedrich, Johann. *Documenta ad illustrandum Concilium Vaticanum.* Nördlingen, 1871 (2 vols.). Vol. I, pp. 129-186 contains a reprint of *La Liberté du Concile et l'infaillibilité,* attributed to Darboy, Archbishop of Paris.

————. *Geschichte des vatikanischen Konzils.* Bonn, 1877-88. Forbidden by Decree of the Holy Office, Dec. 19, 1877.

————. *Tagebuch während des vaticanischen Concils geführt.* Nördlingen, 1873 (2nd edit.). Forbidden by Decree of the Holy Office, Sept. 20, 1871. Friedrich is of first-rate importance.

Frommann, T. *Geschichte und Kritik des Vatikanischen Concils.* Gotha, 1872.

Frond. *Actes et histoire du concile œcuménique de Rome.* Paris, 1869 ff. (8 vols., many illustrations).

Gibbons, James (Cardinal). *A Retrospect of Fifty Years.* Baltimore, John Murphy, 1916 (Vol. I, 335 pp.; Vol. II, 287 pp.). Autobiographical memoirs, containing, especially in the first volume, much information about the Vatican Council, presented in a popular manner from the standpoint of an American prelate who had taken part in the proceedings.

Giles, Edward. *Documents Illustrating Papal Authority, A.D. 96-454.* London, S. P. C. K., 1952. A valuable, annotated translation of the main sources illustrating the development of papal authority in the first centuries.

Gladstone, William Ewert (The Rt. Hon.). *The Vatican Decrees in their Bearing on Civil Allegiance: a political expostulation.* New York, Harper, 1875. Despite the English statesman's strongly anti-Catholic prejudices, he was by no means ill informed about the Vatican Council and its political consequences.

Gore, Charles (Bishop). *Roman Catholic Claims.* London, 1889. From an Anglican standpoint. Dom Chapman wrote a reply, *Bishop Gore and the Catholic Claims.*

Goyau, G. *Bismarck et l'Eglise.* Paris, 1911.

Granderath, Th. (S.J.). *Constitutiones dogmaticæ Sacrosancti Concilii Vaticani ex ipsis ejus actis explicatæ atque illustratæ.* Friburg, 1892. One of the two principal commentaries on the decrees of the Council (see Vacant).

————. *Geschichte des Vaticanischen Konzils.* Friburg, 1903-1906 (3 vols.). The fullest account of the Council. There is a French translation, *Histoire du Concile du Vatican,* edited by C. Kirch, 4 vols., 1907-19.

Gratry, A. *Four Letters to the Bishop of Orléans and the Archbishop of Malines.* Paris, 1870. Translated into several languages and the subject of fierce controversy. Some bishops forbade it; others, including Montalembert, approved it. Pius praised the opponents, and the Archbishop of Malines (Deschamps) replied with *Three Letters to Gratry.*

Guettée, Aimé-François Wladimir (Abbé). *Histoire de l'église de France, composée sur des documents originaux et authentiques.* Lyons, Guyot, 1847-52; Paris, Renouard, 1852-57 (12 vols.). From the Gallican standpoint. Forbidden by Decree, January 22, 1852; also June 11, 1855. The author's Gallican and Jansenist opinions made him a very controversial figure. On the other hand, among his numerous writings is an attack on Renan's also prohibited *Vie de Jésus.*

Hales, E. E. Y. *Pio Nono.* London, Eyre & Spottiswoode, 1954. Sympathetic modern biography of Pius IX; but takes little account of the legal and constitutional aspects of the Council.

Halperin, S. W. *Italy and the Vatican at War: a study of their Relations from the Outbreak of the Franco-Prussian War to the Death of Pius IX.* Chicago, 1939. An important, well-documented work by an American scholar.

Hayward, F. *Pie IX et son temps.* Paris, Plon, 1948. A detailed biography, but lacking annotation.

Hefele, Joseph de. *Causa Honorii Papæ.* Naples, 1870 (28 pp.). Against the infallibilist position. Hefele's *opus maximum* is his *History of the Councils.* (*Infra,* Moss.) He was Bishop of Rothenburg; formerly Professor at Tübingen.

————. *Honorius und das sechste allgemeine Concil.* Tübingen, 1870 (28 pp.). Appendix against Pennachi (*q.v.*). There is an English translation in the *Presbyterian Quarterly and Princeton Review* (N.Y., April 1872) pp. 273 ff.

Hoçedez, E. *Histoire de la Théologie au XIX Siècle.* Paris 1947-48 (3 vols.). A standard Jesuit survey.

Hornstein. *Les Doctrines catholiques, ou Exposition des vérités enseignées dans l'Eglise depuis Nicée jusqu'à la IV⁸ session du concile du Vatican.* Paris, 1872.

Jacob, E. F. *Essays in the Conciliar Epoch.* Manchester, 1943. 2nd edit., augmented, 1952.

Jalland, Trevor Gervase. *The Church and the Papacy.* London, S. P. C. K., 1944. (Bampton Lectures, 1942.) An exceptionally scholarly and readable modern work by an Anglican specialist. Its great merits are recognized by both Anglican and Roman historians.

[Janus]. *The Pope and the Council.* Boston, 1870 (Authorized Eng. trans.; 346 pp.). Attributed mainly to Döllinger, *q.v.;* against the infallibilist position. Original edition, *Der Papst und das Concil, eine weiter ausgeführte und mit dem Quellennachweis versehene Neubearbeitung der in der Augsburger allgemeinen Zeitung erschienen Artikel,* was forbidden by Decree, November 26, 1869.

Kenrick, Peter Richard (Archbishop). *Concio in Concilio Vaticano habenda et non habita.* Naples, typis fratrum de Angelis, 1870. The prefatory note is dated, Rome, June 8, 1870. Against the infallibilist position. Reprinted in Friedrich, *Documenta,* I, pp. 187-226. English translation in L. W. Bacon, *An Inside View of the Vatican Council,* New York, pp. 90-166. It is also printed in Mansi (*q.v.*), but without the valuable appendices. On the title-page the American Archbishop quotes Paschasius Radbert: "Not on Peter only, but on all the apostles and their successors, is built the Church of God." Also 1 Tim. vi. 20, 21. He concludes, paraphrasing St. Jerome: "Major est salus orbis quam urbis." Preferring to predicate inerrancy rather than infallibility even of the Church herself, Kenrick points out that this inerrancy is due not to a *charisma* (as Manning had contended) but only to the tradition that safeguards against errors contrary to revealed truths of the Faith; that is, it is a negative, not a positive attribute of the Church.

Ketteler, (Bishop). *Das unfehlbare Lehramt des Papstes, nach der Entscheidung des Vaticanischen Concils.* Mainz, 1871. From the papalist side.

———. *Quaestio.* Printed in Switzerland, 1870. Against the infallibilist position. An able dissertation prepared during the Vatican Council. Reprinted in Friedrich, *Documenta,* I, pp. 1-128.

Kissling, J. B. *Geschichte der Kulturkampf im Deutschen Reiche.* Friburg, 1911-16.

Lagrange, F. *Vie de Mgr. Dupanloup.* Paris, 1883-84. There is an abridged English version by Lady Herbert (Chapman and Hall, 1885; 2 vols.). A valuable study for the whole period of the reign of Pius IX.

———. *Lettres choisies de Mgr. Dupanloup.* Paris, 1888.

Lamennais, Hugues Félicité Robert de. *Mélanges religieux et philosophiques.* Paris, 1819.

Lecanuet, E. *L'Eglise de France sous la troisième République.* Paris, 1907.

———. *Montalembert d'après son journal et sa correspondance.* Paris, 1895-1902 (3 vols.). The best account of the controversy with Veuillot (*q.v.*). See Lemaître.

Legge, Alfred Owen. *The Growth of the Temporal Power of the Papacy.* London, 1870. Written while the Council was in progress, it has sometimes a journalistic flavor.

Leitner, F. X. *Thomas von Aquino über das unfehlbare Lehramt des Papstes.* Frankfurt, 1872. An important work: it opposes Döllinger.

Lemaître, Jules. *Les Contemporains.* Paris, 1888-98. A defense of Veuillot (*q.v.*). See Lecanuet.

[Leto, Pomponio]. *Otto mesi a Roma durante il concilio,* Florence, 1873. "Pomponio Leto" is the pseudonym of Francesco Vitelleschi-Nobili, a brother of Cardinal Vitelleschi. Forbidden by Decree of the Holy Office, March 29, 1876. English translation, *Rome during the Vatican Council* (John Murray, 1876).

Lutterbeck, J. A. B. *Die Clementinen und ihr Verhältniss zum Unfehlbarkeitsdogma.* Giessen, 1872 (85 pp.).

Magrassi, Antonio. *Lo schema sull' infallibilità personale del Romano Pontefice.* Alexandria, 1870 (64 pp.). Against the infallibilist position.

Maistre, Joseph de. *Du Pape.* Paris, Charpentier, 1819; many later editions. The masterpiece of the famous statesman who, disgusted by the anarchical tendencies of the French Revolution, reacted ardently in favor of the *ancien régime.* But while he desired a temporal monarchy be believed the papacy could provide the conditions necessary for the establishment of the order he desired to see throughout

Europe. Probably the ablest pre-1870 defense of the papalist view. Lord Acton said it forged the "alliance of Religion with absolute Monarchy." The title bears the motto ΕΙΣ ΚΟΙΡΑΝΟΣ ΕΣΤΩ (Homer, *Iliad* II, v, 204).

Manning, Henry Edward (Cardinal). *The True Story of the Vatican Council.* London, 1877.

———. *The Vatican Council and its Definitions.* London, 1887.

———. *The Vatican Decrees in their Bearing on Civil Allegiance.* London, Longmans, 1875. A reply to Gladstone, *q.v.* See Purcell.

Maret, H. L. C. *Du Concile général et de la paix religieuse.* Paris, 1869 (Vol. I, 554 pp., Vol. II, 555 pp.). A defense of Gallicanism; later withdrawn from sale. Maret was Bishop of Sura (*in partibus*) and Dean of the Faculty of Theology in Paris.

Margerie, Amédée de. *Lettre au R. P. Gratry sur le Pape Honorius et le Bréviaire Romain.* Nancy, 1870. From the papalist side.

Martin, C. *Die Arbeiten des vaticanischen Concil.* Paderborn, 1873.

———. *Omnium Concilii Vaticani quæ ad doctrinam et disciplinam pertinent, documentorum collectio.* Paderborn, 1873.

Maurain, J. *La politique ecclésiastique du second Empire de 1852 à 1869.* Paris, 1930. An important work; generally critical of the papalist position.

Mayer, Salesius. *De Summi Pontificis infallibilitate personali.* Naples, 1870 (32 pp.). Distributed in the Council by Cardinal Schwarzenberg. From the Minority side.

Maynard, U. *Mgr. Dupanloup et M. Lagrange son historien.* Paris, 1884 (2nd edit.).

Mirbt, D. Carl. *Geschichte der Katholischen Kirche von der Mitte des 18. Jahrhunderts bis zum Vatikanischen Konzil.* Berlin, Göschen, 1913 (159 pp.).

———. *Quellen zur Geschichte des Papsttums und des römischen Katholizismus.* Tübingen, J. C. B. Mohr, 1911 (514 pp.). A valuable and convenient source book. See also the very full bibliography on the Vatican Council provided by Mirbt in the *Realencyclopädie,* Vol. XX, pp. 445 ff. (Leipzig, 3rd edit., 1908). Mirbt was Professor at Marburg and at Göttingen.

Mollat, G. *La question romaine de Pie VI à Pie IX.* Paris, 1932.

Monsabré, J. M. C. *Conférences de Notre Dame: Concile et jubilé.* Paris, 1890.

Montalembert, C. de. *L'Eglise libre dans l'Etat libre.* Paris, 1863. See Lecanuet.

Monti, A. *Pio IX nel risorgimento italiano.* Bari, 1928. Includes the letters of Pius to his brother, the Conte Gabriele Mastai.

Moss, C. B. *The Old Catholic Movement.* London, S. P. C. K., 1948. Shows how Hefele was compelled, after he had submitted, to falsify his story in a new edition of his *History of the Councils* (*q.v.*).

Mourret, F. *Le Concile du Vatican, d'après des documents inédits.* Paris, 1919. Mourret was Professor at St. Sulpice. Based chiefly on the papers of Icard, who was director of St. Sulpice in 1870 and was in Rome as theological adviser to the Archbishop of Sens, at the Council.

Mozley, T. *Letters from Rome on the Occasion of the Œcumenical Council, 1869-1870.* London, 1891. The letters are sometimes ill informed, but Mozley was the *Times* correspondent and they reflect, at any rate, public opinion in England.

Newman, John Henry (Cardinal). *A Letter to his Grace the Duke of Norfolk, on the occasion of Mr. Gladstone's recent Expostulation.* London, 1874. A mild defense of the infallibilist position, in reply to Gladstone (*q.v.*).

Nielsen, Fredrik Kristian. *The History of the Papacy in the XIXth Century.* London, John Murray, 1906 (2 vols.). Translated by A. J. Mason. Original edition: *Romer-Kirken: det 19. hundredaar* (Copenhagen, Schønberg, 1895-98; 2 vols.).

Nippold, F. *Handbuch der neuesten Kirchengeschichte.* Elberfeld, 1893 (2 vols.).

Ollivier, E. *L'Eglise et l'Etat au Concile du Vatican.* 1877. Ollivier, Napoleon's Premier in 1870, was a Protestant. His account is, however, quite sympathetic to the papalist viewpoint. He was a personal admirer of Pius.

Omodeo, A. *Difesa del Risorgimento.* 1951. From an anticlerical standpoint.

Pelczar, G. S. (Bishop). *Pio IX e il suo pontificato.* Turin, 1911 (3 vols.). Translated from the Polish. For long the standard biography.

Pennachi, Joseph. *De Honorii I Pontificis Romani causa in Concilio VI.* Pennachi was Professor of Church History at Rome. See Hefele.

Perrone, J. *De Romani Pontificis infallibilitate.* Turin, 1874.

Pithou, Pierre. *Les Libertéz de l'église gallicane,* Paris, 1594. Forbidden by Decree, Jan. 15, 1610; Sept. 10, 1610; May 27, 1614.

Pressensé, Edmond de. *Le Concile du Vatican.* Paris, 1870. Forbidden by Decree, March 6, 1876.

Purcell, Edmund Sheridan. *Life of Cardinal Manning.* London, Macmillan, 1896 (Vol. I, 702 pp.; Vol. II, 832 pp.). There are also biographies of Darboy, by Guillermin; Ketteler, by Pfülf; Gasser, by Zöbl.

[Quirinus]. *Letter from Rome on the Council.* London, Rivingtons, 1870. Attributed to Döllinger; reprinted from the *Allgemeine Zeitung,* authorized translation.

Rauscher (Cardinal). *Observationes quædam de infallibilitatis ecclesiæ subjecto.* Naples, 1870 (83 pp.). Against the infallibilist position.

Reinkens, Joseph Hubert. *Über päpstliche Unfehlbarkeit.* Munich, 1870. Against the infallibilist position. The author was Professor of Church History in Breslau.

Renouf, Peter Le Page. *The Case of Pope Honorius*. London, 1869. Against the infallibilist position.

Riess, F., and Weber, K. von. *Das Oekumenische Concil: Stimmen aus Maria-Laach, Neue Folge, No. X. Die päpstliche Unfehlbarkeit des Kirchenoberhauptes nebst Widerlegung der Einwürfe*. Munster, 1870 (110 pp.). From the papalist side, by two Jesuits.

Roskovany, A. V. *Romanus Pontifex*, Vols. VII-XVI, Suppl. 7-10. Nitrae, 1871-79.

Rump, Hermann. *Die Unfehlbarkeit des Papstes und die Stellung der in Deutschland verbreiteten theologischen Lehrbücher zu dieser Lehre*. Munster, 1870 (173 pp.). From the papalist side.

Runciman, Steven. *The Eastern Schism*. Oxford, 1955. The Waynflete Lectures, 1954. Though not directly relevant to the present study, this excellent presentation of the Byzantine case against the Papacy in the eleventh and twelfth centuries has an indirect bearing on it. There is a very good bibliography.

Salmon, George. *The Infallibility of the Church*. London, John Murray, 1888; several later editions; abridgment 1952. A standard polemical work from the Protestant side. Salmon was Provost of Trinity College, Dublin. The *Catholic Encyclopaedia* deemed this work the cleverest attack on the infallibilist position.

Sambin, J. (S.J.). *Histoire du Concile œcuménique et général du Vatican*. Lyons, 1872.

Sauvé, H. *Le Pape et le concile du Vatican*. Laval, 1890.

Scheeben, M. J. *Periodische Blätter zur Mittheilung und Besprechung der Gegenstände welche sich auf die neueste allgemeine Kirchenversammlung beziechen: Das Ökumenische Concil vom Jahre 1869*. Ratisbon, 1870 (2 vols.).

———. *Schulte und Döllinger gegen das Concil: Kritische Beleuchtung, etc.* Regensburg, 1871. From the papalist side.

Schmidlin, J. *Papstgeschichte der neuesten Zeit*. Munich, Kosel & Pustet, 1933-36 (3 vols.). Covers the period 1800-1922; a continuation of Pastor's famous work.

Schmidt, Hermann Joseph. *Das Vatikanische Konzil*. Paderborn, 1927.

Schulte, J. Friedrich Ritter von. *Das Unfehlbarkeits-Decret vom 18 Juli 1870 auf seine Verbindlichkeit geprüft*. Prague, 1870. Against the infallibilist position.

———. *Der Altkatholicismus*. Giessen, 1877. A history of the "Old Catholic" Church after 1870. Schulte was Professor at Prague; later at Bonn.

Sell, K. *Die Entwickelung der Katholischen Kirche im 19. Jahrhundert*. Leipzig, 1898.

Sparrow-Simpson, W. J. *Roman Catholic opposition to Papal Infallibility*. London, John Murray, 1909 (369 pp.). Chiefly concerned to show, from Roman sources, that the doctrine of papal infallibility was widely opposed before 1870.

Sturzo, Don Luigi. *Church and State.* New York, Longmans, 1939. Translated by B. B. Carter from the original French edition, *L'Eglise et l'Etat* (Paris, 1938). Favorably reviewed in the *Civiltà Cattolica.* The author, well known for his opposition to Fascism in Mussolini's day, is a distinguished priest and sociologist. Chapter XIII, on the Vatican Council, admits failings on the "human side," and makes clear the reality of the opposition. Don Sturzo should be read alongside of Dom B. C. Butler (*q.v.*).

Tierney, Brian. *Foundations of the Conciliar Theory.* Cambridge, 1955. This fourth volume in the New Series of Cambridge Studies in Medieval Life and Thought is of first-rate importance for a detailed study of the contribution of the canonists to the development of the conciliar theory, from the time of Gratian till the Great Schism. An admirably lucid exposition, it is furnished with an excellent bibliography of both the manuscript and printed sources.

Ullmann, Walter. *Medieval Papalism: the Political Theories of the Medieval Canonists.* London, Methuen, 1949 (230 pp.). (The Maitland Memorial Lectures, Cambridge, 1948.)

Vacant, J. M. A. *Etudes théologiques sur les constitutions du Concile du Vatican d'après les actes du concile.* Paris, 1895 (2 vols.). One of the two principal commentaries on the decrees of the Council (see Granderath).

Vercesi, E. *Pio IX.* Milan, 1929.

Veuillot, E. *Louis Veuillot.* See especially Vol. III (Paris, 1905) and Vol. IV (Paris, 1913).

Veuillot, Louis. *L'Illusion libérale.* Paris, 1866.

———. *Le Pape et la diplomatie.* Paris, 1861.

———. *Rome pendant le Concile.* Paris, 1872. In *Œuvres Complètes,* Vol. XII (Paris, 1927).

Virginio (Marchese). *Le mie impressioni al Concilio Vaticano.* Saluzzo, 1912.

Ward, Wilfrid. *William George Ward and the Catholic Revival.* London, 1893.

Weninger, P. *L'Infaillibilité du Pape devant la raison et l'écriture, les papes et les conciles, les pères et les théologiens, les rois et les empereurs.* (Translated from German into French by P. Bélet.) From the papalist side, by a Jesuit, and highly commended by Pius IX in a brief, Nov. 17, 1869. Kenrick (*q.v.*) wrote of him as "a pious . . . but ignorant man." Weninger had also written several pamphlets on the subject, one published at Innsbruck, 1841, one at Graz, 1853, and one at Cincinnati, 1868.

Zirngiebl, Eberhard. *Das vaticanische Council mit Rucksicht auf Lord Actons Sendschreiben und Bischof v. Kettelers Antwort kritisch betrachtet.* Forbidden by Decree, Sept. 20, 1871.

D. PERIODICALS

La Civiltà Cattolica, 1868-71, under *Cose spettanti al Concilio. Series 7:*
Vol. IV, pp. 79-91; Vol. V, pp. 210-220, 353-357, 454-467, 590-598,
717-722; Vol. VI, pp. 91-96, 201-207, 350-353, 602-607, 712-721;
Vol. VII, pp. 89-95, 210-217, 342-351, 591-596, 728-731; Vol. VIII,
pp. 93-98, 208-221, 339-350, 483-485, 600-610; Vol. X, pp. 64-90,
208-220, 342-358, 463-484, 589-608, 724-735; Vol. XI, pp. 78-91,
203-222, 350-354, 459-475, 593-599. *Series 8:* Vol. I, pp. 716-730.
See also: *Correspondant, Dublin Review, Français, Tablet, Univers,* for
the last months of 1869 through 1870.
British Quarterly Review, April 1870. Article. "The Council of the
Vatican."

INDEX

Abraham, 26

Acton, John Emerich Dalberg, Baron: considers representative government almost universal in Middle Ages, 94; mentioned, 70, 71

Acton, Sir Richard, Bt., 70

Adam, Fall of, 100

Adrian IV, Pope, 107

Aequitas, 97, 112

Albertus Magnus, 44, 203

Alemany, Joseph Sadoc, Archbishop of San Francisco, 39

Amalfi, 28

Ambrose, Saint, 201, 203

America, 156

Anatolius of Constantinople, 87

Angelis, Filippo de, Cardinal-priest, tit. S. Laurentii in Lucina, President of the Council, 31, 37

Anna, Mother of B. V. Mary, 8

Antonelli, Giacobbe, Cardinal-deacon, S. Mariae in via Lata, 51

Apocalypse of Abraham, 203

Aquinas. *See* Thomas Aquinas

Aristotle, 100

Ascension of Isaiah, 203

Assumption: term used untechnically in patristic writings, 201

Assumption of B. V. Mary: history of the doctrine of the, 9, 201ff; some Vatican Fathers wish Council to define, 203; defined by Pius XII, 203f

Assumption of Saint John the Evangelist, 141f

Assumption of Saint Martin of Tours, 201

Augsburg Gazette, Döllinger's articles in, 66

Augustine, Saint: teaches Mary not exempt from original sin, 9; paraphrased by Strossmayer, 35; considers doubt of Thomas more beneficial to us than Mary's faith, 164; holds common N.T. and patristic doctrine that all have sinned except Christ, 198; calls Mary's flesh sinful, 198; refers to Assumption of Apostles, 201; mentioned, 95ff, 120, 123

Austria, representation of, at Vatican Council, 28

Ave Maria, some Vatican Fathers wish Immaculate Conception mentioned in, 161

Balthazar of Heredia, Bishop: asks Tridentine Fathers not to treat doctrine of Immaculate Conception with pinch of salt, 200

Barili, Lorenzo, Cardinal-priest, tit. S. Agnetis extra moenia: celebrates Low Mass, 1

Basle, Council of, 117

Baxter, Richard, 92

Bede, Venerable, 202

Bedoyère, Michael de la, 63

Belgium, representation of, at Vatican Council, 28

Bellarmine, Saint Robert, S.J., Cardinal, 41, 91, 127, 138

Belsen, 55

Benedict XIV, Pope, 123

Benedictine Order, 101

Berkeley, George, 138

Bernard of Clairvaux, Saint: opposes doctrine of Immaculate Conception, 9; mentioned, 197

Bernini, Giovanni Lorenzo, 26

Bible Societies, classed with Communism, 19

Bilio, Luigi, Cardinal-priest, tit. S. Laurentii in Paneperna: celebrates High Mass, 38